# The Roots of Texas Music

*Number Ninety-three:*
*Centennial Series of*
*the Association of*
*Former Students,*
*Texas A&M University*

# The
# Roots
## of
# Texas
# Music

### Edited by
## Lawrence Clayton
### and
## Joe W. Specht

**Texas A&M University Press**
*College Station*

The paper used in this book meets the minimum
requirements of the American National Standard for
Permanence of Paper for Printed Library Materials, Z39.48-1984.
Binding materials have been chosen for durability.

Library of Congress Cataloging-in-Publication Data
The roots of Texas music / edited by Lawrence Clayton and
Joe W. Specht. — 1st ed.
      p. cm. — (Centennial series of the Association of Former
Students, Texas A&M University ; no. 93) Includes index.
    ISBN 1-58544-221-6 (alk. paper)
    1.   Music—Texas—History and criticism.   I. Clayton,
Lawrence. II. Specht, Joe W., 1945–  III. Series.
ML200.7.T35 R66 2003
780'.9764—dc21
                    2002007119

*This work is dedicated to
the rich musical past and present of
the great state of Texas
and to
those who created and performed
in those varied traditions
and to
Lawrence Clayton, who
so appreciated these traditions.*

# Contents

*List of Illustrations*   *ix*
*Preface*   *xi*

## 1

**The Roots Run Deep**
*An Overview of Texas Music History*
BY GARY HARTMAN
*3*

## 2

**Texan Jazz**
*1920–50*
DAVE OLIPHANT
*37*

## 3

**Put a Nickel in the Jukebox**
*The Texas Tradition in
Country Music, 1922–50*
JOE W. SPECHT
*66*

## 4

**Early Texas Bluesmen**
JOHN LIGHTFOOT
*95*

## 5

**Roots of Classical Music in Texas**
*The German Contribution*
LARRY WOLZ
*119*

**6**

**Make a Joyful Noise**
*Some Popular Religious Music
in Twentieth-Century Texas*
KENNETH W. DAVIS
*138*

**7**

**Chicano Music**
*Evolution and Politics to 1950*
JOSÉ ANGEL GUTIÉRREZ
*146*

**8**

**Czech and Polish Music in
Texas before World War II**
CAROLYN F. GRIFFITH
*175*

**9**

**Black Creoles and
the Evolution of Zydeco
in Southeast Texas**
*The Beginnings to 1950*
ROGER WOOD
*192*

*Contributors   217*

*Index   219*

# List of Illustrations

Oran "Hot Lips" Page
43

The Howell Brothers
Moonshine Dance Orchestra
46

Tex Ritter
74

Cindy Walker
85

Blind Lemon Jefferson
97

Odessa Band
129

Lydia Mendoza
162

John Muszynski and
the White Eagles
178

Zydeco players performing at
The Silver Slipper
198

# Preface

Lawrence Clayton had a love of all things Texan, but he had a special feel for the music of the Lone Star State. Lawrence's musical tastes ranged from plaintive cowboy ballads to the frat-boy party sounds of singer/songwriter Pat Green, to whom his younger daughter Lea had introduced him in recent years. And it is from his life-long interest in Texas music that this project sprang.

In 1998, Lawrence decided to assemble a collection of essays that would bring a fresh look to the subject of Texas music. The focus would be on the beginnings of the music to 1950. To accomplish this goal, he enlisted associates, former students, and colleagues whose interests in Texas music matched his own. Lawrence was excited about the project, and his enthusiasm was contagious. After four years and a series of unforeseen delays, the project is complete. Unfortunately, Lawrence did not live to see it through to fruition. In October, 1999, he was diagnosed with ALS/Lou Gehrig's Disease. Fourteen months later, he died, on December 31, 2000.

A few months before his death, Lawrence asked me to sign on as co-editor. At the time, we discussed the need for an introductory or overview chapter, and Gary Hartman accepted the assignment. I later contacted Dave Oliphant to write a chapter on jazz. With the exception of the Hartman and Oliphant essays, the rest of the chapters were written in 1999, with some slight revisions and updates along the way.

Thanks, then, to the authors of each chapter who stayed the course and to Peggi Gooch, Lawrence's administrative assistant, for her assistance with the preparation of the manuscript. We finally got it done, Lawrence.

—Joe W. Specht
McMurry University

# The Roots of Texas Music

# 1

# The Roots Run Deep
## *An Overview of*
## *Texas Music History*

## Gary Hartman

The roots of Texas music run deep. Although some people may think of Texas music as mainly "country," the music of Texas and the American Southwest is as diverse and distinctive as the many different groups who have lived in the region over the past several centuries. Music also has played a central role in the daily lives of all those who have called the Southwest their home. Native Americans have long used music to mark births, deaths, marriages, harvests, and a variety of other important events in their lives. For Hispanic people living in Texas, corridos, rancheras, cumbias, and other musical forms have played a prominent part in both religious and secular ceremonies. African Americans in Texas have articulated their experiences through gospel, blues, ragtime, jazz, and other types of music. French-speaking blacks and whites in East Texas still celebrate their culture through zydeco and Cajun music. Whether a fiddle breakdown, a polka, a rag, a canción, a *Volkslied,* or any other form of musical expression, music has been vital in shaping and reflecting the historical and cultural development of Anglo, Irish, Scottish, African, German, Czech, Mexican, Polish, Jewish, Asian, Slavic, and other ethnic groups in Texas.

Not only has the Lone Star State served as a crossroads for so many different ethnic groups, but the particular social, political, and economic forces that have shaped the area have helped make the Southwest one of the most complex and diverse regional societies in the

country. Nowhere is this tremendous diversity more apparent than
in Texas music. An astounding variety of musical genres have thrived
in the region, often cross-pollinating to create new subgenres. Blues,
gospel, ragtime, jazz, conjunto, Tejano, Cajun, zydeco, polka, western
swing, rock and roll, and a number of other musical styles have mixed
and mingled in the Southwest as they have nowhere else. Texas also
has contributed some of the most influential artists to modern American music. Scott Joplin, Bob Wills, Buddy Holly, Van Cliburn, Janis
Joplin, Lead Belly, Selena Quintanilla, Charlie Christian, Ornette Coleman, Sippie Wallace, Willie Nelson, Flaco Jiménez, Roy Orbison, Gene
Autry, Lydia Mendoza, Don Henley, Big Mama Thornton, Kenny Rogers,
Stephen Stills, and ZZ Top all are from Texas, and all have had a significant impact on mainstream American music.[1]

Skeptics might question whether the history of Texas music is a
subject worthy of serious academic study. After all, some might argue
that music is little more than a manifestation of popular culture that can
be manufactured, manipulated, and marketed purely for profit. In many
cases, this is certainly true. However, music, especially that which
evolves "organically" from within certain communities or segments of
society, is a profoundly important means of expressing and addressing
the concerns of that particular group.[2] In fact, music may be the most
democratic form of cultural expression available, because it allows
everyone—rich or poor, educated or uneducated—to exchange information and reconcile the issues they face in their daily lives. As an important part of the "cultural vocabulary" through which all societies
communicate, music also serves as a medium of exchange between different groups. Sometimes these groups express ambivalence or even animosity toward each other through music. However, they also have used
music to bridge the distances between them, often exchanging musical
ideas or incorporating each other's musical traditions into their own.

For Texans, both individually and collectively, music has played a
central role in communicating information, addressing important issues, reconciling conflicting notions of ethnic identity, and shaping and
reflecting the society in which we live today. Examining the evolution
of music in the Southwest can provide a more complete understanding
of the unique development of Texas society and the ways in which Texans have viewed themselves and the world around them. This volume
will trace the evolution of Texas music up to the mid-twentieth century
and examine the ways in which music reflects the cultural and historical transformation of the state.

## ⋙ Native American Music ⋙

Many different American Indian groups have lived in the Southwest during the past several centuries. Dozens of tribes, often comprised of smaller bands and extended family units, spoke numerous languages and dialects and interacted through a complex system of intertribal trade, migration, and warfare.[3] However, very few of the Indian groups that inhabited the region when Spanish explorers first arrived in the early 1500s remain today. Most, such as the Karankawa, Atakapan, Coahuiltecan, Jumano, Wichita, and Caddo, either disappeared completely or were displaced by other Indians or by European settlers.[4] Only the Tigua, Kickapoo, and Alabama-Coushatta—three tribes that migrated to Texas from elsewhere—claim permanent residence in the state today.[5]

For most Native American groups, music was essential to communicating information and culture within and among communities. Singing and dancing played a vital role in both secular and religious ceremonies, helping to articulate tribal beliefs and transmit tribal history from one generation to the next.[6] For example, Karankawas used music in a broad range of tribal rituals. As with human societies the world over, dances and musical performances provided the Karankawa with a means for individuals to demonstrate intelligence, physical agility, and emotional sensibility, three basic qualities others within the community certainly would look for in a potential mate. Coahuiltecans also made singing and dancing a regular part of their communal celebrations, sometimes incorporating cannibalism and the use of hallucinogenic substances. Jumano ceremonies often involved choreographed dancing along with vocal impersonations of various musical instruments. Atakapans celebrated victory in battle or a successful hunt with music, singing, and dancing that could last for days.[7]

Caddos, a sedentary agricultural group living in East Texas, organized their musical celebrations around the cultivation and harvesting of corn, their primary food crop.[8] Wichitas and Kiowas of the northern Texas plains took part in a ritual commonly known as the "Ghost Dance," which was widely practiced among Plains Indians in the late nineteenth century as part of an effort to unite Indians politically and culturally in the face of a growing European American presence in the West.[9] Black Seminoles, descended from Seminole Indians and former black slaves, lived along both sides of the Rio Grande and combined elements of Native American, African American, and Hispanic culture in their language and music.[10] Cherokees in East Texas incorporated ritual bathing into their musical celebrations as a symbol of purification and the ongoing cycle of birth, death, and renewal.[11] Comanches, one group that arrived in Texas after Europeans, engaged in "vision quests," or lengthy periods of fasting, in which "guardian spirits" communicated with fasting members through music.[12]

Music continues to play a central role in the communal activities of the Kickapoo, Tigua, and Alabama-Coushatta. The Kickapoo, whose reservation is near Eagle Pass, perform a variety of ritual dances, including a celebration honoring domestic work, in which women dressed in traditional clothing dance in single file around a collection of cooking pots. The Tigua, living in far West Texas near El Paso, have blended their culture with that of Spanish-speaking settlers in the region. For instance, the Catholic church's annual celebration of Saint Anthony has become the Tiguas' single biggest festival each year and combines Catholic rituals with traditional Tigua costumes, dance, and music.[13] In Northeast Texas, many Alabama-Coushatta who converted to Christianity during the nineteenth century have begun to use traditional music and dance to rediscover their ethnic and cultural heritage. For the approximately 60,000 Native Americans still living in Texas, music remains an integral part of celebrating their history and culture. Each year, a number of pow wows, or tribal gatherings, are held throughout the state, and participants take part in singing, dancing, religious rituals, and various educational activities as a way to preserve and promote Native American traditions.[14]

## ≈ Música Tejana ≈

The Hispanic influence on the development of Texas music has been profound. The broad spectrum of Texas Mexican music, often called "música tejana," includes conjunto, Tejano, canciónes, corridos, cumbias, mariachis, orquestas, and a variety of other musical genres and styles.[15] Of course, Spanish-speaking people lived throughout the Southwest three hundred years before the first English-speaking immigrants settled, making Spanish the oldest and most prevalent European culture in the region. This began to change in the 1820s, when a newly independent Mexico allowed some 30,000 primarily English-speaking American settlers to move into the province of Tejas. In 1836, Anglo and Hispanic Texans working together won their independence from Mexico.

Despite U.S. annexation of Texas in 1845, and of most of the rest of the American Southwest by 1848, the United States remained historically and culturally connected to Mexico. What is essentially a permeable border between the two countries has allowed for an almost continuous flow of people, goods, and culture back and forth for generations.

The musical heritage born of these two diverse cultures is a rich and colorful one that brings together European, Mexican, African, Native American, and other influences. Most Tejanos, or Texans of Mexican descent, have an enduring sense of both their Mexican ethnic heritage and their identity as Americans. It would be a mistake, however, to assume that there is one single Mexican American culture or sense of ethnic identity. Like any other ethnic group, the Mexican American community is not at all monolithic. Instead, it has deep internal divisions based on class, gender, age, region, religious and political affiliation, and numerous other issues. In many ways, Texas Mexican music, or música tejana, mirrors the complex internal dynamics of the Texas Mexican community.[16]

Música tejana's roots extend at least as far back as medieval Spain. With much of the Iberian Peninsula under Moorish occupation from A.D. 711 to 1492, Spain absorbed a variety of North African musical influences. After the Spanish reconquista was complete in 1492, a newly united Spain reoriented itself increasingly toward mainland Europe and began to embrace European musical fashions. While the Spanish middle and upper classes tended to prefer formal symphonic orchestras, smaller stringed-instrument groups became the most common form of musical entertainment for the nonelite. In the Spanish colonies of America, a lack of symphonic orchestras meant that Spanish colonists of all classes had to rely on smaller ensembles to replicate the music enjoyed by their peers back in Spain. Following Mexico's independence from Spain in 1821, middle and upper-class Mexicans began turning away from traditional Spanish music and increasingly toward the waltzes, polkas, schottisches, and minuets so popular among their nineteenth-century European counterparts. In most larger Mexican cities the elite could participate in these new musical trends in parlors, salons, and ballrooms. Eventually, working-class Mexicans incorporated many of the same dance steps into their own folk music.[17]

As important as dance music was to all classes of Tejanos at the turn of the century, vocal music also was essential to celebrating culture and exchanging ideas and information within Mexican American society.[18] Two of the most important forms of vocal music among Tejanos at this

time were corridos and rancheras. The corrido, or ballad, usually includes several stanzas that relate an epic story. Because illiteracy rates
were high among the working classes in Northern Mexico and South
Texas, corridos were an effective method of relaying information between villages or transmitting folklore from one generation to the
next.[19] It is important, however, to remember that ballads normally are
not reliable sources of factual information. They usually are highly ro-
manticized—and, sometimes, completely fictionalized—accounts of
events.[20]

For Tejanos, the "corrido trágico," or heroic ballad, was extremely
popular. These usually were epic narratives describing an important
historical event or the life of someone who had had a significant impact
on the community. Often these corridos included larger-than-life characters and an emphasis on tragic or somewhat sensationalized events.
Because they served to express the concerns of many marginalized
working-class Mexican Americans, corridos often celebrated the un-
derdog, for example, by portraying a notorious outlaw or social outcast
as a hero. By glorifying such "Robin Hood" characters, Tejanos, who
faced increasingly systematic discrimination and exploitation, could
articulate their frustrations regarding the legal, political, and social bar-
riers they often were almost powerless to overcome. Like the folk ballads of all ethnic groups, corridos also reflect certain racial or national-
istic biases, which some Mexican Americans harbored toward other
groups. For instance, a recurring theme in corridos along the U.S.-
Mexican border at the turn of the century was the unfair treatment
sometimes inflicted on Tejanos by local "gringos."[21]

Corridos also reveal conflicting attitudes within the Mexican American community regarding gender. Perceptions about gender identity,
and what it means to have "masculine" or "feminine" personality traits,
are highly subjective. Mexican Americans, like all other groups, con-
structed particular notions of gender identity that reflected certain biases within the community. In most corridos, for example, men are portrayed as either brave and noble or cowardly and dishonest. Women
often are passive characters who either represent goodness and virtue
or treachery and wickedness. Sometimes the male protagonist in the
corrido insults his opponent by portraying him not only as disreputable,
but also as having supposedly "feminine" qualities. This "emasculation
through feminization" allows the hero to call into question his opponent's honor as well as his masculinity, but it also unfairly equates fem-
ininity with weakness and treachery.

*The Ballad of Gregorio Cortez,* perhaps the most famous of all Texas-Mexico border ballads, combines all of these elements. Based on the true story of Cortez, who was accused of killing a South Texas sheriff in 1901, the ballad celebrates Cortez as a noble champion of his people who fought valiantly against a discriminatory Anglo-dominated judicial system and eventually prevailed. Those gringos who victimized Cortez, especially the "rinches," or Texas Rangers, are portrayed as cowardly, dishonest, and even "feminine."[22]

The ranchera has been another popular Texas Mexican song style since the late nineteenth century. The ranchera typically is a romantic song set in the idyllic environment of the frontier ranch. It evokes images of the rugged pioneer who embodies such noble characteristics as honesty, self-sufficiency, and patriotism. These rustic, pastoral themes had tremendous appeal to many Mexican Americans who faced a rapid and uneasy transition from a primarily rural agrarian existence to a more urban industrial one. Much like popular English-language songs of the American West, rancheras also allowed audiences to idealize their ancestry and ethnic heritage. Sometimes, this romanticizing reflected deeper class concerns. For example, middle-class rancheras tended to focus on the "charro," or gentleman cowboy and his noble lineage, while working-class rancheras honored the "campesino," or common ranch hand and his reputation for hard work and honesty. In both cases, Tejanos were using folk culture selectively in order to define and articulate their cultural and ancestral heritage as they perceived it.[23]

By the early twentieth century, Mexican folk music in Texas had evolved into two predominant styles based largely on class distinction. The middle and upper classes preferred the "orquesta típica," a medium-sized string ensemble that usually included violins, guitars, contrabass, and mandolins. Because it was bigger and more expensive to hire, the orquesta típica was usually associated with middle- and upper-class festivities, such as "bailes," or formal balls. Working-class Tejanos tended to celebrate through less formal public dances known as "fandangos," and the "conjunto" became their musical ensemble of choice. The accordion, which was borrowed from German and Czech immigrants, was the centerpiece of the conjunto band. A single accordionist could combine melody, bass lines, and a danceable rhythm with enough volume to fill a good-sized dance hall. If the occasion permitted, the accordionist would be joined by a guitar, contrabass, and a "tambora de rancho," a cylindrical drum suspended from the waist and played with mallets. Many conjunto groups also added the "bajo sexto,"

a twelve-string bass guitar, which could either supplement drums or replace them altogether as the percussion section.[24]

Conjunto was primarily instrumental dance music, although, by
the 1940s, vocals became an important part of the conjunto sound. In
addition to boleros, cumbias, and waltzes, polkas and schottisches, borrowed from German and Czech musicians, became standard material
in the conjunto repertoire. In fact, the schottische is one of the best examples in Texas music of cross-cultural hybridization among ethnic
groups. Derived from the German word for "Scottish," the schottische
is a German interpretation of the traditional Scottish Highland fling.
Mexican American musicians reinterpreted it in their own way to fit
the conjunto style. Likewise, many country dance bands in Texas have
added fiddles and steel guitar to the schottische and made it a standard
part of their repertoire.

Bruno Villareal, José Rodríguez, and Jesús Casiano were three
accordionists during the 1920s who helped popularize the accordion
throughout Texas and Northern Mexico, but it was Narciso Martínez and
Santiago Jiménez, Sr., who created the style known as conjunto. Born
in Reynosa, Mexico, just south of McAllen, Martínez grew up as a migrant farm worker in the Rio Grande Valley.[25] Santiago Jiménez, Sr.,
known as "El Flaco" (the Skinny One) was born in San Antonio in 1913.
He learned accordion from his father, who played community dances
and church functions and often took his son to hear the polkas and
oompah music of ethnic German bands in the area.[26]

Although not a conjunto artist, Lydia Mendoza, nicknamed the
"Meadowlark of the Border," was a very influential figure in Texas Mexican music during the 1930s and 1940s. Born into a musical family
in Houston in 1916, Mendoza played a unique role in giving Hispanic
women a voice in a traditionally male-dominated society, because she
was not afraid to speak out against male mistreatment of women through
such songs as "Mal Hombre." She also was one of the first to transform
the ranchera style from merely a romantic ballad to include important
social issues, such as poverty and misogyny. During her lifetime, Mendoza made more than thirty-five albums and toured worldwide.[27]

World War II brought important changes to the Mexican American
community and to música tejana. Traditionally a marginalized ethnic
group, Tejanos found unprecedented opportunity for social and economic advancement during and immediately after the war. Those who
had served in the United States military learned new job skills and had
access to college educations through the G.I. Bill. Also, most felt a new

sense of empowerment from having served their country during its time of crisis. As a result, many Mexican Americans emerged from World War II generally more prosperous, better educated, and less willing to tolerate being treated like second-class citizens.

However, not all Mexican Americans shared equally in the new prosperity. While the middle class grew, achieving upward mobility at an unprecedented rate, many working-class Tejanos still suffered from high unemployment, low levels of education, and continued discrimination. Furthermore, a massive influx of agricultural workers brought in from Mexico through the U.S. government's *Bracero* program helped swell the ranks of the Mexican American working class. Faced with increasing pressure to conform during the early years of the cold war, middle-class Mexican Americans urged this rapidly growing working class to assimilate and demonstrate that they were "100 percent American." However, many working-class Tejanos resented this pressure to become "agringado" or "gringoized" and began accusing the middle class of abandoning its ethnic heritage.[28]

This growing class conflict was reflected in the evolution of música tejana during the late 1940s and early 1950s, as middle-class Tejanos began distancing themselves from working-class conjunto music and began gravitating toward the new "orquestas tejanas," which were patterned after the big swing bands of Glenn Miller, Benny Goodman, and others. Orquestas tejanas still incorporated some traditional Mexican musical styles. However, they shunned the accordion-based sound of conjunto, because, for most middle-class Tejanos, conjunto was too closely associated with the rural, working-class music of Northern Mexico.

Beto Villa, from Falfurrias, Texas, is usually considered the "father" of orquesta tejana. In 1946, he began blending traditional Mexican music with big band swing at Armando Marroquín's Ideal Records studio in Alice, Texas. Orquesta tejana remained very popular among middle-class Tejanos until the late 1950s. However, as the big band sound began to fade in popularity nationwide, Isidro López, a prominent orquesta tejana leader, started mixing orquesta tejana and conjunto to broaden its appeal and attract more listeners.[29] For many working-class Tejanos, on the other hand, conjunto came to symbolize their pride in long-standing cultural traditions and their refusal to "abandon" their ethnic heritage. Consequently, conjunto grew increasingly popular among the working class during the postwar period.[30]

The post–World War II era was important for música tejana in other ways, too. During the 1920s and 1930s, major U.S. record labels had been eager to record and market "race" music, especially African American and Hispanic. However, by World War II, the major labels decided that it would be more profitable to abandon local ethnic recording and focus instead on the already well-established Spanish-language market in Latin America. Consequently, after World War II, Tejanos had to establish their own independent labels, such as Falcon and Ideal Records. Despite the economic burden this placed on these fledgling record companies, they were now free to be more innovative. As a result, these small independent studios allowed musicians to experiment and create new variations of Tejano music. For example, Valerio Longoria, an Ideal conjunto artist, began incorporating vocal duets into his recordings, moving conjunto away from being almost exclusively instrumental.

Paulino and Eloy Bernal, Ideal artists who formed El Conjunto Bernal in 1952, further revolutionized conjunto by introducing the acordeón cromatica, three-part harmonies, and allowing band members to improvise the way jazz musicians did. Tony de la Rosa, from Corpus Christi, began using electric bass, a public address system, and full drum sets. Isidro López, also from Corpus Christi, brought the vocalist to center stage and continued blending pop, blues, and other styles into conjunto. All of these innovations, along with the appearance of rock and roll in the 1950s, helped pave the way for the more vocally oriented and politically conscious "Onda Chicana" music of the 1960s and 1970s, as well as the more synthesizer-driven Tejano style of the 1980s and 1990s.[31] From the colonial period to the present, música tejana has been an important means of expressing economic, political, and cultural concerns and has reflected the important changes that have taken place within Texas Mexican society.

## ☙ African American Music in Texas ☙

African Americans also have had a profound impact on shaping the state's culture and music. African American music in the Southwest encompasses a variety of styles, including gospel, blues, ragtime, jazz, zydeco, rhythm and blues, and others.[32] Most of the earliest African Americans in Texas arrived as slaves, beginning with Moses Austin's settlers in the 1820s and continuing until the end of the Civil War. Following the Civil War, thousands more blacks migrated into the state to work as cowboys, farmers, tradesmen, laborers, and in other occupations.[33] As Texas became the largest cotton-producing state by 1890, many African

Americans came to make their living working as sharecroppers, tenant farmers, or hired hands on larger corporate-owned cotton farms. Twentieth-century industrialization attracted even more African Americans to the Lone Star State. During World War II, the booming petrochemical industry brought dramatic job growth to the upper Texas coast, providing new employment opportunities for black workers. Over the years, African Americans in the Southwest have faced a unique set of experiences, including slavery, institutionalized discrimination, and a rapid transition from a primarily agrarian lifestyle to an urban industrial one.[34] All of these experiences are reflected in the music of African Americans in Texas.

Gospel is one of the oldest African American musical styles, and it is an essential component in nearly all other forms of African American music that have emerged over the past two centuries. Deeply rooted in the experiences of slaves throughout the South before the Civil War, gospel evolved as a unique blend of European religious hymns with traditional African rhythms, dance steps, vocal phrasings, and choral arrangements. Gospel, with its underlying theme of "social deliverance," has been important for many within African American society, not only as a means of religious worship, but also as a way for participants to pass along their values and beliefs from one generation to the next.

One of the most prominent Texas gospel singers was "Blind" Arizona Dranes, born in Dallas around 1904. Dranes, who recorded for OKeh Records during the 1920s, was well known for infusing lively barrelhouse piano and ragtime syncopation into traditionally solemn gospel songs. The Soul Stirrers, formed in Houston in the early 1920s, incorporated energetic, choreographed dance movements into their gospel arrangements. In 1950, a young unknown singer named Sam Cooke briefly joined the group before he went on to become an international singing star.[35]

Blues is another fundamental component of African American culture that emerged as a distinct musical form among black slaves in the American South. The term "blues" probably derived from the old English term "blue devils," which were thought to be mischievous spirits that made people sad. The blues evolved from traditional African rhythmic patterns and singing styles, such as flattening or "bending" certain notes and using "call and response," in which a lead singer called out a verse and others responded in unison.[36] On one level, the blues were very basic, because slaves had few instruments and no formal musical training. On the other hand, blues allowed for a good deal of improvisation in terms of lyrics, vocal arrangements, and the incorporation of additional voices or instruments, thereby allowing blues to cover the full range of complex human emotions. The interactive nature of performing the blues also allowed democratic participation from an audience which, traditionally, had little or no voice in a segregated and racially hierarchical society.

The blues, which had served so well as a medium of expression during slavery, continued to provide an important outlet for black Americans after the Civil War, as they faced crushing poverty and harsh discrimination. By the 1880s, blues had evolved into a predominantly three-verse format, in which the singer would repeat the first line twice and then change the third line to make a particularly emphatic point. This repetitive style allowed the singer to express his emotions very candidly, while customizing each song to fit a particular situation.[37]

By the early twentieth century, thousands of rural blacks had relocated to major Texas cities and found themselves living in segregated neighborhoods. Rural black culture began to change in this more secular, urbanized environment. Gospel, which had been so popular among agrarian communities, was increasingly overshadowed by blues as the preferred form of musical expression for urbanized African Americans. Blind Lemon Jefferson was one of the most influential early Texas blues musicians. Born near Wortham, Texas, on September 24, 1893, Jefferson moved to the predominantly black Dallas neighborhood of Deep Ellum as a young man. He quickly gained fame playing on street corners and in bars, singing everything from gospel to bawdy drinking songs. Blind Lemon's music reflected a wide variety of issues he and other blacks faced, including economic hardship and racial discrimination. Between 1926 and 1929, Jefferson was the best-selling "race" artist in the country. He made more than eighty recordings for Paramount Records, including "See That My Grave Is Kept Clean," later performed by Bob Dylan on his debut album, and "Matchbox Blues," which became a hit for both the Beatles and Carl Perkins. Jefferson's "Teddy Bear Blues," with its line "Let me be your teddy bear/ tie a string on my neck/ I'll follow you everywhere," was reinterpreted by Elvis Presley in his song "Teddy Bear." Jefferson's influence on the blues and on later blues artists was profound. His phenomenal commercial success convinced major record companies of the potential market within the African American community for recorded blues. This helped introduce the blues to a national audience and inspire legions of younger players.[38]

Huddie Ledbetter, better known as Lead Belly, was another influential Texas blues pioneer. Born near Caddo Lake on the Texas-Louisiana border in 1889, Lead Belly often played with Blind Lemon Jefferson in Deep Ellum on street corners, in bars, and in whorehouses. In 1934, Texas folklorist John Lomax and his son Alan ran across Lead Belly in Angola Prison in Louisiana, where he was serving time for assault. Fascinated with his vast and diverse musical repertoire, the Lomaxes produced dozens of recordings of Lead Belly's songs and arranged tours for him across the country.

As the Great Depression brought economic hardship to millions of Americans, Lead Belly became a celebrated spokesman for labor unions, communist organizations, and other groups that championed the rights of the working class. Lead Belly often performed his "Bourgeois Blues" and other songs of class protest at political rallies and other functions sponsored by such organizations. However, apparently he remained somewhat leery of these groups that were dominated mainly by white men, and he never formally enrolled in any labor union or left-leaning political party.[39] Lead Belly died in 1949, but his musical legacy remains strong. He played with Woody Guthrie, Burl Ives, and other popular white singers, inspiring them to incorporate more of the blues influence into mainstream folk music. Lead Belly's best-known songs include "Goodnight Irene," "The Midnight Special," "Cotton Fields At Home," "House of the Rising Sun," and "In the Pines," all of which have been recorded by numerous rock, blues, and country artists.[40]

Mance Lipscomb, another important Texas blues pioneer, was born on April 9, 1895, in Brazos County, Texas. He spent most of his life in rural East Texas, where he worked as a sharecropper and performed at dances and other social events among the black, Czech, and Scots-Irish communities in the area. Two of Lipscomb's biggest musical influences were Blind Lemon Jefferson and Lead Belly. Like Lead Belly and most other "country blues" artists, Lipscomb played much more than just the blues. His broad repertoire included ballads, reels, shouts, and other traditional forms of African American folk music. In 1960, San Francisco–based Arhoolie Records recognized Lipscomb's unique style, which blended traditional blues, folk ballads, and jazz, and began recording him. At the age of sixty-five, Lipscomb moved to Austin, began performing professionally, and became a mentor for younger Texas blues and rock guitarists, such as Stevie Ray Vaughan.[41]

Texas piano players also had an important impact on the early development of blues. One of the major contributions made by Texas musicians was the piano style known as "boogie-woogie." Also known as "barrelhouse," "fast Texas," or "fast western" blues, boogie-woogie developed in the sawmills and turpentine camps of the East Texas Piney Woods. With little else available for entertainment, black lumber workers congregated in the lumber camp's makeshift tavern, known as a "barrelhouse," because the bar consisted of a long plank placed on top of barrels. As the principal form of musical entertainment, piano players had to provide a hard-driving, rocking rhythm in order to accommodate what often was a rather rowdy audience.[42] "Whistlin'" Alex Moore, born in Dallas in 1899, was a pioneer of boogie-woogie who mixed together blues, ragtime, and New Orleans Dixieland jazz. Beulah "Sippie" Wallace, born in Houston in 1898, was perhaps the most influential female singer and pianist to combine boogie-woogie with gospel, blues, and jazz. During her career, Wallace starred in vaudeville shows, toured with Louis Armstrong, and inspired countless younger blues singers.[43]

By the 1930s, the advent of electric guitars, amplifiers, public address systems, and full drum sets took blues in a new direction. One of the era's most influential electric blues guitarists was Aaron Thibeaux "T-Bone" Walker, who grew up in the South Dallas suburb of Oak Cliff. As a young man, Walker frequented Deep Ellum where he met Blind Lemon Jefferson and a young guitarist named Charlie Christian. By 1929, T-Bone was an accomplished musician who toured with Cab Callaway, Ma Rainey, and other jazz and blues stars. Walker became famous for his wild stage antics, such as playing guitar behind his back and gyrating his hips wildly on stage, all movements later borrowed by James Brown, Chuck Berry, Elvis Presley, Jimi Hendrix, and Stevie Ray Vaughan. T-Bone's electrified sound and powerful stage presence helped give birth to a new style known as rhythm and blues. His biggest hit, "They Call It Stormy Monday," epitomizes Walker's unique blending of blues, jazz, and slow ballads with a more brash, electrified sound.[44] Other important "electric blues" artists from Texas include Sam "Lightning" Hopkins, Clarence "Gatemouth" Brown, and Willie Mae "Big Momma" Thornton. Thornton, who was born in Montgomery, Alabama, but moved to Houston as a teenager, had a raw, powerful singing style that made her a national sensation in the 1940s and 1950s. Some of her better-known songs, such as "You Ain't Nothin' But A Hound Dog" and "Ball and Chain," were later repopularized by Elvis Presley and Janis Joplin.[45]

Jazz is another musical genre in which both black and white Texans have played leading roles. The emergence of jazz during the early twentieth century reflected some important changes taking place within the African American community. With the outbreak of World War I, and the onset of a second industrial revolution, millions of black Americans moved from rural areas to industrial cities, where they faced unique challenges in a new, more urbanized environment. These profound changes helped bring about the 1920s "Harlem Renaissance," an extraordinary proliferation of black art, literature, and music. Jazz— whose roots lie in blues, gospel, ragtime, and other predominantly African American traditions—became the musical voice for this cultural movement, although jazz quickly moved beyond the black community and became a powerful creative force that changed mainstream popular culture forever.

Ragtime, a precursor to jazz, was rooted in classical piano technique, but it incorporated an energy and spontaneity based on improvisation, syncopation, and unique phrasing. Scott Joplin, by far the most famous composer of ragtime, was born in Texarkana, Texas, in 1868. Joplin was classically trained but was strongly influenced by the black blues and gospel he heard as a child. As a young man, Joplin formed the Texas Medley Quintet and traveled throughout Northeast Texas performing blues, marches, and minstrel tunes. Eventually, he moved to St. Louis, Missouri, and began playing in saloons and brothels, where he combined his classical training with a broad background in blues, gospel, and show tunes to build a repertoire of spirited dance numbers. Joplin's eclectic style fit perfectly with a new form of lively, syncopated music emerging from within the black community that would become known as ragtime. Soon, Joplin's own "rags" became part of mainstream popular music. In 1899, he published "Maple Leaf Rag," which sold more than one million copies and became the most popular song of the entire ragtime era. Joplin followed this with other successful compositions, such as "The Entertainer," which was reissued as the theme song to the 1973 Robert Redford and Paul Newman movie *The Sting*. Joplin's impact on the careers of other musicians is almost incalculable. Early jazz pioneers, such as Fats Waller, Louis Armstrong, and Jelly Roll Morton, all cite Joplin as one of their most important influences. Furthermore, the ragtime sound can be heard running through a variety of popular musical styles of the twentieth century, including boogie-woogie, western swing, and Broadway show tunes.[46]

Charlie Christian, arguably the most influential jazz guitarist of the twentieth century, was born in Northeast Texas in 1919. As a guitarist for Benny Goodman's sextet, Christian encouraged his fellow players to abandon more structured arrangements and rely on greater spontaneity. Christian's trademark single-string soloing technique eventually became a staple of jazz, rock, and country guitarists.[47] However, it was Eddie Durham, a guitarist from San Marcos, Texas, who taught Christian this new style of playing. Durham, who was perhaps the first jazz musician to record with an electric guitar, became one of the most sought after musicians and arrangers in American jazz during the 1930s. He performed and recorded with Count Basie and Jimmie Lunceford and arranged numerous songs for Glenn Miller and others.[48]

Several other Texas musicians have been very influential in the evolution of jazz.[49] Herb Ellis, born in Farmersville, Texas, in 1921, drew from both his blues roots and the music of Charlie Christian to become a brilliant guitarist who worked with Jimmy Dorsey, Ella Fitzgerald, Joe Pass, Charlie Byrd, and Barney Kessel. Ornette Coleman, born in Fort Worth in 1930, is perhaps the most famous Texas saxophone player. He was a major influence on Miles Davis and other jazz innovators. Henry "Buster" Smith, born near Ennis, Texas, in 1904, wrote, directed, and performed with some of the biggest names in jazz and is considered one of the leading mentors for saxophone great Charlie "Bird" Parker. The great Houston-born tenor saxophonist Arnett Cobb worked with a variety of top-ranked musicians, blending jazz with rhythm and blues to create what some have called "soul jazz." Tex Beneke, born in Fort Worth in 1914, was a vocalist and saxophonist for the Glenn Miller Orchestra; he took over leadership of the band following Miller's death. Dallas-born saxophonist David "Fathead" Newman also has been an important force in blending together jazz with soul and rhythm and blues. Jack Teagarden, from Vernon, Texas, became one of the most creative and innovative trombonists in jazz and recorded with Bing Crosby, Louis Armstrong, and others.[50]

Jazz, like blues, gospel, and ragtime, grew out of the unique experiences of African Americans. In Texas, all of these musical forms played a vital role in the African American community's ability to express its concerns and share its culture with succeeding generations. Likewise, Texans had a profound influence on shaping these important musical styles and making them a permanent part of our nation's musical heritage.

## ⤸   German Music in Texas   ⤸

German immigration to Texas began in the 1830s, but it increased dramatically in the mid-1840s, as political instability, declining economic opportunities, and a shortage of available farmland displaced thousands of ethnic Germans living in Central Europe.[51] Once in Texas, German immigrants, who were fiercely proud of their heritage, worked hard to preserve their long-standing cultural traditions. They established numerous organizations aimed at providing social and economic support for their new German settlements, including schools, newspapers, publishing companies, and a variety of art, music, and educational societies.[52] Music always has been an important part of culture and community bonding for Germans. The importance of musical celebration to the German American communities is apparent in the proliferation of German music clubs and dance halls across the state. Germania, the first German singing society in Texas, was established in New Braunfels on March 2, 1850. Other German communities soon founded their own singing societies, including those in San Antonio and Austin in 1852 and Fredericksburg in 1858. On October 15, 1853, a number of these groups came together in New Braunfels to establish the Texas Sängerbund, or singers' union. The following day, the Texas Sängerbund hosted its first statewide Sängerfest, or singing festival, in New Braunfels.[53]

German Americans tended to preserve German music, whether classical or folk, more or less in its traditional form. There are several factors that might account for this. For one thing, most Germans came to Texas directly from Europe. They usually arrived in family units and sometimes even moved together as entire villages. This allowed their "cultural support system" to remain intact throughout the trans-Atlantic crossing and made it possible for them to establish new settlements quickly, with most of their familiar customs intact. For the most part, they were surrounded by other German immigrants and did not have to deal much outside of their own language or culture. Germans also had one of the highest literacy rates of all immigrant groups in Texas. This was reflected in their extensive use of printed sheet music and published literature, both of which allowed Germans to preserve their culture better in its traditional form.[54]

Despite the general trend among ethnic Germans in Texas to cling to their traditional musical roots, folk music did evolve in important ways among the Texas German communities. In fact, by the early twentieth century, German folk songs performed in the Southwest sometimes included references to shotguns, horse-drawn wagons, or other features of life on the frontier prairie. Traditional love songs might be modified to include specific American place names. By the 1930s, Texas German singing festivals sometimes combined traditional German folk songs with popular American tunes, such as "Oh, Susannah" or "Yellow

Rose of Texas."[55] Perhaps as significant as the impact of the American environment on German culture was the influence German immigrants had on the music of other ethnic communities in Texas, including the fact that so many other ethnic groups in the Southwest adopted the accordion, polka, schottische, yodeling, and other German musical traditions.

### ∾   Czech Music in Texas   ∾

Czechs are another important immigrant group that has helped shape the musical landscape of Texas. Czechs are a Slavic people whose ancestral homeland in East-Central Europe has been occupied at times by Germans, Austrians, and a variety of other groups. Perhaps because they were dominated by others for so many years, Czechs developed a resilient sense of ethnic identity. For those Czechs who came to Texas, this strong sense of ethnic heritage was reflected in the music they celebrated. Czech immigration to Texas started as a trickle in the 1840s, but, by the turn of the century, more than 40,000 Texans listed Czech as their native tongue. Because the German and Czech cultures are so deeply intertwined, early Czech immigrants often settled in established German communities throughout Central Texas. However, Czechs also founded many of their own settlements. The highest concentration of Czechs was in Fayette County, but, by the 1850s, Fayetteville, La Grange, Praha, Rowena, Caldwell, Ennis, Hostyn, Dubina, Corpus Christi, San Antonio, and Taylor all had sizable Czech communities in which Czechs established a variety of newspapers and social and educational societies.[56]

By the early twentieth century, Czech dance halls in Texas rang with the sounds of Czech polkas, country, and blues. Frank Baca established the first Texas Czech band, the Baca Band, in Fayetteville in 1882, which toured throughout the state. Although Baca died in 1907, the band has added new members over the years and continues to tour. The late Adolph Hofner grew up in a Czech family in San Antonio and absorbed both traditional Czech musical influences and Texas western swing. Perhaps best known for his fiddle classic "Cotton-Eyed Joe," Hofner also is believed to be responsible for incorporating the polka into western swing. The Patek family of Shiner, Texas, also has maintained one of the state's most enduring and popular Czech bands for several generations. Each year, Czech celebrations still are held throughout

Texas—including the "Prazka Prout" in Praha, the Czech folk festival in Shiner, and the National Polka Festival in Ennis—and Czech music still can be heard on a variety of radio stations throughout Central Texas.[57]

≈ **French Music in Texas** ≈

Although several groups of French-speaking immigrants have settled in Texas, the two best-known styles of Francophone music in the Southwest are zydeco and Cajun. Both of these musical forms reflect the unique blending of ethnic cultural traditions in the region. France began exploring the Texas-Louisiana coastline in 1682 but did not establish a permanent presence in the area until 1718, when it founded New Orleans at the mouth of the Mississippi River. New Orleans soon became the gateway for commerce along the Mississippi River, which connected the fertile farmlands of the Upper Midwest to the Atlantic Ocean via the Gulf of Mexico. The original French settlers in New Orleans brought with them their art, music, literature, and cuisine. Many also brought black slaves. These slaves, who came from a variety of backgrounds and spoke a number of different dialects, eventually developed a common "patois," or amalgamation of French and their own native languages.[58]

By the time the United States bought New Orleans and the Louisiana Territory in the 1803 Louisiana Purchase, the descendants of these slaves, many of whom had gained their freedom under French rule, were scattered throughout southwestern Louisiana. During the mid-1800s, more and more of these French-speaking blacks moved westward into Texas seeking greater economic opportunity through farming, ranching, and many other trades. When the United States abolished slavery in 1865, another wave of Francophone African Americans crossed the Sabine River into Texas. As World War II brought a boom in the Texas petroleum and petrochemical industries, thousands more relocated along the upper Texas Gulf Coast to fill the growing demand for workers.[59]

Since first arriving in the eighteenth century, these black slaves and their descendants had combined African and French musical traditions, along with blues, gospel, and a variety of other African American musical forms. By the 1940s, the mixing of blues, Cajun, and other French and African American influences within the French-speaking black culture of East Texas and Southwest Louisiana had matured fully into what record companies began to market as "zydeco," a word derived from the French term "Les Haricots," or snap beans. Houston was, and still is, home to some of the most influential zydeco artists, as well as some of the earliest commercial recordings ever made of zydeco.[60]

Clifton Chenier, generally considered the "King of Zydeco," brought the music to national prominence during the post–World War II era. Although born in Louisiana, he spent much of his adult life in the Houston area. Clifton, and his brother Cleveland, combined blues, Cajun, accordion, and guitar with a strong dance rhythm and lyrics in both French and English. They also fashioned a special metal washboard that could be strapped across the chest and strummed with metal thimbles or spoons in order to produce a sharp, staccato rhythm. The Chenier brothers helped define and popularize zydeco as an up-tempo dance music that blended a variety of musical styles drawn from African, French, and Anglo sources.[61] Zydeco remains quite popular in East Texas and Louisiana, where some zydeco bands now are incorporating urban black rap and hip hop into their sound.[62]

Cajuns are another important French-speaking group who have left a distinct musical imprint on the Southwest. The word "Cajun" is derived from the French term "Acadian," meaning a person from the Acadia region of eastern Canada. Their ancestors, mainly from northern France where their musical heritage included both French and Celtic traditions, began settling in Canada as early as 1605. However, following more than a century of war with Great Britain, the British forced France to cede Acadia and the rest of French Canada under the 1713 Treaty of Utrecht. After the Acadians refused to pledge their loyalty to Great Britain, the British eventually expelled about 8,000 of them. Many Acadians fled to New Orleans, but authorities there feared these uprooted French settlers might become a burden to the city. So, they redirected the Acadians toward the sparsely populated swamps and bayous of southwestern Louisiana. In this remote area, the Acadians, or "Cajuns," as some came to call them, rarely encountered anyone else besides local blacks and Indians. This relative isolation helped the Cajuns preserve a good deal of their cultural heritage well into the twentieth century.[63]

By the early twentieth century, thousands of Cajuns had moved from Louisiana into East Texas to work in the lumber camps, rice fields, or burgeoning petrochemical industry. Cajuns kept their musical culture alive through public celebrations, such as the traditional Saturday night dance held in nearly every Cajun community. Because the small children often were placed in a separate room to sleep while the teenagers and adults danced the night away, these celebrations came to be known as "fais dodo," a French term for lullaby. Eventually, Cajun music began to mingle with western swing, honky-tonk, blues, and other musical styles of the Southwest, further broadening the entire spectrum of Texas music.[64]

Although Cajun music originated in Louisiana, Texas musicians have played an important role in the development of Cajun music. For example, "Corrine, Corrina," now considered a Cajun standard, probably was originally an African American blues song. In the 1930s, it was adapted to western swing by Bob Wills, and, from there, worked its way into the standard Cajun repertoire, changing slightly with each transformation.[65] Following World War II, Cajun music continued to evolve in the hands of Texas musicians. Harry Choates, a Houston fiddler of German-Czech ancestry, helped revitalize Cajun music when he recorded the old Cajun song "Jole Blon," giving it an up-tempo western swing beat. It became a huge hit on the national charts, and, country bands across the United States and Canada began adding this and other Cajun tunes to their repertoire.[66]

## Anglo American Music in Texas

Although no single ethnic group can claim to have created an entire musical genre by itself, the Anglo American musical heritage in Texas is, perhaps, best represented by the development of country music. Rooted in the folk music of the British Isles, country has been dramatically influenced by other ethnic forms of music, including African, Mexican, German, French, Czech, and others. As with all other forms of music, country also has been affected by the social, political, and economic forces that have shaped the lives of its listeners. Some of the most influential country artists have come from Texas, and, the unique cultural environment of the Southwest has given birth to some of the most interesting and important genres of country music in history.[67] As large numbers of predominantly Anglo Irish settlers moved from the Deep South into the newly formed Republic of Texas after 1836, they brought with them their traditional folk music. From the time Texas joined the United States in 1845 until the end of the nineteenth century, thousands more land-hungry southerners poured into the state. This massive migration of primarily English-speaking Americans during the nineteenth century brought into Texas an Anglo culture that would absorb a variety of other ethnic influences.[68]

The great cattle drives of the late 1800s had a tremendous impact on the economy and culture of Texas. In addition to bringing dramatic economic and demographic growth, the cattle drives helped make the cowboy an internationally recognized icon of Texas culture. Although he owes much of his prominence in Texas folklore to twentieth-century romance novels and Hollywood movies, the cowboy has played an important role in shaping Texas music.[69] White cowboys drew from the traditional English folk songs they knew, but they also absorbed musical and lyrical influences from the many Hispanic and black cowboys with whom they worked.[70] Cowboys also were influenced by the popular music of their day. Although we might imagine the cowboy as a lone, romantic figure living in near isolation on the prairie, most had access to the traveling musical shows that traversed the South and Southwest. Such traveling shows mixed traditional western songs with tunes from professional songwriters, many of whom had never been out west. Consequently, "cowboy" music included both authentic songs of the working ranch hand and commercially produced tunes written by songwriters who had little or no actual experience as cowboys.[71]

The emergence of radio in the 1920s dramatically changed country music, making it more accessible nationally and increasing its viability as a marketable commodity. Atlanta's WSB radio was probably the first to broadcast country music in 1922. WBAP in Fort Worth was the first to host a "barn dance" in 1923. This format proved so popular that other stations soon copied it, including Nashville's 1925 WSM debut of the "Grand Ole Opry." Radio brought uniformity to what had been a patchwork of country music styles scattered throughout the South and Southwest and helped create a national market for country music. In 1924, Vernon Dalhart, born Marion Try Slaughter II in Jefferson, Texas, recorded the "Wreck of the Old 97," which sold millions of copies and awakened record companies to the commercial potential of country music. Houstonian Carl Sprague's 1925 song "When the Work's All Done This Fall" was a big enough hit for New York's Victor Records label to release an additional twenty-seven songs by Sprague and expand its catalog to include several other cowboy singers.[72]

Hollywood movies also helped popularize country music. The first singing cowboy from Texas to appear on the silver screen was Ken Maynard in the 1930 film *Songs of the Saddle*. Orvon Gene Autry, born in

Tioga, Texas, in 1907, landed a small part in another Maynard film, *Old Santa Fe*. Autry soon became the first Hollywood cowboy superstar, featured in more than one hundred movies as "the Singing Cowboy." The American public's fascination with the romantic image of the crooning cowboy inspired several studios to find their own singing western stars, which would come to include Texans Rex Allen, Dale Evans, and Woodward Maurice "Tex" Ritter. Although born and raised in Mississippi, Jimmie Rodgers spent the final years of his life in Central Texas. Long intrigued by the music and culture of the Texas cowboy, Rodgers blended his southern country music roots with the music of the western cowboys and became one of the most widely imitated singer-songwriters in American musical history.[73]

One of the most important developments in American music during the 1930s and 1940s, the emergence of western swing, took place in Texas and Oklahoma. Western swing, which was a blend of country, jazz, blues, ragtime, polkas, schottisches, and other musical styles, is a dramatic example of how various ethnic influences mixed and mingled in the unique cultural environment of Texas. James Robert "Bob" Wills, a young barber from Turkey, Texas, who moved to Fort Worth in 1929 to become an entertainer, was the leading architect of western swing.[74] As an amateur fiddler in Turkey, Wills was steeped in traditional country music, but he also absorbed a variety of other ethnic musical influences as he grew up. In Fort Worth, Wills found work on radio and in blackface minstrel shows, where he honed his diverse musical skills.[75]

In 1931, Wills formed the Light Crust Doughboys with the other leading pioneer of western swing, vocalist Milton Brown. The Doughboys demonstrated remarkable musical versatility, switching easily from a slow country ballad to a swinging dixieland jazz number. They mixed blues, pop, mariachi, swing, and ragtime with traditional fiddle breakdowns to create one of the most eclectic genres of music ever to achieve national popularity.[76] This diverse repertoire was due partly to Wills's and the other band members' genuine love for a variety of ethnic musical influences. For example, several of the musicians who played with Wills, such as Marvin "Smokey" Montgomery and John "Knocky" Parker, frequented the Dallas neighborhood of Deep Ellum to jam with black jazz musicians. These white artists took what they learned in Deep Ellum and incorporated it into what would become western swing.[77] However, this impressive musical diversity also was, in part, a result of local radio stations and dance halls insisting that performers have a broad repertoire of songs in order to appeal to the largest possible audience. In the depths of the Great Depression, it seems, musicians had to be versatile and able to provide their employers with the maximum in entertainment value in order to remain employed.[78] Wills went on to form Bob Wills and His Texas Playboys, who had a long string of hits, appeared in eight movies, and toured the United States almost continuously until World War II, when the band broke up. Wills died in 1975, but he was a major influence on younger country artists, such as Merle Haggard, Hank Thompson, Willie Nelson, George Strait, Clint Black, Asleep at the Wheel, and countless others.[79]

During the mid-1940s, Texas helped spawn yet another important genre of country music known as "honky-tonk." The honky-tonk style mirrored dramatic changes taking place in post–World War II American society, as large numbers of traditionally agrarian white workers migrated into the cities and faced a new set of challenges, including urbanization, industrialization, and changing social mores. Country always had been primarily a working-class genre of music, but honky-tonk focused on aspects of the blue-collar lifestyle that earlier country music avoided, such as alcoholism, adultery, domestic violence, and depression. Honky-tonk also signaled a dramatic change in the commercial direction of country music. Whereas western swing borrowed the jazz technique of improvisation and extended experimental "jam sessions," honky-tonk songs typically were tightly scripted, three-minute jukebox hits designed to maximize record sales.[80]

Ernest Tubb, born near Crisp, Texas, in 1914, was a pioneer of the honky-tonk sound with hits such as "Walking the Floor Over You." In 1947, Tubb became one of the first country singers to perform at Carnegie Hall in New York City. Hank Thompson, from Waco, was a protégé of Bob Wills. With his Brazos Valley Boys, Thompson took western swing and the traditional Texas two-step and incorporated themes of hard drinking and wild living to produce such hits as "The Wild Side of Life" and "A Six Pack to Go." Other important honky-tonk artists from Texas include Floyd Tillman with "Slippin' Around," Lefty Frizzell with "If You've Got the Money, I've Got the Time" and "That's the Way Love Goes," George Jones with "The Race is On" and "White Lightnin'," Jim Reeves with "He'll Have to Go," and Ray Price with "Crazy Arms" and "Please Release Me." Price's band, the Cherokee Cowboys, also provided a training ground for future Texas country stars, such as Willie Nelson, Johnny Paycheck, and Roger Miller. Alvis Edgar Owens, Jr., more commonly known as "Buck" Owens, from Sherman, Texas, moved to Arizona and then to California during the Great Depression.

Along with Merle Haggard, Owens helped start what came to be known as the "Bakersfield" sound, which influenced artists ranging from the Eagles to Dwight Yoakam. Owens even had one of his songs, "Act Naturally," recorded by the Beatles. These honky-tonk artists helped set the stage for a proliferation of Texas musicians who would continue to bring important changes to country music throughout the remainder of the twentieth century.[81]

### Rock and Roll

Although this chapter focuses on the roots of Texas music up until the mid-twentieth century, it is important to acknowledge at least briefly the importance of early rock and roll as a reflection of dramatic social changes that took place in American society after World War II. Rock and roll is an amalgamation of blues, jazz, swing, folk, rhythm and blues, country, and other musical forms. With increasing pressure on American youth to conform during the early cold war years of the mid-1940s, many teenagers rebelled in a variety of ways, including through music. Texas rock and roll pioneers, such as Buddy Holly and Roy Orbison, combined their musical backgrounds in country with pop and rhythm and blues to help fashion rock and roll into a powerful force that tapped into the restless energy and repressed sexuality of American youth. Other Texans—including J. P. "The Big Bopper" Richardson, Janis Joplin, Doug Sahm, John Denver, Don Henley, ZZ Top, and others—followed, helping Texas to play, once again, a leading role in forging this new genre of music.[82]

Whether conjunto, Tejano, blues, gospel, ragtime, jazz, Cajun, zydeco, polka, country, or rock and roll, music has been an important means of cultural expression for all ethnic communities in Texas. With a unique history and culture, Texans have created a rich and diverse musical heritage that reflects the complexity of their lives, and, in turn, has helped shape mainstream American music.

### Notes

1. For the most complete encyclopedic listing of Texas musicians, musical organizations, and musical events, see the *Handbook of Texas Music*, published jointly by the Texas State Historical Association, the Texas Music Office/Office

of the Governor, and the Center for Texas Music History at Southwest Texas State University, forthcoming in 2003.

2. Manuel Peña, *Música Tejana: The Cultural Economy of Artistic Transformation* (College Station: Texas A&M University Press, 1999), pp. 3–24. Although I agree with Peña's theory of "organic" versus "superorganic" forms of music, I do not believe that he adequately acknowledges the fact that music that is produced primarily for commercial purposes still resonates in some meaningful way with its audience and, therefore, is capable of communicating important cultural information.

3. David La Vere, *Life Among the Texas Indians: The W.P.A. Narratives* (College Station: Texas A&M University Press, 1998), pp. 4–11; Robert A. Calvert and Arnoldo De León, *The History of Texas* (Arlington Heights, Ill.: Harlan Davidson, Inc., 1990), pp. 3–6.

4. Cecile Elkins Carter, *Caddo Indians: Where We Come From* (Norman: University of Oklahoma Press, 1995), pp. 101–24; Thomas F. Schilz, *Lipan Apaches in Texas* (El Paso: Texas Western Press/ University of Texas at El Paso, 1987), pp. 19–39.

5. Jonathan B. Hook, *The Alabama-Coushatta Indians* (College Station: Texas A&M University Press, 1997), pp. 82–98; "Our Native Spirit," booklet (Austin: Texas Music Museum, 1998), p. 3.

6. Reginald and Gladys Laubin, *Indian Dances of North America: Their Importance to Indian Life* (Norman: University of Oklahoma Press, 1977); La Vere, *Life Among the Texas Indians,* pp. 131–139.

7. "Our Native Spirit," p. 4.

8. Carter, *Caddo Indians,* pp. 36–37, 196–98.

9. Mildred P. Mayhall, *The Kiowas* (Norman: University of Oklahoma Press, 1971), pp. 114, 312–13.

10. Kevin Mulroy, *Freedom on the Border: The Seminole Maroons in Florida, the Indian Territory, Coahuila, and Texas* (Lubbock: Texas Tech University Press, 1993), pp. 22–23, 105, 177–79.

11. Dianna Everett, *The Texas Cherokees: A People Between Two Fires, 1819–1840* (Norman: University of Oklahoma Press, 1990), p. 54.

12. "Our Native Spirit," p. 3.

13. Ibid., pp. 8–10.

14. Hook, *The Alabama-Coushatta Indians,* pp. 104–107; "Our Native Spirit," pp. 9–11. For more information on Native Americans and their musical heritage, visit the following websites: www.isjunction.com/places/indians.htm, www.clevernet/cam/cyberindians.htm, www.texasindians.com, www.indians.org.

15. Peña, *Música Tejana,* p. xi. For a broader overview of Texas Mexican culture and music, see "Música Tejana: History and Development of Tejano Music" (booklet published by the Texas Music Museum, Austin, 1996) and *The Mexican Texans* (San Antonio: University of Texas Institute of Texan Cultures at San Antonio, 1986). For some of the most extensive collections of primary

archives relating to música tejana, see the following at the Center for American History at the University of Texas at Austin: UT Folklore Center Archives, Allan Turner Oral History Collection, and the Chris Strachwitz Collection.

16. For a good overview of Texas Mexican music, see Guadalupe San Miguel, Jr., "Música Tejana: Nuestra Música," *Journal of Texas Music History* 1, no. 1 (spring, 2001): 24–35.

17. Robert Stevenson, *Music in Mexico* (New York: Crowell Publishers, 1971) provides one of the most thorough accounts of music in colonial Mexico; José R. Reyna, "Notes on Tejano Music," *Aztlán: International Journal of Chicano Studies Research* 13, nos. 1–2 (spring and fall, 1982): 82–83. See also Manuel Peña, *The Texas-Mexican Conjunto: History of a Working-Class Music* (Austin: University of Texas Press, 1985), pp. 20–24.

18. An older yet still helpful source of information on Texas Mexican folk culture is Mody C. Boatright, *Mexican Border Ballads and Other Lore* (Dallas: Southern Methodist University Press, 1967).

19. These so-called "ballad communities" are quite common among populations with low rates of literacy. For example, traveling troubadours in Medieval Europe carried news and entertainment from place to place in the form of ballads. African American slaves, who were forbidden to learn to read or write, built on ancient African traditions of oral history and ballads to transmit information and culture. Cowboys in the American West often relied on ballads to relay information or celebrate folklore.

20. John Holmes McDowell, "The Corridos of Greater Mexico as Discourse, Music, and Event," *And Other Neighborly Names: Social Process and Cultural Image in Texas Folklore,* edited by Richard Bauman and Roger D. Abrahams (Austin: University of Texas Press, 1981), pp. 45–75. Corridos often are punctuated by "gritos" or shouts from the audience. Because audience members often already know the basic storyline, this is a way of involving themselves in the telling of the tale, perhaps in a similar vein to African American "call and response."

21. For a good discussion of Texas Mexican folksongs and the variety of themes they included, see Américo Paredes, *A Texas-Mexican Cancionero: Folksongs of the Lower Border* (Urbana: University of Illinois Press, 1976).

22. See Américo Paredes, *With His Pistol In His Hand* (Austin: University of Texas Press, 1976), for the most complete discussion of the facts and folklore surrounding Gregorio Cortez.

23. Peña, *Música Tejana,* pp. 50–69. Peña says corridos and rancheras also reflect many Tejanos' difficult transition from a pre-capitalist, agrarian environment to an increasingly capitalist, urban existence. For example, the positive themes in these songs usually center on a simple, rural life, in which people are honest and hard working. By contrast, the negative themes seem to reflect a new mindset in which greedy people, often gringos or "bad" women, cannot be trusted and will take advantage of others in any way possible. Of course, such

songs are highly idealized, because, in a pre-capitalist society, people also could be greedy and dishonest.

24. Peña, *The Texas-Mexican Conjunto,* pp. 29–36; Peña, *Música Tejana,* pp. 27–34; Rick Koster, *Texas Music* (New York: St. Martin's Press, 1998), p. 214; Reyna, "Notes on Tejano Music," pp. 82–85. Scholars disagree as to how the accordion made its way into Texas Mexican folk music, but, as many other ethnic groups discovered, the accordion was the ideal instrument in terms of being highly portable, relatively inexpensive, and capable of filling a large room with as much sound as otherwise might require several instruments to produce. Reyna and Peña acknowledge at least two possible scenarios. Either German immigrants introduced the accordion into Mexico during the mid-1800s, and then the instrument was brought northward into Texas by traveling musicians, or, German and Czech immigrants into Texas at around the same time might have been the first to bring the accordion to Texas Mexican musicians.

25. Manuel Peña, "The Emergence of Conjunto Music, 1935–1955," *And Other Neighborly Names: Social Process and Cultural Image in Texas Folklore,* pp. 281–99. There is still a good deal of debate over which came first, conjunto in Texas or its closely related cousin norteño in Northern Mexico. The overall sound, instrumentation, and dance styles are very similar, and both are generally considered "rural, peasant" music. If norteño developed first, it probably was carried northward into Texas by migrant workers or along trade routes between Monterrey, Mexico, and South Texas. If conjunto originated first, then it is a clear example of how immigrant groups sometimes develop new cultural traditions, which then "ripple back" to the old country and influence culture there.

26. Koster, *Texas Music,* p. 215. Jimenez's two sons, Santiago Jr., and Leonardo "Flaco," have continued playing conjunto long after their father's death in 1984. Santiago, Jr., has worked to preserve and promote a more traditional conjunto style, while the younger Flaco's playing has evolved in a less traditional direction. He has recorded on his own and with such groups as the Grammy Award–winning Texas Tornados, which included Doug Sahm, Freddy Fender, and Augie Myers.

27. Carlos B. Gil, "Lydia Mendoza: Houstonian and First Lady of Mexican American Song," *Houston Review* 3 (summer, 1981): 249–57. See also Lydia Mendoza, *Lydia Mendoza: A Family Autobiography,* compiled by Chris Strachwitz (Houston: Arte Publico Press, 1993), and Louis Barbash and Frederick P. Close, "Lydia Mendoza: The Voice of the People," *Texas Humanist* 6 (Nov.–Dec., 1983).

28. Peña, "The Emergence of Conjunto Music," pp. 286–94.

29. Ramiro Burr, *The Billboard Guide to Tejano and Regional Mexican Music* (New York: Billboard Books, 1999), pp. 214–15; Peña, *The Texas-Mexican Conjunto,* pp. 8–15.

30. Peña, *Música Tejana,* pp. 21–22.

31. Ibid., pp. 118–217; Burr, *The Billboard Guide to Tejano and Regional*

*Mexican Music,* pp. 132–33; Little Joe Hernandez, a pioneer of "La Onda Chicana," is generally considered the father of Tejano music. Born in Temple, Texas, in 1941, he played in rock-and-roll bands as a teenager but later began mixing those influences with the traditional conjunto sounds with which he had been raised. His band, Little Joe y La Familia, blended a variety of styles including conjunto, blues, and rock and roll. His bilingual songs helped bridge the gap between Spanish and non-Spanish-speaking crowds, introducing many non-Hispanics to Mexican American musical traditions for the first time. Hernandez's growing awareness of his ethnic heritage, along with his celebration of a bilingual culture, reflected the increasing sense of ethnic pride and political activism of many young Mexican Americans involved in "La Onda Chicana." In 1992, Hernandez won the first Grammy Award ever given to a Tejano artist for his 1991 album *Dies y Séis de Septiembre.*

32. For a good, brief overview of African American music in Texas, see "Rags to Rap: African-American Contributions to Texas Music" (booklet published by the Texas Music Museum, Austin, 1997). For some of the most extensive collections of primary archives relating to African American music in Texas, see the following at the Center for American History, University of Texas at Austin: Texas Music Collection, UT Folklore Center Archives, John A. Lomax Family Papers, Mance Lipscomb–Glen Alyn Collection, Folk Music Collection, Allan Turner Oral History Collection, William A. Owens Collection, Texas Folklife Resources Collection, and Austin Blues Family Tree Video Collection.

33. See Calvert and De León, *The History of Texas,* pp. 35, 54–55, and 59–60, for a discussion of early black migration into Texas. See also Dave Oliphant, "Eddie Durham and the Texas Contribution to Jazz History," *Southwestern Historical Quarterly* 96, no. 4 (Apr., 1993): 491–525. Oliphant suggests that, as blacks migrated out of the Deep South into Texas, they faced a less rigidly structured system of discrimination and a more ethnically fluid society, in which they were more free to mingle with other ethnic groups. Consequently, blacks in Texas were exposed to a more ethnically diverse music scene, which included a rich mixture of Mexican, German, Czech, French, Polish, Anglo, Irish, and other influences; William A. Owens, *Tell Me a Story, Sing Me a Song: A Texas Chronicle* (Austin: University of Texas Press, 1983), pp. 12–16. Owens agrees that greater cross-pollination of ethnic music occurred in the Southwest than in the Deep South.

34. Neil Foley, *The White Scourge: Mexicans, Blacks, and Poor Whites in Texas Cotton Culture* (Berkeley: University of California Press, 1997), pp. 1, 64–74, 118–40. Foley provides the most thorough examination of Central Texas blacks in the context of the state's multiracial makeup and its transition from an almost exclusively agrarian economy to a more diverse, industrial one.

35. Alan B. Govenar and Jaye F. Brakefield, *Deep Ellum and Central Track: Where the Black and White Worlds of Dallas Converged* (Denton: University of North Texas Press, 1998), pp. 105–106; Koster, *Texas Music,* pp. 259–61.

36. Dave Oliphant, *Texan Jazz* (Austin: University of Texas Press, 1996),

p. 36; Hettie Jones, *Big Star Fallin' Mama: Five Women in Black Music* (New York: Viking Press, 1974), pp. 10–11.

37. See Bill Malone, *Country Music USA* (Austin: University of Texas Press, 1985), pp. 27–30, 80–81. For a discussion of the early development of blues and how it influenced country music. Malone's book still offers the most thorough examination available of the evolution of country and country and western music in Texas and the American South. See also Sheldon Harris, *The Blues Who's Who: A Biographical Dictionary of Blues Singers* (New York: Da Capo Press, 1989) and Bruce Jackson, *Wake Up Dead Man: Afro-American Work Songs of Texas Prisons* (Cambridge: Harvard University Press, 1972).

38. Govenar and Brakefield, *Deep Ellum,* pp. 61–79; Koster, *Texas Music,* pp. 143–44.

39. Charles Wolfe and Kip Lornell, *The Life and Legend of Leadbelly* (New York: HarperCollins Publishers, 1992), pp. 97–99, 200–10.

40. Benjamin Filene, "Our Singing Country: John and Alan Lomax, Leadbelly, and the Construction of the American Past," *American Quarterly* 43, no. 4 (Dec., 1991): 602–24. Filene argues that, as important as they were in helping preserve the music of Lead Belly and many other more obscure musicians, in some cases, the Lomaxes were guilty of questionable practices in their selection of artists and material. For example, at times, they tried to "sanitize" Lead Belly's song lyrics for white audiences, or, they manipulated musicians into performing under artificial conditions in order to obtain recordings the Lomaxes considered appropriate for their purposes. See also Koster, *Texas Music,* pp. 144–45; Govenar and Brakefield, *Deep Ellum,* pp. 63–65; Charles Wolfe and Kip Lornell, *The Life and Legend of Leadbelly;* and the John Lomax Collection at the Center for American History at the University of Texas at Austin.

41. Mack McCormick, "Mance Lipscomb: Texas Sharecropper and Songster," *American Folk Music Occasional, Berkeley, California,* no. 1 (1964): 61–73; Govenar and Brakefield, *Deep Ellum,* p. 66; Koster, *Texas Music,* pp. 146–47; Glen Alyn, *I Say Me For a Parable: The Oral Autobiography of Mance Lipscomb, Texas Bluesman,* as told to and compiled by Glen Alyn (New York: W. W. Norton and Company, 1993).

42. Govenar and Brakefield, *Deep Ellum,* p. 109.

43. Oliphant, *Texan Jazz,* pp. 54–62; Koster, *Texas Music,* p. 150.

44. Helen Oakley Dance, *Stormy Monday: The T-Bone Walker Story* (New York: Da Capo Press, 1987); Govenar and Brakefield, *Deep Ellum,* pp. 67–69, 125, 130; Koster, *Texas Music,* pp. 152–54.

45. Sarah Ann West, *Deep Down Hard Blues: A Tribute to Lightnin' Hopkins* (Lawrenceville, Va.: Brunswick Publishing Corporation, 1995); Koster, *Texas Music,* pp. 163–64.

46. For a good overview of Joplin's life and career, see Edward A. Berlin, *King of Ragtime: Scott Joplin and His Era* (New York: Oxford University Press, 1994); Oliphant, *Texan Jazz,* pp. 10–35; Koster, *Texas Music,* pp. 281–83.

47. Koster, *Texas Music,* pp. 287–88; Oliphant, *Texan Jazz,* pp. 195–203. Most sources indicate that Christian was born in Dallas; however, on page 121 of their book *Deep Ellum and Central Track,* Govenar and Brakefield cite Bonham, Texas, northeast of Dallas, as Christian's birthplace.

48. Oliphant, "Eddie Durham and the Texas Contribution to Jazz History."

49. For a detailed discussion of Texas musicians and "bebop" music, see Dave Oliphant, "Texas Bebop Messengers to the World: Kenny Dorham and Leo Wright," *Journal of Texas Music History* 1, no. 1 (spring, 2001): 15–23.

50. Koster, *Texas Music,* pp. 281–91; John Litweiler, *Ornette Coleman: A Harmolodic Life* (New York: William Morrow, 1992); Oliphant, *Texan Jazz,* pp. 135–39, 225–33, 307–308.

51. For a good overview of German history, see Mary Fulbrook, *A Concise History of Germany* (Cambridge, England: Cambridge University Press, 1990). For a thorough discussion of the social, political, and economic turmoil that helped fuel the massive nineteenth-century German *Auswanderung,* or exodus, see Mack Walker, *Germany and the Emigration, 1816–1885* (Cambridge: Harvard University Press, 1964). Walker argues that most German immigrants coming to the United States during the mid-1800s did not seek to build a new, more modern society in America. Instead, he contends, they actually sought to preserve traditional ways, which they believed were being undermined by German modernization. Most of these social organizations established by German immigrants in Texas were devoted to preserving and promoting traditional German culture.

52. For a good, brief overview of German culture and music in Texas, see "Musikfest: German Contributions to Texas Music," (booklet published by the Texas Music Museum, Austin, 1992). For a more in-depth discussion of Texas German culture, see *German Culture in Texas: A Free Earth; Essays from the 1978 Southwest Symposium,* edited by Glen E. Lich and Dona B. Reeves (Boston: Twayne Publishers, 1980). Also helpful is *The German Texans* (booklet published by the University of Texas Institute of Texan Cultures at San Antonio, 1987).

53. Rudolph L. Biesele, *The History of the German Settlements in Texas* (San Marcos, Tex.: German-Texan Heritage Society, 1987), pp. 222–23; Lota M. Spell, "The Early German Contribution to Music in Texas," *The American-German Review* 12, no. 4 (Apr., 1946): 8–10.

54. Lich and Reeves, *German Culture in Texas,* pp. 157–88.

55. Owens, *Tell Me a Story, Sing Me a Song,* pp. 193–208. See also the Carl Venth Papers at the Center for American History, University of Texas at Austin, for an example of a German Texan composer who incorporated Texas themes into his musical compositions.

56. *The Czech Texans* (booklet published by the University of Texas Institute of Texan Cultures at San Antonio, 1983), pp. 3–10. See also Clinton Machann and James W. Mendl, *Krasna Amerika: A Study of the Texas Czechs,*

*1851–1939* (Austin: Eakin Press, 1983) and Victor Greene, *A Passion for Polka: Old-Time Ethnic Music in America* (Berkeley: University of California Press, 1992).

57. Owens, *Tell Me a Story, Sing Me a Song,* pp. 209–19; *The Czech Texans,* pp. 7–22; Koster, *Texas Music,* pp. 229–30; *The Harmony Illustrated Encyclopedia of Country Music* (New York: Salamander Books, 1986), p. 79; "Muziky, Muziky: Czech Contributions to Texas Music" (booklet published by the Texas Music Museum, Austin, 1995); Roger H. Kolar, *Early Czech Dance Halls in Texas* (Austin: Roger H. Kolar, 1975). At the Center for American History, University of Texas at Austin, see the Allan Turner Oral History Collection, the Kermit Baca Interview, and the Adolph Hofner Recordings.

58. Calvert and De León, *The History of Texas,* pp. 17–21; "The Vieux Carré," on The Official City of New Orleans Website, www.new-orleans.la.us/. See also the William A. Owens Collection at the Center for American History, University of Texas at Austin.

59. Ira Berlin, *Slaves Without Masters: The Free Negro in the Antebellum South* (New York: Pantheon Books, 1975), pp. 109–28, and Leonard Curry, *The Free Black in Urban America, 1800–1850* (Chicago: University of Chicago Press, 1981), pp. 138–40. See also *The French Texans* (booklet published by the University of Texas Institute of Texan Cultures at San Antonio, 1973).

60. Chris Strachwitz, "Zydeco Music, i.e., French Blues," *The American Folk Music Occasional,* edited by Chris Strachwitz and Pete Welding (New York: Oak Publications, 1970), pp. 22–24. See also Michael Tisserand, *The Kingdom of Zydeco* (New York: Arcade Publishing, 1998), pp. 9–21. The most plausible explanation as to how snap beans came to be associated with this particular style of music seems to be that it is in reference to an older song popular among French-speaking blacks entitled "Les Haricots Sont Pas Salés" ("The Snap Beans Are Not Salty"), in which the singer complains that he cannot afford salt meat to flavor his snap beans.

61. Strachwitz, "Zydeco Music, i.e., French Blues," pp. 22–29.

62. Shane K. Bernard, *Swamp Pop: Cajun and Creole Rhythm and Blues* ( Jackson: University Press of Mississippi, 1996), pp. 75–114.

63. See both Paul Tate, "The Cajuns of Louisiana," pp. 8–10, and Harry Oster, "The Louisiana Acadians," *The American Folk Music Occasional,* pp. 18–21.

64. Oster, "The Louisiana Acadians," pp. 20–21. For a good discussion of Cajun music and its many permutations, see Barry Jean Ancelet, *The Makers of Cajun Music* (Austin: University of Texas Press, 1984).

65. Owens, *Tell Me a Story, Sing Me a Song,* pp. 127–28.

66. Chris Strachwitz, "Cajun Country," *The American Folk Music Occasional,* pp. 13–17.

67. From the Center for American History, University of Texas at Austin, see the Texas Music Collection, University of Texas Folklore Center Archives,

John A. Lomax Family Papers, Bill Boyd Papers, Townsend Miller Collection, Marvin Montgomery/Light Crust Doughboys Collection, Allan Turner Oral History Collection, and the William A. Owens Collection.

68. Malone, *Country Music USA,* pp. 5–20.

69. Joe Carr and Alan Munde, *Prairie Nights to Neon Lights: The Story of Country Music in West Texas* (Lubbock: Texas Tech University Press, 1995), pp. 8–31; Archie Green, "Austin's Cosmic Cowboys: Words in Collision," in *And Other Neighborly Names: Social Process and Cultural Image in Texas Folklore,* pp. 153–62.

70. For a good sampling of traditional Texas folk and country songs, see Francis E. Abernethy, *Singin' Texas* (Dallas: E-Heart Press, 1983).

71. Owens, *Tell Me a Story, Sing Me a Song,* p. 106. One of the best examples of this gray area between traditional cowboy folksongs and commercially written, western-themed music is the classic "Home on the Range." Professional Texas songwriter David Guion claims credit for having written the song, but some folklorists believe it is based largely on older cowboy ballads.

72. Malone, *Country Music USA,* pp. 36–37; Koster, *Texas Music,* pp. 4–9.

73. Koster, *Texas Music,* pp. 3–10; Malone, *Country Music USA,* pp. 79–102, 145–83. Malone says this public fascination with the romantic cowboy image reflected deeper social concerns. During the 1930s and 1940s, the United States accelerated its movement toward industrialization and urbanization and from isolationism to internationalism. Country music, and especially the romantic image of the lone cowboy, represented the more traditional lifestyle to which many Americans longed to return. Even though the image of the cowboy was manufactured in Hollywood, it seemed to help Americans reconcile their anxieties over relinquishing their agrarian past to an increasingly urbanized future; For more on Jimmie Rodgers, see Nolan Porterfield, *Jimmie Rodgers: The Life and Times of America's Blue Yodeler* (Urbana: University of Illinois Press, 1992).

74. For a personal view of the life and career of Wills, see Rosetta Wills, *The King of Western Swing: Bob Wills Remembered* (New York: Billboard Books, 1998). See also, Jean A. Boyd, *The Jazz of the Southwest: An Oral History of Western Swing* (Austin: University of Texas Press, 1998).

75. Charles R. Townsend, *San Antonio Rose: The Life and Music of Bob Wills* (Urbana: The University of Illinois Press, 1976), pp. 1–52; Duncan Mc Lean, *Lone Star Swing: On the Trail of Bob Wills and His Texas Playboys* (New York: W. W. Norton and Company, 1997), pp. 234–35.

76. Koster, *Texas Music,* pp. 11–16.

77. Govenar and Brakefield, *Deep Ellum,* pp. 138–63.

78. Mc Lean, *Lone Star Swing,* pp. 77–81. According to some of the musicians who played with Wills, they also had to have extensive song lists so they could play for hours to prevent dancers from stopping long enough to get into fistfights.

79. For a good collection of interviews with Texas singer-songwriters, including information about who influenced their music, see Kathleen Hudson, *Telling Stories, Writing Songs* (Austin: University of Texas Press, 2001).

80. See James Rice, *Texas Honky-Tonk Music* (Austin: Eakin Press, 1985), and Richard A. Peterson, *Creating Country Music: Fabricating Authenticity* (Chicago: University of Chicago Press, 1997).

81. Koster, *Texas Music,* pp. 20–31; "Waltz Across Texas: An Introduction to the Country and Western Music of Texas" (booklet published by the Texas Music Museum, Austin, 1991); Carr and Munde, *Prairie Nights to Neon Lights,* pp. 60–80.

82. For a brief overview of Texas rock and roll, see Koster, *Texas Music,* pp. 79–122. See also Philip Norman, *Rave On: The Biography of Buddy Holly* (New York: Simon and Schuster, 1996), and Ellis Amburn, *Dark Star: The Roy Orbison Story* (New York: Lyle Stewart, 1990). From the Center for American History, University of Texas at Austin, see the Huey P. Meaux Collection, Armadillo World Headquarters Archives, Soap Creek Saloon Archives, Tom Wright Collection, Eric Graham Video Collection, and the Robert N. Simmons Collection.

# 2

## Texan Jazz
### *1920–50*

### Dave Oliphant

Although the most prominent Texas jazz musicians have traditionally left the state for greater exposure in the urban centers of Kansas City, Chicago, New York, and Los Angeles, this should not obscure the fact that Texas has accounted for an impressive number of significant figures over the entire history of the music. Also important in terms of the state's contributions to jazz is evidence that its African American roots reach back in Texas to the music's earliest forms, including worksongs, chants, spirituals, gospel, blues, ragtime, and boogie-woogie. Indeed, all of these musical forms were known and performed in the state in the nineteenth or the early twentieth centuries.

In the case of ragtime and boogie-woogie, these highly influential piano styles are thought to have originated to some extent in East Texas. Texarkana produced Scott Joplin, considered the greatest of all ragtime composers, creator in 1899 of the "Maple Leaf Rag." Hersal Thomas of Houston was deemed a boogie-woogie prodigy from the early and mid-1920s.[1] The blues as well were something of an indigenous product of Texas, developed especially by such rural singer-guitarists as Blind Lemon Jefferson and Huddie Ledbetter (known as Lead Belly), who brought their country blues to the urban settings of Dallas and Houston. Jefferson in the 1920s was even billed as "The King of Country Blues." Female blues singers in Dallas and Houston also were active in the

1920s, including Sippie Wallace and Victoria Spivey. Even before these better-known vocal stars had recorded in the mid- and late 1920s, Fae Barnes of Hillsboro was the earliest Texas blues singer to be recorded, under the name of Maggie Jones, in New York City on July 26, 1923.

As to the rise of jazz in Texas, a number of musicians emerged from towns and cities throughout the state who eventually exerted a national impact on this American music. The first jazz recording was made in 1917 by the Original Dixieland Jazz Band, but jazz had been in existence a decade or more prior to this event, and some of its founding figures, such as Bunk Johnson, Sidney Bechet, Jelly Roll Morton, and Joe "King" Oliver, reportedly had ventured into Texas between 1904 and 1914.[2] The presence of these four jazzmen in Texas may well have stimulated a local interest in the music, and yet a major instrumentalist like Jack Teagarden of Vernon was playing jazz around 1921 without even knowing that it had a name. The white ODJB members and the four black men—Johnson, Bechet, Morton, and Oliver—who are now recognized as jazz masters, all were from Louisiana. Although Louisiana and Oklahoma figure prominently in the development of jazz, Texas is perhaps unique in having produced vital exponents of the music who represent every period and style in its history.

Jazz musicians in Texas unquestionably were aware of blues, ragtime, and boogie-woogie, because these forms of African American music could be heard in most every part of the state. But none of these forms was jazz as it is thought of today. That is, these musical forms were not played primarily with wind instruments (with the exception of ragtime bands and the jazz musicians who accompanied female blues singers), did not develop the contrast or harmonization of brass and reeds, did not emphasize improvisation as an essential feature of the form (although both blues and boogie-woogie did involve improvisation to a limited degree), did not normally include a rhythm section devoted to supporting and stimulating a band's sections and soloists, and did not create a sound and rhythmic drive that are identifiable as distinctively jazz (even though all three of the earlier forms did contribute to the creation of jazz's rhythms, structures, and tonal colors). Clearly jazz does owe much to earlier forms of African American music, and for this reason it is perhaps surprising to discover that certain jazz ensembles emerged in areas of Texas that are not generally associated with ragtime, blues, or boogie-woogie. This is the case with such groups as Gene Coy's Happy Black Aces of Amarillo and the Real Jazz Orchestra of Laredo, which were active as early as 1921 and the mid-1920s, respectively. Of course, jazz had by this time already spread around the world, as indicated by the fact that in Chile a group called The Royal Orchestra had formed in 1924 and that circa 1926 a recording was made in that South American country of a "shimmy" entitled "Y tenía un lunar (And She Had a Mole)."[3] In Houston in 1925, Fatty Martin's Orchestra also recorded a "shimmy" foxtrot entitled "End O' Main," on which composer Earl Church takes two fine muted trumpet breaks.[4] Pablo Garrido, the organizer in Chile of the Royal Orchestra, noted in an article published in 1935 that Chilean jazz musicians were influenced by Paul Whiteman's recordings, which had first appeared in 1920 with his "Whispering" and "Wang-Wang Blues." The Whiteman recordings represented something of a watered-down version of black jazz, while Gene Coy's Happy Black Aces of Amarillo were playing original tunes "built on the structure of the blues" and at tempos slower than were typical of the one- and two-step dances of the period.[5] Obviously the blues were fundamental even to a group located in an area known more for cattle ranching than for an African American musical form. This seems to reveal that even in Amarillo a black jazz group at the beginnings of the 1920s was performing in the blues mode that would be characteristic of most all Texas jazz musicians. This is especially true of the many black Texans who would have such a marked influence on the evolution of jazz.

White musicians in Texas, like their black counterparts, were playing jazz at least by 1920, and probably much earlier.[6] In 1922 "almost certainly the first jazz festival on the books" was held in Houston, where pianist Peck Kelley and his Bad Boys had been performing since 1921.[7] Trombonist Jack Teagarden, born in 1905, left his Vernon home in 1921 at age sixteen and joined his uncle's band in San Angelo. In that same year Teagarden moved on to San Antonio, where he played with Cotton Bailey's band at the Horn Palace, afterward working in Shreveport, Louisiana, before becoming a member of Kelley's Bad Boys in Houston.[8] Like his black colleagues, Teagarden had been affected by hearing the blues, in his case as sung by Bessie Smith, not on her recordings but in person in Galveston. The trombonist also heard spirituals as a boy and reported being able to sing along "with no trouble at all."[9] After touring the Southwest as far as California and into Mexico—first with R. J. Marin's Southern Trumpeters and then in 1924 with Doc Ross and his Jazz Bandits—Teagarden headed for New York City in the fall of 1927. As they say, the rest is history, for "Big T" revolutionized the role of the trombone in jazz through his recordings with any number of prominent groups in New York, from the orchestras of Roger Wolfe Kahn and Ben

Pollack to studio bands led by Red Nichols, Benny Goodman, and even Louis Armstrong.

Technique-wise, Teagarden was the most advanced player on his instrument. When he arrived in New York, he brought with him a smoothness of execution on the trombone that had not been seen or heard before. Not even trombonist Jimmy Harrison of the Fletcher Henderson Orchestra, who was simultaneously developing a similar technical facility, was in the same category with Teagarden, who had been advertised even five years before as "The South's Greatest Sensational Trombone Wonder."[10] Teagarden's advanced, blues-based conception has even been compared with the revolutionary melodic and harmonic developments of bebop as conceived by Charlie Parker in the 1940s. In terms of the sheer number of recordings, Teagarden's more than one thousand sides makes his discography "one of the most extensive in jazz, comparable to Louis Armstrong, Fats Waller, Duke Ellington, and Coleman Hawkins."[11] And as a vocalist, Teagarden has been considered the greatest white singer of the blues in the entire history of jazz.

Future research into the development of Teagarden's jazz artistry will be aided significantly by an archive of the jazzman's life and music, compiled assiduously by Joe Showler of Toronto, Canada. Working with Robert Gibbona and Stephen La Vere, Showler spent two years in producing a 121-minute documentary of Teagarden's career, entitled *It's Time for "T": The Story of Trombonist Jack Teagarden* (1996), which was shown in the spring of 2001 to interested viewers on the campus of the University of Texas at Austin. Teagarden's career spanned the period from 1921 to his death in 1964 and took him around the world to acclaim in Europe and the Far East. One particular segment of the Showler film is representative of the kinds of materials in the collector's archive that are unknown to most students of jazz: a radio series played by the Ben Pollack Orchestra for the Whiz antifreeze company of Canada.[12] On the classic dixieland number "That's a Plenty," both Jack and his trumpet-playing brother Charlie contribute the finest solos on the side. Jack's extended ride is filled with his trademark turns that no other trombonist of the period could quite duplicate. His improvisation begins with a held and then repeated note that swings with the greatest intensity. His virtuosity is exhibited through phrases that shift direction abruptly, even as he maintains a tremendous drive and phenomenal control. It is to be hoped that the Showler archive will eventually come to the trombonist's home state as a resource for the study of the history of jazz as it developed in Texas and in particular in the work of one of the music's major artists.

Charlie Teagarden, like his older brother Jack, also made a name for himself in the annals of jazz. As demonstrated by the Whiz radio program recording from 1930, Charlie was by that year already a full-fledged jazz trumpeter. In addition to recording with his brother as part of the Ben Pollack Orchestra, the Mills Merry Makers, and one of the many Five Pennies aggregations led by Red Nichols, Charlie also joined Jack in the Paul Whiteman Orchestra, in which both men were featured soloists during the mid- to late 1930s. Charlie Teagarden is said never to have taken a bad solo, and in the 1950s he was playing as well if not better than he had in the '30s when even then he could at times upstage his more famous sibling. This is true, for example, of Charlie's playing on *Jack Teagarden and His Band—1951, Live at the Royal Room, Hollywood,* another compact disc produced by Joe Showler.[13] One other member of the Teagarden family, Clois Lee, a drummer known as Cub, joined brother Jack in the orchestra he formed in 1939. Sister Norma, a pianist, also performed with her brothers on occasion, including the 1951 Royal Room appearance, at which even Helen "Mama" Teagarden was present as a guest pianist. Jazz was clearly a family affair with the Teagardens, as it was for many other Texas musicians, white and black, such as Eddie Durham and his cousins Allen Durham and Herschel Evans and brothers Budd and Keg Johnson. But before moving on to jazz musicians like these who made a name for themselves in the 1930s, it is instructive to mention a few others in the 1920s, black and white, who, though not in the same class historically with the Teagardens, lend additional insight into the early awareness of jazz by Texas musicians and their ability to create this type of music on a level comparable with—or at least imitative of—that of such legendary jazzmen as King Oliver, Louis Armstrong, and Bix Beiderbecke.

Like Scott Joplin, cornetist-trumpeter Lammar Wright was born in Texarkana but made his reputation in Missouri, where Wright was a key member of the Bennie Moten band. Recording in 1923—the first year that both King Oliver and Louis Armstrong were immortalized on wax—the Moten band cut two sides, "Crawdad Blues" and "Elephant Wobble," on which Wright performs with a cup mute after the manner of King Oliver. Because Wright was only sixteen at the time, and Oliver had been a major figure for a decade, it seems clear that Wright was aware of the King either from having heard him on riverboats or during the older musician's reported trips through Texas and Missouri. But even if Wright was influenced by Oliver, the younger musician could hold his own by comparison, especially in terms of a blues-inflected sound and style. Of Wright's playing on the 1923 "Crawdad Blues," one critic has declared, "It is doubtful if anything he has done since 1923 can surpass the beauty of the cornet work on this record; even the poor recording possible at this time cannot dim the immediacy of his searing, stabbing style."[14] Later, in 1929, Wright would record with the Missourians, a group that in the next year became the orchestra of singing star Cab Calloway. On the Calloway unit's recording of "Some of These Days," from December 23, 1930, Wright is the featured soloist on this side that critic Gunther Schuller has considered "amazing to this day for its hell-bent break-away tempo, upwards of 300 to the quarter-note beat . . . a staggering technical achievement . . . and . . . the fastest tempo achieved by any orchestra up to that time."[15] Wright remained with the Calloway organization until 1947, contributing throughout the 1930s a number of powerhouse solos in the King Oliver vein and serving throughout his years with Calloway as a strong section leader.

After King Oliver, the next great cornetist-trumpeter was Louis Armstrong, who many consider the most important figure in jazz history owing to his role in making the music primarily an art of the improvised solo. On June 28, 1928, Armstrong and pianist Earl "Fatha" Hines recorded King Oliver's tune, "West End Blues," and Armstrong's cadenza on this occasion demonstrated his, up to that moment, unmatched virtuosity. On December 5, 1928, Leroy Williams and his Dallas Band recorded "Going Away Blues," on which Williams plays a cornet cadenza which, as discographer Brian Rust has noted, "suggests that we have a potential rival to Louis Armstrong," although Rust goes on to assert that Williams's "other known records by no means bear this out."[16] As a matter of fact, another side with a tune entitled "Tampa Shout," on which Williams leads the same ensemble and solos to fine effect, reveals that what Rust calls an "effortless introduction" to "Going Away Blues" was no fluke, that indeed Williams was an impressive soloist in the New Orleans tradition.[17] Williams and his band may well have come from the Crescent City to Dallas, for the style of their jazz is in keeping with that of New Orleans, both from the point of view of their note choices and phrasing and of the group's instrumentation, which included banjo and brass tuba. The other soloists include alto saxophonist Lawson Brooks, who may have been related to Alva Brooks, an altoist in the 1930s with the outstanding San Antonio band of Boots Douglas, and Octave Gaspard, the brass tuba player who the year before, in December, 1927, had recorded with Dallas blues singer Lillian Glinn.[18] The name Gaspard, like that of trombonist Fred Millet, is of French derivation and again suggests that this group probably originated in New Orleans. Their presence in Texas certainly must have contributed to an early awareness in the state

*Oran "Hot Lips" Page.*
*From the collection of Dave Oliphant*

of the grand tradition of New Orleans jazz, and especially in Dallas, which already by 1927 was the home of a number of future impact players at the national level, including saxophonists Budd Johnson and Buster Smith and trumpeter Oran "Hot Lips" Page.

Although Austin has never been thought of as a jazz center, the state's capital city was in fact the birthplace of two notable jazzmen and the home for an important early period of two others: pianist Teddy Wilson, bassist Gene Ramey, and trumpeters Hot Lips Page and Kenny Dorham. A native of Dallas, Page was discovered working in Austin in 1927 by the Oklahoma Blue Devils band, which hired him away from the band of Eddie and Sugar Lou. During 1929 and 1931 Eddie and

Sugar Lou's Hotel Tyler Orchestra recorded several sides, but it is clear from the group's October, 1929, recording of "There'll Be Some Changes Made," that the trumpeter who replaced Page, either Henry Thompson or Stanley Hardee, was neither technically nor imaginatively on a par with Hot Lips.[19] Fortunately, in 1929, Lips Page, with his powerful drive and highly inventive, blues-tinged improvisations, would also be captured on wax, when the Blue Devils made their only recordings, two tunes entitled "Squabblin'" and "Blue Devil Blues."

Hot Lips Page's opening solo on "Blue Devil Blues" has been acclaimed as exhibiting "great rhythmic freedom" and as "a remarkably cohesive solo built on two ideas, both constantly varied."[20] In 1932 Hot Lips would record with the Bennie Moten Orchestra on a session that produced what critics have judged to have been "one of the dozen or so most thrilling single sessions in this history of jazz. Here is the epitome of the Kansas City big band sound before it became absorbed into the swing movement."[21] As one of the principal soloists in the Moten unit, Hot Lips can be heard in a classic, blues-inflected performance on the "hair-raising, exciting 'Toby,'" a Kansas City riff "certainly known to all the black musicians of the day." Also on "Moten's Swing," a piece arranged by Texan Eddie Durham, Hot Lips has been praised for producing a solo of "pure melodic essence" and limiting himself to "a minimum of activity with a maximum of expression, a lesson Lester Young was to extend several years later."[22] In 1937 Page led his own shortlived band at Smalls' Paradise in New York, promoted as another trumpeter-singer in the Louis Armstrong mold by none other than Armstrong's own manager, Joe Glaser. Later, in 1941, Page would become the featured soloist for the highly popular swing-era orchestra of Artie Shaw.

In the year following Hot Lips Page's first recording date of 1929, Tom Howell, another trumpet (or cornet) player, and his brother, trombonist Lee Howell, recorded in San Antonio with a group billed as Fred Gardner's Texas University Troubadours. The Howells took part in a recording session on June 9, 1930, at which the Troubadours performed four tunes: "Loveless Love," "Papa's Gone," "No Trumps," and "Daniel's Blues."[23] Of Tom Howell, little had been known other than the information supplied by Brian Rust in his discography for recording sessions in 1929 and 1930 and in his notes to a 1997 CD:

> Many years ago, someone in a defunct magazine tried a leg-pull suggesting that British reedman Freddy Gardner, on holiday in Texas, had gathered a band together in a recording studio and

made these four numbers—and the cornetist was Bix Beiderbecke. It was in fact Tom Howell, a brilliant musician who later
worked with Sunny Clapp and his Band o' Sunshine, and who
may well have been a student at Texas at the time, along with
his colleagues in the band.[24]

Although the registrar's records at the University of Texas at Austin
are unclear, Howell was on the campus as early as 1924. In 1929, he was
photographed for the university's student annual, *The Cactus,* as part
of Steve Gardner's Hokum Kings, which was composed of "university
students, the pick of the campus musicians, and each man master of numerous instruments." Fred Gardner also appears in the photo, along
with Steve Gardner, who is identified as the "manager and director of
the Hokum Kings," which the annual reports is "well known in musical
circles. [Steve Gardner] is master and teacher of all instruments and
head of the Department of Band, Orchestra and Public School Music
in the University Conservatory of Music."[25] Other members of the unit
are Chester Seekatz, who plays saxophone, clarinet, soprano sax, and
double clarinet; F. N. "Tommy" Howell on saxophone, clarinet, soprano
sax, banjo, trumpet, and piano; and Leland H. "Freshman" Adams on
banjo, trombone, bass, trumpet, and piano.[26] Adding to the confusion
in the historical record is the presence among this group of two musicians with the name Howell, the one referred to as "Tommy" and
the other Thomas A., both able to play the trumpet. But it is clear that
the principal instrument of Thomas A. was the trumpet or cornet, and
it seems evident that the trumpeter-cornetist on the 1930 recordings
made in San Antonio was the same Thomas A., who was born Thomas
Alva Howell, Jr., on May 6, 1906, in Belton, Texas, and died on July 5,
1989, in Bexar County. Howell's father, Thomas Alva, Sr., owned a music store in Cameron, Texas, a town midway between Temple and Bryan,
and Tom Howell, Jr., was the youngest of five brothers who in 1921
formed the Howell Brothers Moonshine Orchestra, which played regularly for dances at the University of Texas in Austin and in the Central
Texas area.[27]

The idea that Tom Howell was jokingly identified as the legendary
cornetist Bix Beiderbecke is not surprising. His performance on "No
Trumps" can easily be taken for the work of Beiderbecke, who died on
August 7, 1931, slightly more than a year after this side was recorded by
the Texas University Troubadors. Howell's cornet tone, his upward rips,
and his phrasing all recall Beiderbecke on this tune that is itself remi-

*The Howell Brothers Moonshine Dance Orchestra, photographed in 1922
by the Jordan Co., Austin, Texas. Pictured from left to right are:
Lee on trombone, Jay on clarinet, Bill on drums, Hilton on piano,
and Tommy (the youngest at 16) on cornet.
Reproduced with permission by Pat Howell Crutsinger*

niscent of "At the Jazz Band Ball" as recorded by Bix and His Gang on October 5, 1927. Also, the way that Fred Gardner bends his notes on tenor saxophone sounds close to the work of C-melody saxophonist Frankie Trumbauer, who in 1928 had recorded two classics with Bix, "I'm Coming Virginia" and "Singin' the Blues." Furthermore, either pianist Tom Donahue or Tommy Howell plays in the style of Frank Signorelli, pianist on the 1927 Bix session that produced "At the Jazz Band Ball." While Howell was undeniably influenced by Beiderbecke, the Texan has his own peculiar manner within the dixieland style. His notes are cleanly played, as Beiderbecke's were, and Howell executes some tricky phrases typical of Bix, even if on a couple of these he does not quite have the latter's control. Howell's second solo break on "No Trumps," on which he uses a mute, is in imitation of Beiderbecke yet contains touches that are purely the Texan's; on both solos Howell drives with the same forcefulness and swing that were characteristic of Bix. Present as well on the Texas University Troubadors recording is a violin break by Lew Bray, a very proficient soloist who forecasts the coming of western swing. The brass tuba player, John Gardner, pumps away quite wonderfully, and the overall ensemble renders this a splendid, swinging piece.

Another of the four sides also merits mention: "Daniel's Blues," with a vocal by drummer Jay "Bird" Thomas. What is striking about this tune is that its opening is basically a recasting of Duke Ellington's "Mood Indigo," which the composer first recorded on October 30, 1930, five months *after* the Troubadors' session. Obviously Gardner and his men had heard the Ellington tune through radio broadcasts prior to their recording, which reveals how up to the minute Texas jazz musicians were, as well as their good taste in picking up so early on this classic Ellington composition. The group captures perfectly the *misterio* quality of the piece, and even after the side shifts to become more of a straight blues, tenorist Fred Gardner especially echoes the opening strains of Ellington's work. Howell's cornet again sounds like Beiderbecke, even though in more of a blues vein. Another notable feature of this side is that the vocal by Thomas includes the phrase "Honey, raise your window high," which would be made famous by blues shouter Jimmy Rushing of the Count Basie Orchestra, but only much later in the 1930s.

As Brian Rust observes in his insert notes to *Jazz in Texas 1924–1930,* the compact disc on which the four sides from 1930 have been reissued, Howell also recorded with Sunny Clapp and His Band o' Sunshine. The Clapp band, with New Orleans clarinetist Sidney Arodin, recorded several sides on July 23, 1929, also in San Antonio.[28] On two of these sides, according to the Rust discography, Howell would be the second trumpet along with Bob Hutchingson, even though *Texas & Tennessee Territory Bands,* the compact disc that reissues the sides, does not include Howell among the personnel.[29] Nonetheless, it seems certain that Howell is present on both "Down on Biscayne Bay" and "We Can't Use Each Other Any More," where he must be the cornetist backing up the vocals credited to Hutchingson, who obviously cannot be singing and simultaneously playing the muted obbligatos. Also, the sound of the cornetist behind Hutchingson is clearly in Howell's Bix-inspired style. Shedding further doubt on the reliability of the insert notes for the personnel is the fact that there is no trombone listed, and yet Rust includes in his discography trombonist Lee Howell, who must be the soloist on his instrument who takes breaks on both sides.[30] The Clapp band also recorded in New York in 1931, but the fine trumpet on the two sides from July first, "Come Easy, Go Easy Love" and "When I Can't Be With You," included on *Texas & Tennessee Territory Bands,* does not at all sound like Howell, or Beiderbecke, and apparently is the work of Bob Hutchingson.[31] In the end, however, none of these Texans from the bands of Fred Gardner and Sunny Clapp has survived in the mainstream history of great jazz, unlike a number of the black jazzmen from Texas who would have a profound impact on this music.

Budd and Keg Johnson of Dallas were members in the 1920s of several territory bands in Texas, including the Blue Moon Chasers, Ben Smith's Music Makers, and Gene Coy's Happy Black Aces. Both Budd and Keg had studied music in Dallas with Portia Pittman, the daughter of famed black author and educator Booker T. Washington. By 1929 the brothers were in Kansas City with the band of George Lee, with which Budd recorded in that year his first tenor solo, on "Paseo Street (Strut)."[32] In 1933, the Johnson brothers formed part of the Louis Armstrong Orchestra, which recorded several sides that have been singled out as exceptional, both for Armstrong's solos and for the contributions made by Budd on tenor and Keg on trombone. While critic James Lincoln Collier has lamented that an "excellent jazz player" like Keg Johnson "did not record often enough to receive the recognition he deserved," Keg did contribute fine outings on the Armstrong recordings of "Basin Street Blues," "Mahogany Hall Stomp," and "Laughin' Louie." Of Keg's break on "Basin Street Blues," critic Gunther Schuller states that it is a "soulful open-toned, unfancy solo."[33] Keg's solos on the other two Armstrong sides exhibit the trombonist's exceptional work in the upper register of his instrument.[34] Keg also recorded impressively with the Benny Carter, Fletcher Henderson, and Cab Calloway Orchestras, but of the two brothers, it is Budd Johnson whose name is more fully a part of the story of jazz.[35]

As a multi-reed man, Budd Johnson made a lasting contribution through his recordings with the Earl "Fatha" Hines Orchestra, for which during the late 1930s and early 1940s Budd was the straw boss and an important arranger and soloist on clarinet, alto, and tenor. Budd also was involved in and helped organize the first bebop recording, made on February 16, 1944. His solo work on tenor could be confused at times with that of Lester Young, even though the two men developed their styles independently during the mid-1930s. On alto Budd could sound at times like a forerunner of the great Charlie Parker. One of Budd's

most unusual and even startling solos was taken on clarinet with the
Hines Orchestra on December 2, 1940, on the tune "Jelly Jelly."[36] In
Budd's clarinet solo there are no frills, no Benny Goodman romanti-
cism, only an intensely direct, penetrating, bluesy sound that goes
straight to the soul. In the mid-1960s, Budd Johnson was still performing at the highest artistic level with an Earl Hines combo that included
Budd's fellow Texan Gene Ramey on bass. First recording in 1929, as did
the various white university musicians who were active at the time but
who were essentially never heard from thereafter, Budd demonstrated
his staying power in 1965 by giving a five-minute, masterclass solo on
"Sometimes I'm Happy," full of his "Texas honks" and his unending variations on the song's timeless theme.[37] Before his death on October 20,
1984, Budd Johnson had performed with a variety of important groups,
among them the orchestras of Count Basie, Billy Eckstine, Dizzy Gillespie, Woody Herman, and Gil Evans. However, as Gunther Schuller acknowledges, the Texas reedman had gotten his start and "had grown up
with all the great Southwestern territory bands," and in many ways that
made him the soulful, straight-ahead, exuberant soloist and the highly
adventuresome arranger that he was, qualities he possessed in common
with so many of his Texas compatriots.[38]

Another Dallas reedman who would play a significant role in the development of jazz was Buster Smith, whom critic Ross Russell characterized as the nearest thing to an "archetypal jazzman of the Southwest."[39] Like the Johnson brothers, Smith was active in the 1920s, but
aside from local medicine show bands, he was principally a member of
only one band between 1925 and 1933, the legendary Blue Devils. This
group only recorded once, in 1929, with, as we have seen, Hot Lips Page
on trumpet. Gunther Schuller has judged Smith's alto solos from this
date to be "advanced for their time."[40] After a brief period with the Bennie Moten band in 1933 and with the Count Basie band of 1935, Smith
went off to form his own group that in 1938 included the major new jazz
stylist to be, altoist Charlie Parker. Much has been written about the influence of Smith's alto approach on Parker, who clearly absorbed it from
sitting next to "The Professor," as Smith was called. This seems unde-
niable in light of Buster's solos recorded, not with his own band, which
never cut a single side, but with Hot Lips Page and pianist Pete Johnson,
from June 30, 1939. Smith's performance on "Baby, Look at You," is
truly a new sound on his instrument—harder, more pristine, with no vi-
brato to speak of, unadorned, yet with a flexibility and flow that had not
been heard before but which would be mastered by Parker, who,

however, did not record for the first time until 1940.[41] Previous to Parker's inaugural recording in November, 1940, Smith also soloed on another side with Page—on a remarkable version of "I Ain't Got Nobody," recorded January 1, 1940.[42] As Budd Johnson once declared, and the evidence seems to support his claim, "[Charlie] Bird [Parker] really came from Buster Smith. Because when I was a kid Buster Smith was playing like that then. Way before Bird was ever born. In Dallas, Texas."[43] Indeed, Buster Smith, like Budd Johnson and Lips Page, had begun his career in the southwestern, Dallas tradition of a blues-driven, searing, direct-to-the-heart delivery.

Yet another highly influential jazz musician associated with Dallas was electric guitarist Charlie Christian, who was born on July 29, 1916, apparently in Bonham.[44] Christian first played string bass with the Dallas orchestra of Alphonse Trent, but once he began to concentrate on the electric guitar, in his hands it became a major jazz instrument, capable of long, flowing melodic improvisations filled with a combination of blues inflections and an expanded harmonic vocabulary. In his use of the amplified guitar, Christian was preceded by several performers on this type of instrument, among them Eddie Durham of San Marcos, Bob Dunn of Braggs, Oklahoma, and Leon McAuliffe from the Houston area. Durham was probably the first to amplify a standard guitar, placing a resonator inside it to project his sound, employing this homemade instrument as early as 1932. As a true jazz musician, Durham had first recorded on acoustic guitar in 1929 with Bennie Moten's band, and even then his solos looked forward to some extent to Charlie Christian's long-lined, single-note production. Durham initially recorded on electric guitar on September 30, 1935, with the Jimmie Lunceford Orchestra on Durham's own arrangement entitled "Hittin' the Bottle," but his most advanced guitar style can be heard on his arrangement entitled "Time Out," recorded with the Count Basie Orchestra on August 9, 1937.[45]

Prior to Durham's first recorded performance, Bob Dunn had recorded with the Texas Western Swing unit of Milton Brown and His Musical Brownies on January 27 and 28, 1935. On this date, Dunn played an amplified steel guitar, which primarily was utilized for Hawaiian music.[46] "Taking Off," from January 28, features Dunn's honking, trombone-like sound, and while his solo work is in a way swinging, one is hard put to call it jazz in the traditional sense of the word, because it leans toward a more countrified and Hawaiian tonality and phrasing.[47] As early as 1933, Leon McAuliffe also was playing steel guitar, and in 1935 he joined Bob Wills and His Texas Playboys, recording with the latter his own composition, "Steel Guitar Rag," during a session of September 29–30, 1936.[48] Again, McAuliffe's steel guitar, like that of Dunn, is far from traditional jazz, and certainly McAuliffe's sound is light years away from the smooth drive, rich harmony, and imaginative contours of Charlie Christian's proto-bebop conception.

It is quite likely that Dunn and McAuliffe's steel guitars were heard by Christian on radio or on record and may have had an effect on his development of the jazz electric guitar. But Durham undoubtedly was an early influence on Christian; this is evident from the latter's solo on "Gone With What Draft" (or "Gilly"), from December 19, 1940.[49] Durham reported that Christian had approached him about his interest in learning the electric guitar, but even if this account is unconfirmed by any reference to Durham in Christian's essay on jazz guitar, published in December, 1939,[50] the fact that Christian knew Durham's work is indicated by his quotation from Durham's solo on the latter's own arrangement of "Avalon," recorded with the Jimmie Lunceford Orchestra on September 30, 1935.[51] Yet even if Durham is more in the mainstream jazz tradition than either Dunn or McAuliffe, Durham's notes and his overall style are essentially different from Christian's. Charlie is simply a more fluent performer than all three of these predecessors on amplified guitar.

What critic Bill Simon has said of the contrast between French jazz guitarist Django Reinhardt and Charlie Christian holds true in part for the difference between Christian and his three southwestern contemporaries: "[Django] brought new, exotic and showy elements into jazz; still he himself never came close to the core of jazz. One has only to compare [Django's] frothy, though fertile, inventions with the driving, earthy improvisations of young Christian to understand the difference."[52] Gunther Schuller has concisely summarized the relationship between Christian and his roots in the Southwest by answering a question asked by Teddy Hill, manager of the original bebop venue, Minton's Playhouse, in Harlem. Hill asked of Christian, "Where did he come from?" Schuller has replied in print by referring to "the kind of musical origins that could produce such a major innovative talent. The simple short answer is that the Southwest is guitar country and blues country, the Texas blues tradition particularly being one of the oldest indigenous traditions and probably much older than the New Orleans idiom that is generally thought to be the primary fountainhead of jazz. And Christian embraced all of that: a guitarist who brought the Southwestern blues into modern jazz—and more."[53]

But one of many recordings that reveals Christian's very bluesy feel-ing—as well as his ability to quote phrases from various sources and incorporate them into his improvisation, and his tendency to imitate through his electric guitar the sound of the tenor saxophone—is his version of "Star Dust," from early March, 1940. This particular perfor-mance was taped in Minneapolis with Jerry Jerome on tenor (a regular at the time with the Benny Goodman Orchestra, with which Christian was featured on "Solo Flight" from March 4, 1941, in addition to his many recordings with the Goodman Sextet), Frankie Hines on piano, and an unidentified bass and drums.[54] Here Christian quotes from the pop tune "Pretty Baby" and Duke Ellington's "I Let a Song Go Out of My Heart," sounding at times like Jerome's tenor, even as Charlie creates his trademark long, melodic lines laced with surprising leaps and swing-ing runs. Another standout side is entitled "Blues in B," which was a fully improvised performance captured on March 13, 1941, while the Benny Goodman Sextet members were awaiting the leader's arrival for a recording session. One can hear Christian modulate into the unusual key of B at the suggestion of another of the sidemen, and then begin to chord the blues with an extraordinary drive that does, as Gunther Schuller suggests, bring the grand tradition of Texas blues guitar—from Blind Lemon Jefferson to Eddie Durham—to bear on developments in jazz that at the time were characterized by a piece entitled "Swing to Bop," which marked a change to which Charlie Christian fundamen-tally contributed.[55]

There were other, innumerable Texans who also made important contributions to the swing and bebop movements. To name but a few: Clarence Hutchenrider of Waco, who, during his years with the Casa Loma Orchestra from 1931 to 1943, was "a superb clarinetist" able to take his place "alongside the best jazzmen";[56] Carl "Tatti" Smith of Mar-shall, who, unfortunately—based on his presence on the first record-ings by tenor great Lester Young in 1936—was but a rarely recorded trumpeter with an expressiveness and fluidity of execution close to those of Young;[57] Harry James of Beaumont, who, as a member of the Benny Goodman Orchestra and the leader of his own band, was prob-ably the most popular trumpeter of the swing era;[58] and Herschel Evans of Denton, who starred in the late 1930s with the Count Basie Orches-tra, his bursting-at-the-seams, big-toned tenor a foil to tenorist Lester Young's lean, lithe, ethereal approach.[59]

Clarence Hutchenrider, born June 13, 1908, led his own band at age fourteen and in the late 1920s played at Dallas's Adolphus Hotel in the band of Jack Gardner, who himself would later in 1939 play piano in Harry James's first big band. Like so many Texans in jazz, Hutchenrider and Gardner were active early in the history of the music, performing during its first decade in territory bands, and then in the 1930s as members of some of the prominent units of the swing era. Tatti Smith also was born in 1908 and also was a member of a number of territory bands, including those of Alphonse Trent, Terrence Holder, and Gene Coy. In 1936 Smith became a sideman with the Count Basie Orchestra, serving as well in that year as the nominal co-leader of Jones-Smith, Inc., for the first recordings by Lester Young. Born March 15, 1916, in Albany, Georgia, Harry James got his start in 1931 when his circus family settled in Beaumont and he began playing with local groups like the Old Phillips Friars and the bands of Logan Hancock and Herman Waldman, before being picked up by Ben Pollack in 1935 and later joining Benny Goodman in 1937. Herschel Evans, born in 1909, first recorded in San Antonio in 1929 with the Troy Floyd Orchestra, which cut two sides of a tune entitled "Dreamland Blues, Parts 1 and 2."[60] One commentator has noted that even at this early date, "Herschel Evans's first recorded solo is a minor landmark in tenor saxophone style and shows that he was securely rooted in the Texas blues tradition."[61] But it was as a member of the Basie band, beginning in 1935, that Evans, as one of the band's two tenor stars, helped establish what became known as "the Texas tenor" sound.

The Texas tenor tradition that derived from Herschel Evans was principally carried on by tenor saxophonist Buddy Tate of Sherman and two tenorists from Houston, Illinois Jacquet and Arnett Cobb.[62] Tate, born February 22, 1914, took Evans's chair in the Basie band on Herschel's death of a cardiac condition in 1939. Evans and Tate had played together in the San Antonio band of Troy Floyd, and Tate, like both Evans and Tatti Smith, had been with a number of territory bands. Tate's solos with the Basie band are perhaps even bigger-toned than Evans's, and much more daring, as evidenced by his improvisation on "Seventh Avenue Express" from October 19, 1947.[63]

Both Illinois Jacquet (born in Louisiana in 1922 but from age one a resident of Houston) and Arnett Cobb (born in Houston in 1918) were members of the Houston band of Milt Larkin, who was born in the Bayou City on October 10, 1910, was inspired to take up the trumpet by New Orleans cornetist Bunk Johnson, and was to form his own unit in 1936. The Larkin outfit has been considered "probably the last of the great Texas bands."[64] Possibly even before Larkin was born, Houston was visited by the self-proclaimed inventor of jazz, Ferdinand "Jelly Roll" Morton, who looked up the piano players in Houston and declared in his autobiography that "they were all terrible."[65] While this may have been true at the time, in the early 1920s Hersal Thomas and his father George W. Thomas of Houston would prove important boogie-woogie pianists, and Houston also would produce a number of vital blues singers who recorded in the 1920s with the leading jazzmen of the era, including King Oliver and Louis Armstrong.[66] By the late 1930s, when the nationally known orchestras of Jimmie Lunceford and Cab Calloway came through Houston, they received "rough treatment" at the hands of the local Milt Larkin band, which battled other units "every Sunday for years at the old Harlem Square Club in Houston."[67] In 1942, Illinois Jacquet left the Larkin band to become the star tenor soloist with the Lionel Hampton Orchestra, with which he recorded in New York what has been called a chorus on "Flying Home" that "triggered a whole generation of big-toned, extrovert sax solos."[68] Jacquet also would be a featured soloist with the Count Basie Orchestra from 1945 to 1946.

Following in the same tenor tradition of Herschel Evans, Buddy Tate, and Illinois Jacquet, Arnett Cobb starred as well with the Hampton Orchestra, soloing on "Flying Home No. 2" in 1944, but adding to Jacquet's honks, squeals, shakes, and stratospheric high notes Cobb's own "vocal and drawling" sound full of "grunts, hoots, and wrenching wails," all of which would characterize the Texas tenor style.[69] Cobb once described the origins of his full-toned, Texas sound as deriving from the fact that he would practice in a large field near his home in Houston's Fifth Ward, which required him "to fill up the open space."[70]

Other important figures from Houston who were associated with Milt Larkin include alto saxophonist Eddie "Cleanhead" Vinson, pianist-arranger Cedric Haywood, and altoist Jimmy Ford. Vinson would make a name for himself both as an altoist and a blues singer, principally through his hit song, "Kidney Stew Blues," recorded in 1945 with his own band. Vinson's group at the time included tenorist John Coltrane and Dallas pianist Red Garland, both of whom would in the 1950s star with the Miles Davis Quintet. Cedric Haywood's tune "Hot Rod" would be recorded in 1947 by Illinois Jacquet's own unit, which included Jacquet's brother, Russell, who also had been a member of the Larkin band. Jimmy Ford had played the Eldorado, Houston's jazz ballroom, in 1947, and, after a short time in New York, he was back in Houston working with Milt Larkin. In 1948 Ford returned to New York and joined the Tadd Dameron band, which included some of the giants of bebop, among them Fats Navarro and Kenny Clarke. Russell Jacquet, like a number of Texans, would study at Wiley College in Marshall, Texas, and it was with Russell's own California band that one of the central bebop figures from Texas, trumpeter Kenny Dorham, landed his first important job. Dorham too had studied at Wiley College, as did pianist-arranger Wild Bill Davis (who worked with the Milt Larkin band beginning in 1939) and trombonist Henry Coker of Dallas (a soloist in the 1950s with the Count Basie band). Nearby Galveston also produced two fine musicians in drummer G. T. Hogan and trumpeter Richard "Notes" Williams, the latter featured with the Charlie Mingus Jazz Workshop in the late 1950s and early '60s. Born in Houston between 1938 and 1940 and students at Texas Southern University, Stix Hooper, Hubert Laws, Wilton Felder, and Joe Sample were members of the Jazz Crusaders who would create a type of early fusion jazz in the 1960s.

After working with Russell Jacquet in California, Kenny Dorham moved on to New York where he joined the Dizzy Gillespie big band in 1945, and in January, 1946, was recorded with the Billy Eckstine Orchestra, soloing on his own composition, "The Jitney Man."[71] Dorham, who was born in Post Oak, Texas, on August 30, 1924, first played the piano at age seven but then switched to trumpet when he attended high school in Austin. Like Arnett Cobb, Dorham seems to have been influenced in his style by the Texas landscape, as critic Doug Ramsey suggests when he comments that "a hallmark of [Dorham's] playing was an expansiveness that reflected the open spaces and freedom of his youth."[72] Dorham's "Fragments of an Autobiography," which appeared in *Down Beat Music '70,* is a revealing account of his early years when he took part in cattle roundups and later was first exposed to jazz through the music of Louis Armstrong. Once in New York, Dorham's style developed quickly, especially under the tutelage of bebop genius Charlie Parker, who took the Texan into his quintet with the departure in 1948 of Miles Davis. Remaining with Parker for two years, Dorham would during that time perform in Paris at the first international jazz festival. Dorham also recorded with many other leaders of the bebop movement, including Bud Powell, Kenny Clarke, Fats Navarro, and Milt Jackson. While with the Eckstine Orchestra, Dorham worked with drummer Art Blakey, with whom in the 1950s Dorham and Horace Silver would form the original Jazz Messengers. Dorham first recorded with a Blakey group in December, 1947, when the latter's octet—called simply the Messengers—cut four sides, one of which was Dorham's original tune, "The Thin Man."[73] As trumpet soloist, ensemble player, leader of his own group, The Jazz Prophets, and composer and arranger, Dorham left a rich legacy that is still being discovered and rereleased on countless compact discs.[74]

Prior to Kenny Dorham's arrival in Austin in the 1930s, Gene Ramey, born in the capital city on April 4, 1913, had already been active in the local band of George Corley, which in 1930 also included tenorist Herschel Evans. Corley, who was born in Austin on September 12, 1912, played trombone in the high school band, along with his brothers Wilford on tenor sax and John on trumpet, with whom he formed the Royal Aces. Later in 1937 and '38, Corley would record with the San Antonio band of drummer Clifford "Boots" Douglas (born in Temple on September 7, 1908), but the trombonist never made it in the big time as did Gene Ramey.[75] Originally playing sousaphone with the Royal Aces, Ramey moved on to Kansas City in 1932 and studied the string bass with Walter Page, who in 1936 would become part of the Count Basie "All-American Rhythm Section." In Kansas City, Ramey regularly practiced with Charlie Parker and would serve as the bassist for the Jay McShann Orchestra, the last great Kansas City big band, with which Parker made his first recordings accompanied by Ramey on bass and drummer Gus Johnson, a native of Tyler, Texas, who was born there on November 15, 1913. Ramey would later record on some of the first sessions of the modern jazz giant Thelonious Monk, as well as with a wide variety of big bands and smaller ensembles, including the combo of Lester Young. Johnson would subsequently become the drummer of the Count Basie band in the early 1950s.

Oscar Moore, another Austinite, played a prominent role in the jazz scene of the 1940s. Born on December 25, 1912, Moore, as an advanced guitarist in his own right who developed independently of Charlie Christian, served as a vital member of the Nat King Cole Trio. Yet another outstanding Austin-born jazz musician was Teddy Wilson, star of the Benny Goodman Trio and Quartet. Like Oscar Moore, Wilson, who was born in Austin on November 24, 1912, left Texas at an early age, although in Wilson's case he seemed attracted throughout his career to groups whose members included such Texans as Budd and Keg Johnson, Harry James, Jack Teagarden, Herschel Evans, and Eddie Durham. Like Gene Ramey and Gus Johnson with the McShann Orchestra, Wilson and other natives of the state often teamed up and seemed mutually inspired by the Texas origins they shared.

Along with Dallas, Houston, and Austin, Fort Worth is the other Texas city whose many musicians have made an enduring mark on the history of jazz. One of the earliest natives of Cowtown to figure in the story of jazz was Euday L. Bowman, who was born in Fort Worth on November 9, 1887. Bowman's famous "12th Street Rag" was recorded by almost every important swing band of the 1930s, and on many occasions the recordings involved evolutionary improvisations by such soloists as Louis Armstrong and Lester Young.[76] Other Fort Worth musicians who contributed to various developments in the history of jazz include two members of the Glenn Miller Orchestra: tenor saxophonist and vocalist Tex Beneke (born February 12, 1914) and trumpeter Clyde Hurley (born September 3, 1916). Both of these men were often featured by Miller, most famously on "In the Mood" in 1939 when Hurley, who had studied music at Texas Christian University in Fort Worth, performed the tune's memorable trumpet solo.[77] Drummer Ray McKinley, born on June 18, 1910, in Cowtown, formed part of the Miller organization during World War II.

The most significant figure in jazz history to hail from Cowtown is indisputably Ornette Coleman, who was born there on March 19, 1930. Coleman, who would make a profound impact on jazz beginning in the late 1950s, got his start at Fort Worth's I. M. Terrell High School, where a number of other figures associated with the so-called free jazz movement also began their careers, among them Dewey Redman, born May 17, 1931, in Fort Worth. Coleman was influenced early on by the blues, Mexican American, and country-western sounds that he heard around him, but also by the bebop tradition, which he had mastered by 1947 and which, when he improvised in this vein in high school on John Philip Sousa's "Washington Post March," resulted in his being hooted out of the band. Coleman would go on to revolutionize jazz through his keyless compositions and extended improvisations full of southwestern "harmolodics." According to another alumni of I. M. Terrell and a classmate of Ornette Coleman—clarinetist John Carter, who was born September 24, 1939, in Fort Worth—Coleman, Cowtown drummer Charles Moffett (born September 11, 1929), and Carter would practice together in "an upstairs joint" in Fort Worth where they would "work hard on [their] bop repertoire and at the same time develop [their] personal styles." Carter reported that in the 1940s they "were all stone boppers."[78] Dewey Redman similarly worked on his jazz in the area of Rosedale Street on Fort Worth's southeast side where dozens of "uniquely trained young musicians . . . were either born or weaned musically."[79]

Other Texas cities and towns also produced jazz musicians who made a name for themselves. Like so many of the other figures

mentioned here, Emilio and Ernie Caceres and their cousin Johnny Gomez of South Texas were relatives who formed a family group, in their
case a string trio that created "some of the hottest music around San
Antonio."[80] Later, the trio recorded in 1937 in New York City after having
appeared on Benny Goodman's "Camel Caravan" radio show. Born November 22, 1911, in Rockport, Ernie would subsequently become an important sideman in the orchestras of Glenn Miller and Jack Teagarden.
Yet another musician who would figure prominently in major orchestras
was trombonist Tyree Glenn, who was born November 23, 1912, in Corsi-
cana, Texas. Glenn was a featured soloist during his tenure with the orchestras of Cab Calloway, Benny Carter, and Duke Ellington. During his
five years with the Ellington orchestra, beginning in 1946, Glenn not
only carried on the tradition of Ellington's earlier trombonists, Charlie
Irvis and Tricky Sam Nanton, but he also soloed on vibraharp, notably
for the Carnegie Hall premiere of Ellington's "Liberian Suite," on December 26, 1947.

Although this essay must end with 1950, the story of Texans in jazz
has continued to the present day with the contributions after that date
of a number of vital figures. Booker Ervin of Denison and John Handy
of Dallas, along with Richard "Notes" Williams, were members of and
recorded frequently with the important Charles Mingus Workshop, and
Leo Wright of Wichita Falls starred with the Dizzy Gillespie Quintet
and Orchestra.[81] The part played by these and other Texans has been
considerable, and was even indispensable to the types of jazz created by
Ellington, Mingus, Monk, Parker, Basie, and so many other giants of this
music. Yet even without including any discussion here of the Texans
who came after 1950, there were, as we have seen, numerous sidemen
from Texas who were active from the beginnings of recorded jazz up to
mid-century and who deeply affected the artistry and appeal of this
American music.[82]

While it is possible to list Texans from almost every part of the state
who were members of the leading jazz units from the 1930s on, it is
perhaps difficult to determine in many cases how their Texas roots
contributed to the kinds of jazz that were produced by the various ensembles in which they performed. Nonetheless, it seems clear that at the
very least the Texas blues tradition has been inherent to the creativity
of most every Texas jazz musician. Also, it appears evident that the state
was in no way isolated from but played a seminal role in the creation of
every phase of jazz, from hot to swing to bebop and beyond. High school
and college music programs, local jazz units, inspiring individual per-

formers, and access to traveling shows, radio broadcasts, and recordings made it possible for aspiring Texas jazz musicians to imitate and even excel as creative artists. While Texas may be better known today as a crucible for country, conjunto, and western swing music, the state has equally been the home of some of the most remarkable figures in the history of jazz. And once again, most every section of the state can lay claim to a jazz musician whose roots were formed in its peculiar climate and terrain and whose place in the annals of jazz has been documented by the encyclopedias and histories of this native American music recognized around the world as one of the greatest forms of twentieth-century art.

## ⤞   Notes   ⤝

1. See, for example, E. Simms Campbell's "Blues," in *Jazzmen,* edited by Frederic Ramsey, Jr., and Charles Edward Smith (London: Sidgwick and Jackson, 1958), p. 112.

2. Rudi Blesh, *Shining Trumpets: A History of Jazz* (New York: Alfred A. Knopf, 1946; Reprint, New York: Da Capo Press, 1980), p. 184. Bunk Johnson is said to have played in Dallas in 1904, Sidney Bechet in Plantersville in 1911, and Jelly Roll Morton a few years later in Houston and "more towns" than he could remember, while King Oliver toured Texas in 1914. See Dave Oliphant, *Texan Jazz* (Austin: The University of Texas Press, 1996), pp. 86 and 88.

3. *Jazz and Hot Dance in Chile, 1926–1959* (Harlequin HQ 2083, 1991).

4. *Jazz in Texas, 1924–1930* (Timeless Records, CBC 1-033, 1997). In his *Jazz Style in Kansas City and the Southwest* (Berkeley: University of California Press, 1973), Ross Russell claims that "There is no record of an outstanding band in the Houston area during the twenties" (p. 59), but this Fatty Martin side, as well as another of "Jimtown Blues," on which Martin takes a fine piano solo, suggests that perhaps Russell was unaware of this band.

5. Andy Kirk, *Twenty Years on Wheels* (Ann Arbor: The University of Michigan Press, 1989), p. 46.

6. According to Jim Fisher, former curator of the O'Henry Museum in Austin, there was a band playing jazz in Taylor, Texas, in 1904. Fisher told me in conversation that he had seen more than one reference to this band but could not recall where. In Austin itself, there were a number of groups active from 1920 on. In the University of Texas student newspaper, *The Daily Texan,* an article dated April 21, 1925, surveys on page six the popular bands of the period. For this piece, entitled "'Fire Hall Five' One of Many Former Campus Jazz Orchestras of Varsity," author Lyra Haisley interviewed bandleader William Besserer, whose group had played in 1918 and 1919 for the University's German

Club dances. Besserer remembered that in 1920 "along came the jazz—and Paul Whiteman and his 'tin-can' orchestra." Haisley observes that since Besserer's group "did not realize what jazz was all about," it "disbanded, and Shakey's orchestra, directed by Jack Tobin, became the ruling favorites in University circles. If it wasn't Shakey's, according to some, it wasn't jazz. Jack and his men played the unadulterated, primitive jazz." Haisley then reports that "About 1920, Pharr's Fire Hall Five, directed by Blondy Pharr, was quite well-known for its particular kind of 'jazzmania.'" After this, Haisley writes, "Jimmie's Joys, directed by Jimmy Maloney, was the leading campus dance band for about two years. In 1921–22, six [sic] brothers formed Howell's Moonshiners and played for some of the dances." Another campus group, the Texas Collegians Varsity Peacocks, traveled as far as Laredo to perform. One member of this group was drummer Jay "Bird" Thomas, who, as we shall see, also formed part in 1930 of Steve Gardner's Texas University Troubadours, which recorded four sides that feature cornetist Tom Howell. For making me aware of Lyra Haisley's article in *The Daily Texan,* I am indebted to the unpublished doctoral thesis of Margaret Catherine Berry, *Student Life and Customs, 1883–1933* (New York: Columbia University, 1965), vol. 2, p. 598. A recording entitled *The Best from the Southwest: Jimmie Joy and His Orchestra* includes examples of this group from the years 1923–32 (Arcadia, 2017D, 1985). I am grateful to Dave Laczko of Austin's Tower Records for supplying me with a copy of this recording. Three of these sides are available on *Jazz in Texas, 1924–1930.*

7. Richard Hadlock, *Jazz Masters of the Twenties* (New York: Macmillan, 1965; Reprint, New York: Collier Books, 1974), p. 174.

8. In *Texan Jazz,* I give Teagarden's birth date as August 29, following the standard sources, but this has been corrected by archivist Joe Showler of Toronto, who gives the day as August 20.

9. Quoted in H. J. Waters, Jr., *Jack Teagarden's Music: His Career and Recordings* (Stanhope, N.J.: Walter C. Allen, 1960), p. 3.

10. Jay D. Smith and Len Guttridge, *Jack Teagarden: The Story of a Jazz Maverick* (London: Cassell and Company, 1960), p. 42.

11. Hadlock, *Jazz Masters of the Twenties,* p. 183.

12. The music for this radio series is now available from Showler's compact disc label, Vernon Music. See *Jack Teagarden—1930 with Ben Pollack and his Orchestra: Whiz Radio Programs* (Vernon Music, VMCD-62901, 2001). Most of the music on this compact disc is not jazz, and unfortunately Teagarden is heard from only rarely.

13. *Jack Teagarden and His Band—1951: Live at the Royal Room, Hollywood* (Vernon Music, VMCD-83199, 1999).

14. Ed Steane, liner notes, *Bennie Moten's Kansas City Orchestra 1923–1929* (Historical Records, vol. 9, ASC-5829-9, n.d.).

15. Gunther Schuller, *The Swing Era: The Development of Jazz 1930–1945* (New York: Oxford University Press, 1989), p. 336.

16. Brian Rust, insert notes, *Jazz in Texas, 1924–1930*.

17. *Jazz in Texas, 1924–1930*.

18. See *Lillian Glinn: Complete Recorded Works in Chronological Order 1927–1929* (Document Records, COCD-5184, 1993). The most impressive side by Glinn is entitled "Shake It Down" and was recorded in New Orleans in April, 1928, with an unidentified ensemble.

19. *Blue Rhythm Stomp: Texas Jazz* ( Jazz Greats CD 073, 1999). Because so many jazz musicians tended to be kin to one another, one would think that Stanley Hardee might have been related to tenorist John Hardee of Wichita Falls, who recorded extensively in the mid-1940s.

20. Gunther Schuller, *Early Jazz: Its Roots and Musical Development* (New York: Oxford University Press, 1968), p. 296.

21. John McDonough, "A Century With Count Basie," *Down Beat* 57 ( Jan., 1990): 36.

22. Schuller, *Early Jazz,* p. 316.

23. *Jazz in Texas, 1924–1930*.

24. Rust, insert notes, *Jazz in Texas, 1924–1930*. See also *Jazz Records, 1897–1942,* Vol. 1 A-Kar, compiled by Brian Rust (London: Storyville Publishers and Co., 1975).

25. *The Cactus* (Austin: Texas Student Publications, Inc., 1929), p. 357.

26. Chester Seekatz is listed in *Jazz in Texas, 1924–1930,* as Chester Skeekatz.

27. *Matchless Milam: History of Milam County Texas,* compiled and edited by Milam County Heritage Preservation Society (A Texas Sesquicentennial Edition, 1984), pp. 134–35. The middle name of Thomas Howell, Sr., is mistakenly given as Andrew but is Alva, after Thomas Alva Edison.

28. *Texas & Tennessee Territory Bands* (Retrieval Recordings, RTR 79006, 1997).

29. *Jazz Records 1897–1942,* p. 343. Rust reports in this discography that "Sunny Clapp himself claims that Bix Beiderbecke is on 'Come Easy, Go Easy Love,' but he is not on the issued take of this number, and there is no evidence of his presence on any of the other sides from the three sessions at which this was recorded" (p. 343).

30. See *Jazz Records 1897–1942,* p. 342, as well as Tom Lord's *The Jazz Discography* (West Vancouver, Canada: Lord Music Reference, 1992), Vol. 4, p. 344.

31. "Come Easy, Go Easy Love" is a song credited to Hoagy Carmichael and Sunny Clapp, with a vocal by Carmichael. There is a truly impressive trombone solo on "When I Can't Be With You," but again no trombonist is listed in the compact disc insert notes, while Rust identifies the trombonist as Lee Howell. Also included on *Texas & Tennessee Territory Bands* are four sides by Phil Baxter and his Orchestra, recorded at the Park Hotel Ballroom in Dallas, on October 20, 1929. One of the trumpets here, either Roy Nooner or Al Hann, takes an

excellent solo on "Down Where the Blue Bonnets Grow," and the accordionist, Davy Crocker, also solos wonderfully. The alto soloist on "Honey Child," either Ken Naylor or Jack Jones, has a very professional sound and flow. All four songs were written by Baxter, who is perhaps best known in Texas music circles as the composer of "I'm a Ding Dong Daddy From Dumas."

32. *The Real Kansas City* (Columbia/Legacy CK 64855, 1996).

33. Schuller, *The Swing Era,* p. 184.

34. These three sides were reissued on *Louis Armstrong: The Complete RCA Victor Recordings* (BMG Classics, 09026-68682-2, 1997).

35. Keg Johnson can be heard soloing on "Blue Lou" with the Benny Carter Orchestra from 1933, as reissued on *Benny Carter and His Orchestra 1933–1936* (Classics 530, 1990). He was with the Fletcher Henderson Orchestra of 1934 but does not solo on the sides reissued on *Fletcher Henderson & His Orchestra: The Father of the Big Band 1925/1937* ( Jazz Archives No. 137, 159352, 1998). Keg was with the Calloway Orchestra from 1936 into the 1940s and is present on the numerous recordings reissued for those years on the Classics compact disc series. Hear, for example, his solo on "At the Clambake Carnival," recorded on March 23, 1938 (Classics, 576, 1991).

36. *Earl Hines—Piano Man: Earl Hines, His Piano and His Orchestra* (RCA Victor Bluebird 6750-2-RB, 1989).

37. *Earl Hines Live at the Village Vanguard* (Columbia, CK 44197, 1988).

38. Schuller, *The Swing Era,* p. 285.

39. Russell, *Jazz Style in Kansas City and the Southwest,* p. 74.

40. Schuller, *Early Jazz,* p. 298.

41. "Baby, Look at You" is included on *The Real Kansas City.*

42. *Hot Lips Page and His Band 1938–1940* (Classics, 561, 1991). Parker's first full-length solos appear on *Early Bird: Charlie Parker with Jay McShann and His Orchestra* (Stash Records, St-CD-542, 1991). One poorly recorded side from August, 1940, is also included on this compact disc and may contain a solo by Parker.

43. Quoted in Ira Gitler, *Swing to Bop* (New York: Oxford University Press, 1985), p. 60.

44. Christian's birthplace has always been given as Dallas, but in Alan Govenar and Jaye Brakefield's *Deep Ellum and Central Track: Where the Black and White Worlds of Dallas Converged* (Denton: University of North Texas Press, 1996), the authors identify his birthplace as Bonham (see p. 121).

45. Hear Durham's guitar on "New Vine Street Blues," which is included on *Count Basie in Kansas City: Bennie Moten's Great Band of 1930–1932* (RCA Victor, LPV-514, 1965). "Hittin' the Bottle" is on *Swingsation: Jimmie Lunceford* (GRP Records, GRD-9923, 1998), and "Time Out" is included on *One O'Clock Jump: An Album of Classic "Swing" by Count Basie and His Orchestra 1927* (Decca, MCA-42324, 1990).

46. See Jean A. Boyd, *The Jazz of the Southwest: An Oral History of West-*

*ern Swing* (Austin: University of Texas Press, 1998), where this musicologist quotes from an interview with Leon McAuliffe, who recalled that he had "learned to play Hawaiian music because that's what the steel guitar was primarily used for" (p. 117).

47. *The Complete Recordings of the Father of Western Swing: Milton Brown and the Musical Brownies 1932–1937* (Texas Rose Records, TXRCD1–5, 1995).

48. *Bob Wills and His Texas Playboys: 'The King of Western Swing' 25 Hits 1935–1945* (Living Era, AJA 5250, 1998).

49. *Charlie Christian Volume 6 1940–1941* (Média 7, MJCD 68, 1994).

50. Charlie Christian, "Guitarmen, Wake Up and Pluck!" *Down Beat,* Dec. 1, 1939 (Reprint, July 10, 1969, p. 19).

51. *Jimmie Lunceford 2: "Harlem Shout" (1935–1936)* (MCA Records, 1305, 1980).

52. Bill Simon, "Charlie Christian," in *The Jazz Makers: Essays on the Greats of Jazz,* edited by Nat Shapiro & Nat Hentoff (New York: Holt, Rinehart and Winston, 1957; Reprint, New York: Da Capo Press, 1979), p. 318.

53. Schuller, *The Swing Era,* p. 563.

54. *Solo Flight: The Genius of Charlie Christian* (Columbia, CG30779, 1972).

55. "Swing to Bop," with Charlie Christian and Thelonious Monk, was recorded May, 1941. This piece is essentially a retitled version of Eddie Durham's "Topsy," and Christian's solo work here has been called "a condensed history of jazz as riff after riff from the swing age are laid down until the complex [bebop] phrases are reached" (Dean Tudor and Nancy Tudor, in *Jazz* [Littleton, Colorado: Libraries Unlimited, 1979], p. 144). The side is included on *Charlie Christian—Guest Artists: Dizzy Gillespie and Thelonious Monk* (Everest Records, FS-219, n.d.).

56. François Billard, insert notes to *Casa Loma Orchestra 1930/1934* (Jazz Archives No. 54, 157692, 1992).

57. Smith's sides with Lester Young are included on *Count Basie/Harry James: Basie Rhythm* (HEP Records, 1032, 1991).

58. Much of James's work with Goodman is reproduced on two compact discs, *The Harry James Years, Volume 1* (Bluebird, 66155-2, 1993) and *Wrappin' It Up: The Harry James Years Part 2* (Bluebird, 66549-2, 1995).

59. Some of Herschel's most memorable solos, such as those on "Blue and Sentimental," "Jumpin' at the Woodside," and his own tune "Doggin' Around," can be heard on *Count Basie: His Best Recordings 1936–1944* (Best of Jazz, 4026, 1995).

60. *Jazz in Texas, 1924–1930.*

61. Russell, *Jazz Style in Kansas City and the Southwest,* pp. 56–57.

62. A later exponent of this tenor style was Don Wilkerson, who attended Houston's Jack Yates High School in the late 1940s, recorded with the Ray

Charles Orchestra in 1954, and made three albums with Blue Note in the early 1960s. See *Don Wilkerson: The Complete Blue Note Sessions* (Blue Note, 24555, 2001).

63. *Seventh Avenue Express* is included on *Basie's Basement* (RCA Camden, CAL-497, 1959).

64. Albert McCarthy, *Big Band Jazz* (London: Barrie and Jenkins, 1974), p. 109.

65. Alan Lomax, in his classic version of Morton's autobiography, *Mister Jelly Roll: The Fortunes of Jelly Roll Morton, New Orleans Creole and "Inventor of Jazz"* (New York: Grosset & Dunlap, 1950), reports that in Morton's account of his life and times he mentioned having been active in Memphis during the year 1908, before his travels started again, at which point "Jelly Roll's story began to move so fast that we gave up trying for exact chronology" (p. 143n). After touring the East Coast and ending up in Jacksonville, where Morton stayed for about two months, he returned to Memphis and then traveled with a show that was stranded in Hot Springs, Arkansas, after which he accepted an offer to appear at the Pastime Theatre in Houston (p. 145).

66. For a fuller account of these figures, see *Texan Jazz*, especially chapter three on classic blues and chapter four on boogie-woogie.

67. Frank Driggs, "Kansas City and the Southwest," in *Jazz: New Perspectives on the History of Jazz by Twelve of the World's Foremost Jazz Critics and Scholars*, edited by Nat Hentoff and Albert McCarthy (New York: Holt, Rinehart and Winston, 1959; Reprint, New York: Da Capo Press, 1975), p. 223.

68. Leonard Feather, liner notes, *Lionel Hampton "Steppin' Out," vol. 1, 1942–1945* (Decca Records, DL 79244, n.d.).

69. See *Texan Jazz*, p. 226, and footnotes 34 and 35 to chapter 15. "Flying Home No. 2" is included on *Lionel Hampton "Steppin' Out," vol. 1, 1942–1945*.

70. Kenneth Randall, liner notes, *The Wild Man From Texas: Arnett Cobb* (Home Cooking Records, HCS-114, 1989).

71. "The Jitney Man" is included on *Kenny Dorham: Blues in Bebop* (Savoy, SVY-17028, 1998).

72. Ibid., liner notes, p. 4. Two albums by Dallas natives James Clay and David "Fathead" Newman are entitled *Wide Open Spaces* and *Return to the Wide Open Spaces*. See *Texan Jazz*, pp. 313–14.

73. *New Sounds: Art Blakey's Messengers/James Moody & His Modernists* (Blue Note, CDP 7 84436 2, 1991).

74. For more on Dorham's career, see Dave Oliphant, "Texas Bebop Messengers to the World: Kenny Dorham and Leo Wright," *The Journal of Texas Music History* 1, no. 1 (spring, 2001): [15]-23.

75. George Corley can be heard on *Boots and His Buddies 1935–1937* (Classics, 723, 1993) and *Boots and His Buddies 1937–1938* (Classics, 738, 1993).

76. For a full discussion of Bowman and the Fort Worth source of his most famous tune, see *Texan Jazz*, p. 29.

77. *Glenn Miller: Moonlight Serenade* (Bluebird, 61072, 1992).

78. Quoted by Michael James, liner notes, *Seeking/The New Art Jazz Ensemble* (Revelation Records, REV-9, 1969).

79. Christopher Evans, interview with Dewey Redman, *Fort Worth Star-Telegram,* Feb. 13, 1994, sections A & E.

80. Tony Baldwin, liner notes, *Hot Violins* (ABC Records, 836 049-2, 1988).

81. Ervin and Handy's "duel" on the Mingus recording of "No Private Income Blues" (on *Jazz Portraits: Mingus in Wonderland* [Blue Note, CDP7243 8 27325 2 5, 1994]) is an amazing performance unmatched by anything of its kind. For information on the career of Leo Wright, see note 74 above.

82. Among Texas women instrumentalists, trumpeter Clora Bryant, born in Denison, Texas, on May 30, 1929, was a member of an all-girl orchestra at Prairie View A&M, before establishing herself in Los Angeles as "one of the most respected trumpet players on the West Coast." See Sally Placksin, *American Women in Jazz, 1900 to the Present: Their Words, Lives, and Music* (New York: Putnam Wideview Books, 1982), p. 152. Bryant's one album, issued originally in 1957, is *Clora Bryant . . . Gal With a Horn* (Mode 106, V.S.O.P. #42, 1995). Her autobiographical sketch is included in Clora Bryant, et al., eds., *Central Avenue Sounds: Jazz in Los Angeles* (Berkeley: University of California Press, 1998).

# 3

# Put a Nickel in the Jukebox
## *The Texas Tradition in Country Music, 1922–50*

## Joe W. Specht

When Cindy Walker was inducted into the Country Music Hall of Fame in 1997, she became the sixty-fifth member and nineteenth Texan to be so honored. No other state has been singled out for more recognition. With more than one-fourth of the members of the Hall of Fame either Texas-born or Texas-raised, it is apparent that the Texas contribution to the development of country music has been significant. Historians and writers knowledgeable of the history of the music have long accepted this fact, too. Texas is recognized as the birthplace of western swing and honky-tonk music as well as the home of the singing cowboy. Country music scholars have also clearly documented the accomplishments or "firsts" of individual Texas performers. This essay will highlight some of these achievements from the period 1922–50 by focusing primarily on Texans in the Country Music Hall of Fame, and while the story will be familiar to many, one can only continue to be impressed with the richness of the Texas tradition in country music.[1]

If there is one word to describe the Lone Star State, it is diversity. Its sheer size, varied environment, distinct physical terrain, and multicultural population makes Texas a place of contrasts, and it is important to keep in mind this mix between land and people, particularly when discussing the music of the state. The settlers who came to Texas in the nineteenth century, primarily whites, blacks, and Hispanics, brought with them Anglo American folksong and minstrelsy, black blues, German and Czech polkas and waltzes, Cajun sounds of the Louisiana French, and *norteño* music of Mexico. For some, music was second only to language as a way of maintaining a link to their cultural roots and past. In addition, these groups brought a strong dance tradition, or as one writer has put it, they arrived in Texas "with dancing shoes ready." It is this mingling and blending of different music and dance styles that has given the state's music a great deal of its character and uniqueness, and at least in the 1920s and 1930s, this is what set off much of Texas country music from its counterparts in the Southeast United States.[2]

During the 1920s and 1930s, Texas country musicians also exhibited a willingness to adapt to and use new media and technology. In these two decades, the phonograph record, radio, motion picture, jukebox, and amplified and electrical musical instruments all became integral parts of the entertainment business. Texans were among the first, if not the first, in many instances to explore the possibilities of utilizing this technology to enhance or better promote their music. Some commentators trace the beginnings of country music to one of these Texas technological pioneers, and although Eck Robertson is not in the Country Music Hall of Fame, his importance cannot be overlooked.[3]

On June 30, 1922, Eck Robertson made country music history when he entered the New York City studio of the Victor Talking Machine Company and recorded a fiddle duet, "Arkansas Traveler," with his friend Henry Gilliland. Robertson's appearance at the Victor studios was unsolicited. He was there to see how phonograph records could be used to further his career as a professional musician. Most historians now agree that the fiddle tunes he made on that day and the next were the first commercial country music records ever recorded, and "Arkansas Traveler" backed with "Sallie Gooden" was the first commercial country music record to be released. Although it was Robertson's western clothes and Gilliland's Confederate uniform that seemed to create the most stir, the music is what counted. "Sallie Gooden," which Eck recorded alone, has been called "one of the finest recorded examples of old-time fiddling" and a "stunning, dynamic fiddling masterpiece." It brought the distinctive Texas fiddle style to the national scene, permanently recording it on wax for the first time. The impact, though not immediate, would percolate through country music for years to come.[4]

Alexander Campbell "Eck" Robertson was born in Delaney, Arkansas, in 1887. When he was three, his family moved to Texas, first Hamlin and then Vernon. Taking to the fiddle at an early age, Eck left home before he was seventeen, determined to make his living from music. By 1907, he was apparently wearing western clothes and promoting himself as "the cowboy fiddler" even though his ranching background was minimal. In fact, he had to be given his first pair of boots and a western hat because neither was part of his regular garb. Eck later claimed he was the first musician to wear western clothes on stage, and he was undoubtedly the first musician to record while dressed as a cowboy. This linking of cowboy and music is something that would not become commonplace in country music until a decade later. Robertson's decision to present himself in western attire is even more noteworthy when one understands that suit and tie, "going-to-town clothes," were what country music performers normally wore during this period. Eck's choice of outfit clearly shows that he understood the importance of his cowboy persona, which had stood him in good stead on the movie house circuit in Texas, and it offers one of the earliest examples of a country musician deliberately creating an image—"fabricating authenticity" as sociologist Richard Peterson has termed it—in selling himself and his music to a new audience.[5]

Robertson's list of other accomplishments is also noteworthy. Just two months before his visit to New York City and the Victor studios, the Fox News Service filmed the Vernon Fiddlers, of which Eck was a member. The Fiddlers' reputation apparently justified the travel of a Fox crew to Vernon in April, 1922, to film the trio for possible showing in movie houses across the country. Another first perhaps? Besides recordings, Robertson also looked to radio as means of advancing his career, at least for a while. On March 29, 1923, he performed "Sallie Gooden" and "Arkansas Traveler" on Fort Worth radio station WBAP. Country music historian Bill Malone has suggested that this could well have been the first radio performance by a country music recording artist, and in addition, Eck could have been the first country musician to promote or "plug" his records on the air. About this same time while living in Dallas, he also did radio work on KRLD for almost a year.[6]

Surprisingly, even though Robertson had composed his own radio theme song and continued to advertise himself as a "Radio Artist," he did not broadcast on radio again except for a brief, four-month stint in Wichita Falls in 1941. Even more curious is the fact that after his initial Victor session in 1922 it was seven years before he returned to the recording studio. In the interim, while Eck continued making personal appearances and competing in fiddle contests throughout the state, several other Texas fiddlers were recorded, including W. B. Chenoweth

("The Texas Fiddling Wampus Cat"), Confederate veteran Captain M. J. Bonner, and the still legendary Prince Albert Hunt. Robertson's two 1929 sessions that were held in Dallas in August and October found him in his prime, yet these would be his last recordings except for some transcription work for J. E. Sellers in 1940 and some home taping in 1963. Charles Wolfe, who has written knowledgeably about Eck's recording career, attributes Robertson's failure to follow up on his initial success to "a series of misfortunes, poor timing, and missed opportunities." Whatever the reasons were, nothing changes the facts that Robertson, a seasoned professional, went to New York City on his own initiative specifically to record, and his groundbreaking session blazed a trail for a long line of Texans to follow. And follow they did.[7]

Another Texas country music pioneer, Vernon Dalhart, did not have to travel far at all to make his mark on the music. In fact, he was already in New York City—actually the Bronx—where he had been living since 1910. He was born Marion Try Slaughter in the East Texas town of Jefferson in 1883. Trained as a singer at the Dallas Conservatory of Music, he took his professional name from two Texas towns, Vernon and Dalhart, both of which were close to ranches where he had worked in the mid-to-late 1890s. After moving from Dallas to New York intent on a career in music, he eventually appeared in several operettas including *H.M.S. Pinafore* and *Madame Butterfly*.[8]

In 1915, Dalhart responded to an advertisement soliciting singers to record, and a second career as a recording artist was soon underway. One of his earliest releases, "Can't Yo Heah Me Callin'," was sung in black dialect, an accent he later attributed to his Jefferson, Texas, childhood experience. Scottish novelist Duncan McLean has posed the question: "So was Dalhart the first white singer to make records in the style of blacks?" Whether he was or not, this song is just one example of how Dalhart drew on his Texas roots and incorporated them into his singing style. From 1917–23, he recorded a variety of pop songs, fox-trots, Hawaiian harmonies, as well as songs in black dialect for Edison, Columbia, and Victor, most of which sold well. By 1924, however, with his pop sales declining, Dalhart approached Victor to record country songs, and an unlikely country music superstar was about to be born.[9]

Victor officials at first were reluctant to allow their pop star to test the country market, but they finally agreed, giving a boost to Dalhart's slumping recording career and also a financial shot in the arm for the company. His choice for his first country release, "The Wreck of the Old '97," had previously been recorded by several country performers and in fact had already been recorded by Dalhart himself just two months earlier for Edison. To this point, country music sales had been largely regional, confined primarily to states in the Southeast. With the release of "The Wreck of the Old '97" backed with "The Prisoner's Song," commercial country music really was born. The Victor record was the first country music disc to sell a million copies, and the pairing of these two songs, which was eventually released on close to fifty different labels, produced sales totaling 25 million worldwide.

For the next four years, Dalhart not only dominated the country music field but he was also most likely the best-selling vocalist in the pop market as well. His songs were in such demand that it was not unusual for him to record up to three sessions a day during this period. Other million-selling releases included "The Death of Floyd Collins" and "My Blue Ridge Mountain Home." His record sales have been estimated at more than 75 million, of which two-thirds were country songs. One factor contributing to these sales figures was the propensity of Dalhart and the recording companies to rerecord and release the same songs under a bewildering variety of pseudonyms. For example, Mack Allen, another tip of the hat to a Texas town (McAllen), was his third-most-used recording name. By the early 1930s, however, his inability to change with the times as radio and live performances became more important resulted in declining sales and growing disinterest on the part of the record companies. Although he attempted several comebacks, Dalhart was never again a force in the music.[10]

In 1981, Dalhart was elected to the Country Music Hall of Fame, and his plaque reads in part: "the first popular singer to demonstrate the wide appeal and economic potential of country music." There can be no doubt that his success did open the eyes of record company executives to a largely untapped market, something the recording industry needed since the latest media rage, the radio, had drastically reduced record purchases. The tremendous sales of Dalhart's records clearly demonstrated that country music could appeal to more than just southern listeners, too. As Ralph Peer, the Victor producer who first recorded Jimmie Rodgers and the Carter Family, pointed out: "Dalhart had the peculiar ability to adapt hillbilly music to suit the taste of the nonhillbilly audience." Even at this early stage in the music's development, the crossover potential was already present. In fact, "The Prisoner's Song" is a precursor of sorts to the country pop style that has periodically flourished in country music. One can view Dalhart's decision to record country music, then, as either cynical and opportunistic or as a natural and logical career move given his background. In either case, and no matter what one thinks about his conservatory-trained voice, it should not obscure the fact that by drawing on his Texas roots he was able to sing songs that appealed to a country music audience, and in so doing, he was the first country music recording performer to become a world-wide star.[11]

The two singing cowboys in the Country Music Hall of Fame are also from the Lone Star State. Tex Ritter was elected in 1964, and Gene Autry was inducted four years later. The careers of Autry and Ritter offer some insight into how the phenomenon of the movie singing cowboy affected country music particularly during the 1930s and 1940s.[12]

Orvon Gene Autry was born in 1907 in Tioga, Texas. While growing up on ranches in Texas and Oklahoma, his interest in music was fostered by his mother who also taught him how to play the guitar. After one failed attempt, Autry began his recording career in New York City in 1929 by making records for a variety of labels. Later signing with American Record Corporation (known as ARC) and producer Art Satherley, his first hit in 1931, "That Silver Haired Daddy of Mine," proved to be one of the most popular country songs of the decade. This led to an invitation to join the WLS National Barn Dance as Oklahoma's Singing Cowboy. Three years later, because of his popularity on records and radio and through the efforts of Satherley, Autry was in Hollywood at Republic Pictures. The next year, 1935, he had his first staring role in the feature-length western *Tumbling Tumbleweeds.* The public could not get enough of this unassuming screen hero, and other movie studios scrambled to find their own singing cowboys. By 1937, Gene was the number-one western star at the box office. In 1940, he contracted with CBS to do a weekly radio show, *Melody Ranch,* which was broadcast nationally and ran until 1956. Autry's utilization of the three principal entertainment media of the time—records, radio, and movies—was unmatched in the country field and rivaled in the pop arena only by Bing Crosby. Later he expanded into television as well.[13]

For country music, at least two aspects of Autry's multi-faceted career are important: the songs he sang and the clothes he wore. Many of his earliest recordings were done in the style of the popular Blue Yodeler, Jimmie Rodgers, but he proved to be more than just a Rodgers clone. His recorded output in the early 1930s ranges from sentimental tunes to the blues, many of which he wrote himself. His first hit, "That Silver Haired Daddy of Mine," was in fact an Autry original, co-written with his friend and recording partner Jimmy Long. The song, which conjured up turn-of-the-century images of Appalachian mountains, sold half a million records and provided him with a nonwestern theme he returned to often. His eclectic approach to the music fit in well on the WLS National Barn Dance, which, unlike many of the radio barn dances of the day, offered its listeners a wide variety of musical styles. Soon after joining WLS, Autry also had his own morning program, *Conqueror Record Time,* which featured Gene as a cowboy singing western songs. Oddly enough, he had to be convinced by Satherley to adopt this format. At the time, he was more interested in crooning romantic ballads in the Rudy Vallee mode, and he would utilize these pop style leanings later.

By the time he left for the West Coast in 1934, Autry was a star on the rise, but it was his movies in combination with his records that made him such an important factor in taking country music to a larger audience. No other singing cowboy or country performer packed this dual punch. Hits from the Hollywood years included "Tumbling Tumbleweeds," "Mexicali Rose," "Back in the Saddle Again," and "South of the Border." Many of the songs he recorded and sang in his movies were self-penned, but professional songwriters of the Tin Pan Alley variety were crafting most of the tunes he sang on screen. While incorporating western themes, the emphasis was on romantic and escapist lyrics, so the songs in actuality had little to do with the music of real-life cowboys. Of course, the movies he sang them in were pure fantasy as well. Film historian Jon Tuska has described Autry's films as "not so much musical Westerns as Western musicals" which became even more the case as orchestra and choruses were added to the mix. He continued to record songs of a nonwestern nature, too, and some observers see the roots of the country pop or, as Gene called it, the "soft-country" sound in some of his songs, the 1935 hit "You're the Only Star in My Blue Heaven" being an often-cited example. No one has ever claimed Autry had a great voice, and his genial singing style has been described as warm and mellow as well as innocuous. There can be no doubt, however, that his smooth vocals struck a responsive chord with the movie-going and record-buying public. Increasingly, western and country or country and western, if you will, came to be associated together.[14]

The way Autry and the other movie singing cowboys dressed also influenced country music. Although I have chosen to use the inclusive term country music in this essay, during the first twenty-five years of its recorded history, country music most often was called hillbilly music by the press and marketed as such by the record companies. By the time Autry gained prominence in the mid-to-late 1930s, there was growing disenchantment among many country music performers, especially Texans, with the negative connotations of the hillbilly moniker. As we will see later, both Bob Wills and Ernest Tubb often expressed displeasure with the hillbilly label.[15]

Even though the gaudy garb of Autry and the other silver screen singing cowboys had little connection with the real life of the working cowboy, the clothes came to embody much of the romance and mystique of the Old West. Earlier in the decade, Jimmie Rodgers had shown the possibilities of mixing western dress and country music, but it was not until the Hollywood singing cowboy phenomenon swept the nation that western-cut outfits really caught the attention of country performers. By the late 1930s and early 1940s, cowboy duds, boots, and Stetson hats had been adopted by many country music artists who had little or no western background. It is important to remember, though, that the change in clothing did not necessarily mean a change in the music. Still, cowboy shirts and suits like the ones worn by Autry and his fellow riders of the screen offered a viable alternative to the hillbilly stereotype and an opportunity for country musicians to change their image, if not completely in the public's eye, at least in their own.[16]

The other singing cowboy in the Country Music Hall of Fame, Tex Ritter, was born Woodward Maurice Ritter in 1906 in Panola County near Murvaul, Texas. Growing up in East Texas did not give him much of a chance to sample cowboy life firsthand, but he still collected cowboy songs as a hobby. This interest later was heightened when he entered the University of Texas in 1922. Here he came under the tutelage of English professor and southwestern folklorist J. Frank Dobie, noted ballad collector John Lomax, and composer and voice teacher Oscar J. Fox. Ritter's years at the university provided him with a scholar's interest in cowboy lore that lasted a lifetime, and the ballads Lomax had collected and first published in 1910, *Cowboy Songs and Other Frontier Ballads,* proved to be of particular importance.[17]

From Austin, Tex headed to Houston in 1929 and tried his hand at radio work on KPRC singing cowboy songs. He then moved to New York City and began his acting career on Broadway appearing in several productions including *Green Grow the Lilacs.* During his stay in the Big Apple, besides picking up the nickname Tex, he had his own radio show, *Cowboy Tom's Roundup,* plus he co-hosted the WHN National Barn Dance. With the growing popularity of Gene Autry's movies and the demand for other singing cowboys, Ritter's Hollywood call came from

*Tex Ritter. From the Lomax (John Avery)*
*Family Papers, 1842–1986.*
*Courtesy Center for American History, UT-Austin*

producer Edward Finney in 1936. After a successful audition, Tex was off to star in Grand National's *Song of the Gringo,* the first of his more than sixty movies. Finney said later he wanted to make real westerns with someone who could sing a good song, and after listening to some of Ritter's Decca recordings, he knew he had found his man.

Although Tex had signed with Decca Records in 1935, his recording career had actually begun two years earlier with ARC. The first song he recorded for ARC in 1932, "The Cowboy's Christmas Ball," was never released, but it is important, nevertheless, because it came from Lomax's *Cowboy Songs and Other Frontier Ballads.* When Tex returned to the ARC studio the next year, two of the four songs he recorded, "Goodbye Old Paint" and "Jack O Diamonds," were also from the Lomax collection. "Jack O Diamonds" he called "Rye Whiskey." Art

Satherley, the producer at these sessions, recognized even then that "Rye Whiskey" was special and encouraged Tex to continue singing it whenever he had the chance. Ritter did just that, and "Rye Whiskey" became one of his signature songs. He would record it again for Capitol Records in 1945 and 1959.

The ARC sessions were recorded with just Ritter and his guitar and find Tex drawling and yipping his way through the songs with guitar and voice seemingly out of sync at times. Not surprisingly, the records did not sell well, but they do offer the listener the opportunity to hear authentic cowboy ballads being sung like a working cowboy might have sung them. That Ritter's ARC recordings actually were released commercially makes them even more unique. When he began recording for Decca in 1935, Tex cut two more of the Lomax collected ballads, "Sam Hall" and "Git Along Little Dogies," at his first session. "Sam Hall," which was again just Ritter and his guitar, is probably one of the Decca records that Edward Finney heard, because Tex sings it along with "Rye Whiskey" in *Song of the Gringo.* This was not the last time Ritter sang traditional cowboy ballads on screen either. He sprinkled selections from the Lomax collection into eleven of his other movies, which lent the musical content of the films even more authenticity particularly when compared with the westerns being made at Republic by Gene Autry and Roy Rogers.[18]

Even though he is considered the most believable and genuine of the movie singing cowboys, budget restrictions imposed on his films by producers, like Edward Finney, prevented Ritter from becoming a movie star of the magnitude of an Autry or Rogers. His recording career was something else, however. After signing with newly formed Capitol Records in 1942, Tex racked up top-ten country jukebox hits with regularity throughout the decade while at the same time continuing to record cowboy songs including those found in *Cowboy Songs and Other Frontier Ballads.* Writer and critic John Morthland has described Ritter as "an unlikely combination of ethnomusicologist and recording artist." He was also an educator of sorts who throughout his long career regularly exposed his audiences to the life and lore of the cowboy. Many of the songs he sang on record and on the silver screen offered listeners and viewers alike a taste of what cowboy songs were all about. In his own way, then, Tex Ritter helped keep the songs of the American West alive in commercial media not known for a sense of tradition.[19]

Of course, there was more to country music in the 1930s than singing cowboys. In Texas, a musical hybrid, later to be dubbed western swing, was about to burst forth on the national scene with two Texans, Milton Brown and Bob Wills, its primary shapers. Brown continues to receive belated recognition; Wills, on the other hand, was elected to the Country Music Hall of Fame in 1968. James Robert Wills was born in 1905 near Kosse, Texas, in Limestone County. His family moved west to Hall County in 1913, eventually settling on a farm between the Big Red and Little Red Rivers. Wills's musical roots lie in the breakdown fiddle tradition that he learned from his father, John Wills, a respected contest fiddler, and the music he heard most often on records and radio, especially blues and dixieland jazz. Willie Milton Brown was born in 1903 in Stephenville, Texas. In 1918, his family moved to Fort Worth. Milton's father, Barty Brown, was also a breakdown fiddler who played for house dances; however, the younger Brown's musical background, which came primarily from singing in vocal groups, tended to put more emphasis on the popular music of the day.[20]

Wills and Brown met in Fort Worth in 1930 and soon joined forces playing for dances and performing on the radio, first as the Aladdin Laddies, then as the Light Crust Doughboys. Milton handled most of the singing chores, and Bob was on fiddle along with guitarists Herman Arnspiger and Derwood Brown. The inclusion of vocals in a string band lineup, while it might not seem revolutionary today, had seldom been tried before. Certainly it had never been done by a singer as versatile as Milton who could toss off a risqué blues number as easily as the latest pop song. The Doughboys soon became one of the hottest attractions in the area. The one recording the Wills-Brown aggregation made together in 1932 (as the Fort Worth Doughboys) offers a hint as to what they might have sounded like in person.

Milton left the Light Crust Doughboys in 1932 and formed his own band, the Musical Brownies. In short order, he added a doghouse bass to help beef up the fiddle–guitar–tenor banjo lineup. Even more important was his hiring of a piano player with a jazz background and the adding of a second fiddle to the band. In 1934 when Bob Dunn came on board with his amplified steel guitar, another first in country music, all the ingredients were in place. The recordings the Brownies made for Bluebird in 1934, and especially those for Decca in 1935 and 1936, give the listener a chance to sample their jazzy take-off solos as well as the variety of their blues and pop-tinged oeuvre. A daily radio show, first on KTAT and later on WBAP, along with constant touring, made them the most popular dance band in the state during this period. Unfortunately, at the height of their popularity in 1936, Brown died as the result of a car accident. He was only thirty-two years old. The Brownies disbanded the next year.

Milton Brown's role in the development of western swing was significant. He brought certain essential elements to the string band music of the day that permitted it to evolve into what is now called western swing. These innovations included the use of pop vocals, slapped bass, jazz-oriented piano, twin fiddles, and amplified steel guitar. Because of his tragic and premature death, we will never know what else Brown might have accomplished with his music. Even so, there can be no doubt that the Musical Brownies were the prototype western swing outfit with an influence that resonated throughout Texas and the Southwest well into the next decade.[21]

Bob Wills remained with the Light Crust Doughboys until 1933. After a couple of tries in Waco and Oklahoma City, he and his own band, the Texas Playboys, settled down in Tulsa in 1934 and began daily radio broadcasts on KVOO. With stellar musicians like Leon McAuliffe and Al Stricklin plus the singing talents of Tommy Duncan, the Texas Playboys quickly established themselves as an organization with which to be reckoned. By the time the band recorded for the first time in 1935, Bob had made some significant additions to the string band lineup himself. Drums and horns, both foreign to country music, were now an integral part of the Texas Playboys. He continued to add more fiddles, horns, and electric guitars until by the early 1940s the Playboys numbered as many as twenty-two pieces. It was during this period, particularly after he relocated to the West Coast in 1943, that Wills's fame soared, spilling over onto the national scene. The Texas Playboys' recordings on Vocalion, OKeh, and Columbia were both popular sellers and jukebox favorites. His 1940 hit, "New San Antonio Rose," was reaching millions of listeners via Bing Crosby's cover version. All of this plus screen roles in a series of westerns (his first movie was with Tex Ritter), write-ups in national magazines like *Time,* and sold-out dances for crowds numbering in the thousands spread the Wills name across the country, making him the catalyst for popularizing western swing.

Brown and Wills tower over the Texas western swing scene of the 1930s and early 1940s, but there were others who made their mark as well, including Bill Boyd, Roy Newman, Adolph Hofner, Jimmie Revard, and Cliff Bruner. Country music discographer Tony Russell has estimated that during the period 1932 to 1942 "western swing was defined by about 50 bands who made 2,000 sides." Of course the music these bands were playing was not called western swing. That term or phrase would not appear until the mid-1940s out on the West Coast when it first was used to refer to Spade Cooley's music. During this earlier period, record companies applied a variety of descriptions such as "Hot String Band with Singing" and "Novelty Hot Dance." Vocalion, Wills's recording label, often listed the Texas Playboys' records in the "Folk Music" section. Researcher Bob Pinson has reported that in 1941 the *Victor Record Review* used the term "Texas Swing" for the latest releases by several Texas and Louisiana groups, which points out just how closely this type of music was associated with the Lone Star State.[22]

Even before there was a commonly accepted name for the music, two things were apparent. First and foremost, western swing was music for dancing. Unlike the country music being played in the Southeast where the norm was to sit and listen, the audiences in the Southwest came expecting to dance, and as the setting moved from house parties to dance halls, the bands changed to accommodate the larger and louder crowds. Second, the music itself was a diverse, eclectic mixture of blues, jazz, pop, swing, western, Tin Pan Alley, norteño music, fiddle tunes, Czech and German schottisches and waltzes, something old or something new. You name it. Whatever worked was acceptable. It should be noted here that some contemporary writers continue to confuse the differences between jazz and swing or dance music and attempt to place western swing within the jazz mainstream. Take-off solos and instrumental improvisation long associated with jazz are certainly part of the mix, but the variety of musical styles and repertory along with the number of musicians and bands involved make such attempts difficult, indeed futile. Western swing was fusion music in every sense of the word, perhaps the ultimate fusion music, but it was definitely part of the country music family.[23]

Despite the contrasts between western swing and the country music being played in the Southeast, to the news media and much of the general public it was still hillbilly music and worthy of only patronizing recognition at best. Being stuck with the hillbilly or "Okie" tag was particularly rankling to Wills as he was quick to remind a writer for *Time:* "Please don't anybody confuse us with none of them hillbilly outfits." However, there can be no confusion about one aspect of the music: western swing, particularly as played by the Texas Playboys, was music with a beat. Testimony from musicians, fans, and impartial observers all attest to this fact, and it was never more apparent than in 1944 when Bob and the Playboys made one of their rare guest appearances on the Grand Ole Opry. Country music legend Eddy Arnold was standing off stage: "They just stopped the show cold. They had a good heavy dance beat. And in that old building [Ryman Auditorium], which had great acoustics, it was just overpowering." Western swing will of course always be remembered for bringing electric guitars, drums, etc. to country music, but it just might be the rock solid dance beat that is the most important legacy. This is surely one of the reasons that Bob Wills and his Texas Playboys were inducted in 1999 into, yes, the Rock and Roll Hall of Fame in the Early Influences category.[24]

As western swing reached its height of popularity during World War II, another offshoot of the Texas dance tradition, honky-tonk music, was making its presence known. Nick Tosches has tracked the term "honky-tonk" as far back as 1893 to the East Texas–Oklahoma–Louisiana region. Honky-tonk later popped up in a Tin Pan Alley tune in 1916, but it was not until Texan Al Dexter recorded "Honky-Tonk Blues" in 1936 that the phrase first appeared in a country song. By the time honky-tonk became part of the country music vocabulary, it not only referred to the beer joints where the music was played but also to a sound or style as well as a state of mind. In a sense, the sound was just a downsized version of western swing. Because musicians playing in honky-tonk roadhouses— like those who performed in western swing dance halls—had to cope with the noise of the crowd, electric steel and standard guitars became the featured instruments of the honky-tonk combos. String bass and piano, if available, were also part of the mix, but tenor banjo, a mainstay of western swing rhythm sections, gradually disappeared; in its place, acoustic guitar supplied a closed-chord or sock rhythm. Drums were not to become commonplace until the 1950s.[25]

While western swing was first and foremost music for dancing, honky-tonk music wedded the beat to the lyric with increasing emphasis on the singer. The songs were at first primarily upbeat and seemingly lightweight, Al Dexter's "Pistol Packin' Mama" serves as a good example. With the coming of World War II, the lyrics began to focus more on the dilemmas and problems facing a population on the move from the farm to the city. Honky-tonk songs expressed the fears, frustration, and even anger of many Americans as they attempted to adjust to the changes brought on by the war and its aftermath. Seldom before in country music had subjects such as alcoholism, infidelity, and divorce been dealt with so openly and with such candor and directness.

If any one city can be singled out as the spawning ground for honky-tonk music, it is undoubtedly Houston. The Bayou City was a hotbed of musical activity and opportunity, and it was here in the late 1930s that bands like the Blue Ridge Playboys and Cliff Bruner's Texas Wanderers began making the transition from swing to honky-tonk. Several pioneers of the new sounds came out of these bands including Ted Daffan, Moon Mullican, and Floyd Tillman. Steel guitar wizard Bob Dunn had also moved to the area, and he—along with a host of other talented musicians such as Leo Raley, the music's first electric mandolinist—formed an interchangeable group of players who moved back and forth from one band to another.[26]

Of all the musicians who were part of the Houston music scene, few could match Floyd Tillman's triple-threat talents as guitarist, songwriter, and vocal stylist. Tillman was born in 1914 in Ryan, Oklahoma, but grew up in Post, Texas, where his family moved when he was less than a year old. As a teenager, Floyd got his musical education playing mandolin and then guitar in a family band. He later purchased a guitar with a metal resonator inside it that provided acoustic amplification, and he also began to experiment with improvised single-string solos. By the time Tillman relocated to Houston in 1934 and joined the Blue Ridge Playboys, according to fellow band mate Ted Daffan, he was playing "the most innovative lead guitar I have ever heard." Daffan, who then was also the owner of a radio repair shop, made an electric pickup for Floyd's guitar so it could be electrically amplified. When the Blue Ridge Playboys recorded for the first time in 1936, Tillman's electric lead guitar licks made him one of the earliest exponents of the instrument on record and placed him in the electric vanguard that was beginning to sweep through Texas and the Southwest.[27]

By 1939, after a stint with a Houston pop orchestra and a brief return to the Blue Ridge Playboys, Floyd was recording and touring on his own. He had already begun writing songs and, in fact, sang three of his compositions on the 1936 Blue Ridge Playboys' session. His songwriting prowess soon caught the attention of the Houston music community, and in 1938 Cliff Bruner's Texas Wanderers recorded two of Floyd's songs, "I'll Keep on Loving You," and "It Makes No Difference Now." Both sold well, but "It Makes No Difference Now" began to take on a life of its own. Jimmie Davis, Gene Autry, and, perhaps most importantly, Bing Crosby also recorded the song. Crosby's version, paired with "New San Antonio Rose," was one of the top-selling records of 1941, and its success provided the first indication that Tillman's tunes possessed pop appeal, too. During World War II, Floyd wrote and recorded several jukebox hits for Decca, but his songs would have their greatest impact and success in the postwar years.

Honky-tonk music had been incubating in the roadhouses of the Lone Star State since the late 1930s, but partly because of the 1942–43 strike of the American Federation of Musicians, which resulted in a recording ban, the music's first real flowering on disc did not come until the mid-to-late 1940s. Texans Ted Daffan and Cindy Walker were among the songwriters who brought the honky-tonk consciousness to the nation with classic odes like Daffan's "Born to Lose" and "Headin' Down the Wrong Highway" and Walker's "Bubbles in My Beer" and "Warm Red Wine." However, the songwriting high priest of hurtin' and cheatin' anthems could well have been Tillman. Nick Tosches has called Floyd's "Slippin' Around" the "granddaddy of all country cheating songs." Both Tillman on Columbia and Ernest Tubb on Decca had best-selling versions, but it was Margaret Whiting and Jimmy Wakley's duet recording on Capitol that became the runaway hit, reaching number one in 1949 on both the pop and country best-seller and jukebox charts. Floyd's pop-tinged lyrics that were mixed with a healthy dose of realism continued to make his songs perfect crossover candidates for pop producers who were looking increasingly to rhythm and blues and country music recordings for material to cover and sell to a pop audience. During a span of two years (1947–49), in addition to "Slippin' Around," Tillman also wrote and recorded a trio of songs that, while closely associated with the period, transcend the honky-tonk genre. "I Love You So Much, It Hurts," "This Cold War with You," and "I Gotta Have My Baby Back" rank with some of the finest songwriting of the era, and these songs remain standards to this day.[28]

If Tillman's songwriting abilities had not made him special, the way he sang the songs certainly would have. At a time when country music abounded with unique stylists, no one sounded more unique than Floyd. His voice has been described as lazy and drawling, and just plain bad, but whether he was slurring a word or singing behind or ahead of the beat, there was no mistaking the Tillman touch. His roots in the Houston swing scene and the early influence of Bing Crosby also set his style apart. Willie Nelson, a long-time admirer whose singing has sometimes been compared to Tillman's, sums it up this way: "Floyd has an individual phrasing, a western-type jazz way of doing things." Tillman also took an individual approach when it came to his career. Instead of following the growing migration to Nashville, he chose instead to remain in Texas and Houston. For many years, he did not even have a manager, preferring to handle his own bookings. This independent stance, which was never fully understood or appreciated by the Nashville country

music establishment, did not go unnoticed in his home state where
Floyd has been dubbed the Original Outlaw and the Legendary Cosmic
Cowboy. When he finally received official recognition for all his contri-
butions to the music and was inducted into the Country Music Hall of
Fame in 1984, it was more than appropriate for another Texas maver-
ick, Willie Nelson, to present Tillman with the award.[29]

None of the early honky-tonk heroes would have a greater or a
longer lasting impact than Ernest Dale Tubb, a member of the Country
Music Hall of Fame since 1965. The son of a rowdy, sharecropping father
and a religious, hardworking mother, he was born in Crisp, Texas, in
1914. Tubb discovered the music of Jimmie Rodgers when he was thirteen years old, and the Blue Yodeler proved to be Tubb's inspiration to
pursue a music career. Perhaps just as important in this quest was the
role played by Rodgers's widow, Carrie, whom Ernest first met in San
Antonio in 1936. She quickly became both a friend and patron, and
it was through her efforts that he secured a recording contract with
Rodgers's own label, Victor Records. Her support in these early years
was crucial, and it is just one of the reasons why throughout his long career Tubb did his best to ensure that Jimmie Rodgers's legacy to country music was never forgotten.[30]

The influence of Rodgers was readily apparent in the recordings
Ernest made for Victor in 1936 and 1937. He not only yodeled but also
accompanied himself on one of Jimmie's guitars that Mrs. Rodgers had
loaned to him; however, neither of the two records released at the time
sold well. Tubb spent the next four years on the move, struggling to keep
his fledgling career alive before finally catching on in 1940 on Fort Worth
radio station KGKO, where he soon became known as the Gold Chain
Troubadour (Gold Chain Flour was his sponsor). Earlier that same year,
and again with the assistance of Carrie Rodgers, he signed with Decca
Records. By this time, a tonsillectomy had forced him to drop the yodel
and develop his own singing style. In addition, he was still just using
acoustic guitar accompaniment, and this proved to be a problem when
his records were played on jukeboxes in Texas honky-tonks. As Tubb re-
counted to his biographer Ronnie Pugh in a often-repeated story, a Fort
Worth jukebox operator told him: "as soon as the crowd gets in there and
gets noisy, they start dancing, they can't hear your records, they start
playing Bob Wills: you need to make them louder."[31]

Because jukebox sales accounted for more than half of all the
records sold at the time, Ernest could not afford to ignore the advice. At
his next Decca session, held in Dallas in 1941, he added both an elec-

tric guitar and a string bass to make his records louder, and it was not long before a little four-note turnaround developed by his lead guitar player became one of the most recognizable sounds in country music and a Tubb calling card. While western swing bands had been using electric amplification since the mid-1930s, both in person and on record, Tubb's early, almost tentative, experiments illustrate how slowly other country musicians, even in Texas, adopted these innovations. The jukebox was an important catalyst, then, for not only taking honky-tonk music out of the Lone Star State but also for bringing electric instruments more into the country music mainstream.[32]

The 1941 Dallas session also produced the song that made Tubb a star. "Walking the Floor Over You," one of his own compositions, quickly became a jukebox favorite and proved to be just the thing he needed to kick his career into high gear. Throughout the rest of the decade, he was one of the undisputed country music kings of the jukebox with hits like "You Nearly Lose Your Mind," "Soldier's Last Letter," "Slippin' Around," and "Warm Red Wine." After filming two Hollywood westerns in 1942 with Charles Starrett, Ernest joined the cast of the Grand Ole Opry in 1943 and brought the Texas honky-tonk sounds east of the Mississippi River and to the Opry stage for the first time. Just as importantly, the Opry radio broadcasts on WSM, a clear-channel, 50,000-watt station, took the new sounds of Tubb and his Texas Troubadours directly into the homes of country music listeners throughout the South and Midwest. With his ever-increasing record sales, jukebox popularity, and regular exposure on the Opry and WSM, there was no bigger star in country music during the 1940s.[33]

One of the things that undoubtedly contributed to his success was the fact that Tubb was another of the era's unique stylists. A singer he was not, as he readily admitted on more than one occasion, but even when he sang a quarter step flat or seemed to drag down the tempo, no one had the ability to convey a full range of emotions any better than Ernest. Fellow Texan Willie Nelson has said: "I would compare Ernest Tubb to Frank Sinatra in that they both had distinctive styles that you couldn't confuse with anybody else." As unlikely as it might seem, Tubb was often compared with Sinatra, the rage of the bobby-soxers, even when it came to sex appeal. This is how one of Ernest's female fans described him in 1945: "Ernest Tubb is my Frank Sinatra. I cry and swoon when he sings." He also had an impact on the boys, too, inspiring a host of would-be male country vocalists including a young Hank Williams.[34]

In 1947, at perhaps the height of his popularity, Tubb appeared at

Carnegie Hall in New York City. One of the highlights of his career, it also was important for bringing an Opry troupe to the stage of the hallowed hall for the first time. Not everyone viewed this event as a triumph, however. The headline in *Down Beat,* a leading music magazine, read: "Hillbillies Take Over Carnegie Hall, But Good." The reporter continued: "Getta long little doggie and saddle ol' Paint! Darned if the hillbillies didn't gross some $12,000 in the big 57th St. barn sometimes called Carnegie Hall." Country music entertainers had endured this type of condescending, sarcastic coverage in the press for many years; the *Down Beat* article provides a sense of the second-class status still accorded to country music by much of the public and the media.[35]

Intent on reversing this negative attitude, Tubb approached Dave Kapp, his producer at Decca, with the suggestion that the company stop using the term "hillbilly" in its promotional material and catalogs. The type of ridicule, even contempt, associated with this term obviously was meant as much for the performers as it was for the music, and Ernest clearly understood the class connotations that it involved. It was all a matter of respect. Because his record sales for Decca were second only to Bing Crosby's at the time, Kapp was more than willing to listen. With input from Tubb, Decca ditched the hillbilly tag and adopted "country and western" in its place. The rest of the industry followed, and even though the music had not changed, the perception eventually did. As for the respect, it came too, if a little slower, but the Texas Troubadour never forgot what had been at stake. Thirty years later, he would remind journalist and author Peter Guralnick: "When you call me hillbilly, just smile."[36]

Another Texan directly involved in the changing landscape of country music in the 1940s was Cindy Walker. Born in Mart, Texas, Walker began her show business career as a youngster by singing and dancing in Texas stage shows. She already had begun to write songs, too. In 1940, she and her mother accompanied her father on a business trip to Los Angeles, and Cindy went there prepared: "L.A. meant music to me. Mamma worried about clothes while I worried about getting all my songs in one briefcase." The rest of the story reads like a Hollywood movie script. Within the year, Walker successfully pitched a song, "Lone Star Trail," to Bing Crosby, who had a top-ten pop hit with it. She appeared in the Gene Autry western *Ride Tenderfoot Ride.* And she recorded several songs for Decca with Texas Jim Lewis and His Lone Star Cowboys, including "Seven Beers with the Wrong Man," which was also filmed as a "Soundie," a precursor of today's music video. Her talents

*Cindy Walker.*
*From the collection of Cindy Walker*

obviously made an impression. What began as a visit turned out to be a thirteen-year stay in Tinsel Town.[37]

When Cindy recorded for Decca again in 1941, this time on her own, she was accompanied by members of Spike Jones's City Slickers. Two of the songs she recorded, "He Knew All the Answers" and "Don't Talk to Me About Men," gave some indication that Walker already understood something about the male-oriented business in which she was operating. Two other Decca sessions followed, and the second one in 1944 produced her only jukebox hit, "When My Blue Moon Turns to Gold Again." Interestingly enough, the song was not even a Walker composition. She recorded only occasionally after this, instead devoting her energies primarily to songwriting, and for good reason. Her songs were in demand by both singers and music publishers alike.[38]

Walker's arrival in Hollywood in 1940 could not have come at a more opportune time for a young songwriter just getting established. Because of a dispute with the American Society of Composers, Authors and Publishers over music-licensing fees, the National Association of Broadcasters had recently established a rival organization, namely Broadcast Music Incorporated. Although Gene Autry and Bob Wills were both members, ASCAP had virtually excluded blues and country music songwriters from its ranks. On the other hand, BMI was actively courting these outsiders to supply its needs for new songs to license for radio airplay, both live and on record. For the first time, music publishers and record companies began regularly turning to a growing cadre of country music songwriting professionals to provide a steady stream of original material. Cindy quickly proved she was one of the best of this new breed.[39]

Although Walker's songs have been recorded by a variety of pop and country singers, the ties she established during her early years in Hollywood with a group of fellow Texans, all songwriters in their own right, proved to be especially satisfying both personally and professionally. These Texas connections helped her to become one of the best-selling songwriters of the decade. After appearing with Gene Autry in *Ride Tenderfoot Ride,* Cindy collaborated with him on several songs including "Silver Spurs (On the Golden Stairs)," which was a top-five jukebox hit for Autry in 1946. Gene later recorded her "Blue Canadian Rockies" in 1950. She also met and became lifelong friends with Tex Ritter and his wife, Dorothy Fay. Tex not only used a few of her tunes in his films but also recorded an entire album of her songs. Undoubtedly Cindy's two favorite Texans, at least in the recording studio, were Bob Wills and Ernest Tubb. After recording four of her compositions at a session in 1941, Wills became such an enthusiastic supporter that he helped Walker secure a contract with Columbia Pictures to write the songs for eight westerns he was preparing to film with Russell Hayden. "Cherokee Maiden," "Dusty Skies," "Miss Molly," "Sugar Moon," and "Bubbles in My Beer" are just a few of Cindy's tunes that Bob recorded during the decade, and she continued to supply him with material for the next thirty years. Her association with Ernest Tubb began a year later, in 1942, when Tubb was in Hollywood filming his first western. The two toured together in 1944, but it was not until 1949 that the Texas Troubadour hit pay dirt with a Walker original, "Warm Red Wine," which includes the memorable first line: "Put a nickel in the jukebox and let it play." Over the next decade, Ernest regularly returned to the Walker song bag and eventually recorded eighteen of her compositions.[40]

One of the things that made Walker's song writing so special was her ability to compose what she called "tailor-made songs," and, as her track record shows, she was able to match songs to singers quite nicely. Few in the profession were as versatile as Cindy when it came to composing western-flavored tunes for the movies, honky-tonk anthems for the jukebox, and country pop ballads. Clearly ahead of the times, she was a professional songwriter before there were many in country music. She was also a woman playing a leading role when women in country music were still largely confined to the supporting cast. Words like gumption, gutsy, and pluck have been used to describe Walker, and she certainly needed all of these traits to succeed in such a demanding business. Yet any mention of the potential problems a female songsmith might face because of her gender brings a quick retort from Cindy: "That's a bunch of baloney. Recording artists don't care if you're a man, woman, or monkey. What they're looking for is a hit song." It was this attitude that made Cindy Walker one of the most respected and admired songwriters in country music. She was elected to the Country Music Hall of Fame in 1997.[41]

By 1950, country music was more popular than ever before, and there can be no doubt that Texans played important roles in bringing the music to audiences all over the nation. The experimentation and creativity that was so much a part of the Texas music scene also helped to shape and change the music permanently. In the decades since 1950, the Lone Star State has remained a source of musical energy and innovation. Lefty Frizzell, Hank Thompson, Ray Price, Jim Reeves, George Jones, Willie Nelson, and Waylon Jennings—all members of the Country Music Hall of Fame—are just a few of the Texans who have left their mark. And now with "younger" performers such as George Strait leading the way, the Texas tradition in country music is assured of continuing well into the twenty-first century.

## ⮞ Notes ⮜

1. In addition to Walker in 1997, the other Texans in the Country Music Hall of Fame are Tex Ritter (1964), Ernest Tubb (1965), Jim Reeves (1967), Bob Wills (1968), Gene Autry (1969), Hubert Long (1979), Hugh and Karl Farr as members of the Original Sons of the Pioneers (1980), Vernon Dalhart (1981), Grant Turner (1981), Lefty Frizzell (1982), Floyd Tillman (1984), Hank Thompson (1989), George Jones (1992), Willie Nelson (1993), Ray Price (1996), and most recently Waylon Jennings (2001). I did not include Buck

Owens on the list, even though he was born in Sherman, Texas, because he moved with his family to Arizona at an early age. Much has been written about country music in Texas, but there is no comprehensive history. Until someone rises to the challenge, Bill C. Malone, *Country Music USA*, Rev. ed. (Austin: University of Texas Press, 1985) is still the best place to begin. Throughout his seminal work, Malone emphasizes the importance of the music and musicians of the Southwest, but chapter five, "The Cowboy Image and the Growth of Western Music," is of particular relevance. The bibliographical essay found at the back of the book should not be overlooked either. Other useful overviews of the impact Texans have had and continue to have on the music are included in Paul Kingsbury, ed., *Country: The Music and the Musicians, From the Beginnings to the '90s* (Nashville: Country Music Foundation; New York: Abbeville Press, 1994); Douglas B. Green, *Country Roots: The Origins of Country Music* (New York: Hawthorn Books, 1976); Patrick Carr, ed., *The Illustrated History of Country Music* [2nd ed.] (New York: Times Books, 1995) especially the chapter by Bob Pinson and Douglas Green, "Music From the Lone Star State"; John Morthland, *The Best of Country Music* (Garden City: Doubleday, 1984); and Nick Tosches, *Country: The Twisted Roots of Rock 'n' Roll,* [3rd ed.] (New York: Da Capo Press, 1996).

2. The cultural, economic, historical, and physical geography of the state is covered in D. W. Meinig, *Imperial Texas: An Interpretive Essay in Cultural Geography* (Austin: University of Texas Press, 1969) and Terry G. Jordan, *Texas: A Geography* (Boulder: Westview Press, 1984). The quote is from Betty Casey, *Dance Across Texas* (Austin: University of Texas Press, 1985), p. 1, who offers a concise and readable history of dance in Texas.

3. I agree with Norm Cohen that it is "convenient and not too misleading" to date the beginnings of country music to the years 1922–24 "when it was first captured in the grooves of phonograph records." Norm Cohen, "Early Pioneers," *Stars of Country Music: Uncle Dave Macon to Johnny Rodriguez,* edited by Bill C. Malone and Judith McCulloh (Urbana: University of Illinois Press, 1975), p. 3. For more on this point see William Howland Kenney, *Recorded Music in American Life: The Phonograph and Popular Memory, 1890–1950* (New York: Oxford University Press, 1999).

4. The best source for biographical information on Robertson, including excerpts from an interview with him, is Blanton Owen's notes to *Eck Robertson: Famous Cowboy Fiddler* (County Records 202, 1991). Robertson's recording career is assessed in Charles Wolfe, *The Devil's Box: Masters of Southern Fiddling* (Nashville: Country Music Foundation Press & Vanderbilt University Press, 1997). The chapter, "The Recording Career of Eck Robertson," first appeared as "What Ever Happened to Country's First Recording Artist? The Career of Eck Robertson," *Journal of Country Music* 16, no. 1 (1993): 33–41. The West Texas ranch dance and fiddle contest tradition of which Robertson was so much a part is discussed in the first two chapters of Joe Carr and Alan Munde, *Prairie Nights to Neon Lights: The Story of Country Music in West Texas* (Lub-

bock: Texas Tech University Press, 1995). The quotes are from Cohen, "Early Pioneers," p. 12 and Charles Wolfe's notes to *Old-Time Texas Fiddler* (County Records 3525, 1998) which reissues all of Robertson's 1922 and 1929 recordings for Victor. For a sampling of the sounds of other Texas fiddlers from this period, see *Old Time Texas String Bands, vol. 1* (County Records 3524, 2001) and *Old Time Texas String Bands, vol. 2* (County Records 3525, 2001).

5. Richard A. Peterson, *Creating Country Music: Fabricating Authenticity* (Chicago: University of Chicago Press, 1997), pp. 5–6, 66. In what is otherwise an excellent book, Peterson completely ignores Eck Robertson mentioning him only in a footnote, and even then not by name. The author chooses to begin his study instead in 1923 with Fiddling John Carson.

6. Malone, *Country Music USA,* pp. 35–36. Malone also points out that on January 4, 1923, with fiddler Captain M. J. Bonner behind the microphone, WBAP "inaugurated" the radio barn dance format, another Texas first. During this period, particularly in the 1930s and early 1940s, the role of radio in the development and dissemination of country music can not be overstated. While this essay concentrates to a great extent on the recording aspects of the music, regular live exposure on radio often was more important for a country music performer's career than were recording opportunities. In addition to Malone, see Charles Wolfe, "The Triumph of the Hills: Country Radio, 1920–1950," *Country: The Music and the Musicians,* pp. 41–63. Gregory A. Waller explores the interaction between country music and local radio stations and motion picture theaters in Kentucky during the 1930s in "Hillbilly Music and Will Rogers: Small-town Picture Shows in the 1930s," *American Movie Audiences: From the Turn of the Century to the Early Sound Era,* edited by Melvyn Stokes and Richard Maltby (London: BFI Publishing, 1999), pp. 164–79. Background on the major events of the first fifty years of Texas broadcasting is provided by Richard Schroeder, *Texas Signs On: The Early Days of Radio and Television* (College Station: Texas A&M Press, 1998). The flavor and colorful history of the all important Mexican border radio stations is captured in Gene Fowler and Bill Crawford, *Border Radio* (Austin: Texas Monthly Press, 1987), but the authors only scratch the surface when it comes to chronicling the music and musicians who were such an integral part of this history.

7. Wolfe, *The Devil's Box,* p. 28.

8. Walter Darrell Haden, "Vernon Dalhart," *Stars of Country Music,* pp. 64–85, is still the best overview of Dalhart's career. See also Charles Wolfe, "Vernon Dalhart," *Journal of the American Academy for the Preservation of Old-Time Country Music* 27 ( June, 1995): 9–11.

9. Duncan McLean, *Lone Star Swing: On the Trail of Bob Wills and His Texas Playboys* (New York: Norton, 1998), p. 17.

10. Haden, "Vernon Dalhart," pp. 76–77. Haden lists all the known Dalhart pseudonyms in "Vernon Dalhart: Names to be Reckoned With," *Journal of Country Music* 13, no. 1 (1989): 10.

11. The Peer quote is from Haden, "Vernon Dalhart," p. 78.

12. Another Texan, Carl T. Sprague, is generally credited with being the first singing cowboy on record. Sprague's 1925 recording of "When the Work's All Done This Fall" sold over 900,000 copies and was primarily responsible for sparking the interest of record companies in cowboy songs. For a better understanding of the songs the cowboy sang and the role Texans played in shaping a tradition, see John I. White, *Git Along Little Dogies: Songs and Songmakers of the American West* (Urbana: University of Illinois Press, 1975), Jim Bob Tinsley, *He Was Singin' This Song* (Orlando: University Presses of Florida, 1981), and *"The Whorehouse Bells Were Ringing" and Other Songs Cowboys Sing,* collected and edited by Guy Logsdon (Urbana: University of Illinois Press, 1989) particularly the last chapter, "A Singing Cowboy Roundup." Besides Autry and Ritter, two other Texans closely associated with western music are in the Country Music Hall of Fame as members of the Original Sons of the Pioneers. Hugh Farr was born in Llano, Texas, in 1903, and his brother Karl was born in Rochelle, Texas, in 1909. Together they supplied the hot jazzy and bluesy fiddle and guitar licks that were such an integral part of the Pioneers' sound.

13. In addition to the sources cited in footnote 2, the following are useful in assessing Autry's life and career: Gene Autry with Mickey Herskowitz, *Back in the Saddle Again* (Garden City: Doubleday, 1978), Douglas Green, "Gene Autry," *Stars of Country Music,* pp. 142–56, Douglas Green, "The Singing Cowboy," *Journal of Country Music* 7, no. 2 (1978): 12–20, and Peter Stanfield, "Dixie Cowboys and Blue Yodels: The Strange History of the Singing Cowboy, *Back in the Saddle Again: New Essays on the Western,* edited by Edward Buscombe and Roberta E. Pearson (London: BFI Publishing, 1998), pp. 96–118.

14. Jon Tuska, *The Filming of the West* (Garden City: Doubleday, 1976), p. 303. Autry, *Back in the Saddle Again,* p. 59.

15. The two best sources on the origins of how the music came to be called hillbilly and later country music are Archie Green, "Hillbilly Music: Source and Symbol," *Journal of American Folklore* 76 (July–Sept., 1965): 204–28, and Ronnie Pugh, "Country Music Is Here to Stay," *Journal of Country Music* 19, no. 1 (1997): 32–38.

16. Bill C. Malone, *Singing Cowboys and Musical Mountaineers: Southern Culture and the Roots of Country Music* (Athens: University of Georgia Press, 1993), and Peterson, *Creating Country Music* are especially insightful on the integration of the cowboy image into country music.

17. Bill O'Neal, *Tex Ritter: America's Beloved Cowboy* (Austin: Eakin Press, 1998) offers the most up-to-date overview of Ritter's life and career. Johnny Bond, *The Tex Ritter Story* (New York: Chappell & Co., 1976) is a loosely organized and anecdotal account, lovingly and warmly told by a longtime friend.

18. Information on the songs Ritter recorded and the songs he sang in his movies comes from the discography and filmography in Bond, *The Tex Ritter Story.* The John Lomax connection is covered in more detail in Joe W. Specht, "Jack O' Diamonds, Jack O' Diamonds: Tex Ritter and the Lomax Cowboy Bal-

lads," paper presented at the Texas State Historical Association annual meeting, March 5, 1988.

19. Morthland, *The Best of Country Music,* p. 107.

20. Charles R. Townsend, *San Antonio Rose: The Life and Music of Bob Wills* (Urbana: University of Illinois Press, 1976) is still the place to begin for an understanding of Wills and his music, although it might be time for another extended look at Wills that would incorporate all the western swing scholarship of the last twenty-five years. Ruth Sheldon, *Hubbin' It: The Life of Bob Wills* (Nashville: Country Music Foundation Press, 1995), first published in 1938, is a pioneering biography as well as a unique social document, but it must be used with caution. Rosetta Wills, *The King of Western Swing: Bob Wills Remembered* (New York: Billboard Books, 1998) is both her autobiography as well as biography of her father. Charles Wolfe provides background on the fiddle style and tradition that was so much a part of Wills's music in "Bob Wills, Fiddler," in his *The Devil's Box.* Milton Brown finally found a biographer that did him justice in Cary Ginell, *Milton Brown and the Founding of Western Swing* (Urbana: University of Illinois Press, 1994). To better place Wills and Brown within the larger context of country music, refer to the sources cited in footnote 2.

21. Because of Milton Brown's early death, his role in the development of western swing has often been obscured, certainly in much of the general public's mind, and as a result, Bob Wills has received the majority of the attention. Kevin Coffey's review of Ginell's biography of Milton Brown, "Who Is Western Swing's Father," *Journal of Country Music* 17 no. 1 (1994): 56–60 gives the most balanced account to date of assessing not only the roles of Wills and Brown in the development of western swing but also the part their two biographers, Townsend and Ginell, respectively, have played in assigning credit,

22. Tom Dunbar, *From Bob Wills to Ray Benson: A History of Western Swing Music, Vol. 1* (Austin: Term Publications, 1988) provides basic information on several of the Texas bands playing western swing. Special mention should also be given to Kevin Coffey's ongoing research into western swing and honky-tonk music which has been published in a variety of magazine and journal articles as well as in numerous compact disc liner notes. The quote is from Tony Russell's notes to *Beer Parlor Jive* (String 801, 1975). For an interesting exchange between Ken Griffis, Steve Hathaway, Cary Ginell, and Hank Penny on the origins of the term western swing, see the letters column in *JEMF Quarterly* 17, no. 62; 17, no. 63; 17, no. 64; and 18, nos. 67–68. Even though there are differences of opinion, all the correspondents seem to agree that the term came into existence in 1942 and was first used by Spade Cooley. Bob Pinson's findings on "Texas Swing" are in his notes to *Bill Boyd's Cowboy Ramblers* (RCA Bluebird AXM2-5503, 1975).

23. The latest attempt to classify western swing solely as jazz is Jean Boyd, *The Jazz of the Southwest: An Oral History of Western Swing* (Austin: University of Texas Press, 1998). In her efforts to show "that western swing was, and

is, jazz—swing jazz" and "not country music," Boyd inadvertently demonstrates the dangers of what can happen to a new convert who embarks on a project with little background and even less preparation. To understand better all the issues involved when discussing jazz and swing or dance music see Lewis A. Erenberg, *Swingin' the Dream: Big Band Jazz and the Rebirth of American Culture* (Chicago: University of Chicago Press, 1998), Gunther Schuller, *Early Jazz: Its Roots and Music* (New York: Oxford University Press, 1968), Gunther Schuller, *The Swing Era: The Development of Jazz 1930–1945* (New York: Oxford University Press, 1989), and David W. Stowe, *Swing Changes: Big-Band Jazz in New Deal America* (Cambridge: Harvard University Press, 1994).

24. The Wills quote is from "Strictly By Ear," *Time,* Feb. 11, 1946, p. 50. The Arnold quote is from Rich Kienzle's notes to *Bob Wills* (Time-Life Records TLCW-07, 1982), p. 2.

25. Nick Tosches's account of his research into the origin of the phrase honky-tonk and how it became a part of the language and the music is found in his *Country: The Twisted Roots of Rock 'n' Roll,* pp. 26–27, and also in "Honky-Tonkin': Ernest Tubb, Hank Williams, and the Bartender's Muse," *Country: The Musicians and the Musicians,* pp. 153–55. Bill C. Malone in his doctoral dissertation was the first writer to use the term honky-tonk to describe a subgenre of country music. In addition to *Country Music USA,* see also his "Honky Tonk: The Music of the Southern Working Class," *Folk Music and Modern Sound,* edited by William Ferris and Mary L. Hart (Jackson: University Press of Mississippi, 1982) and his notes to *Honky-Tonkin'* (Time-Life Records TLCW-12, 1983).

26. Garna L. Christian, "It Beats Picking Cotton: The Origins of Houston Country Music," *Red River Historical Review* 7 (summer, 1982): 37–50 was a groundbreaking essay based on interviews with many of the participants of the 1930s and 1940s Houston music scene. Kevin Coffey's notes to *Cliff Bruner and His Texas Wanderers* (Bear Family BCD 15932E1, 1997) touch on many of the important Houston area performers as do Andrew Brown and Kevin Coffey's notes to *Heading Back to Houston: Texas C&W 1950–1951* (Krazy Kat KKCD 12, 1997). The important contributions Bob Dunn made to the development of the electric steel guitar are discussed in Kevin Coffey, "Steel Colossus: The Bob Dunn Story," *Journal of Country Music* 17, no. 2 (1995): 91–109.

27. Tillman's life and career is covered in Kevin Coffey, "Floyd Tillman," *Journal of the American Academy for the Preservation of Old-time Country Music* 30 (Dec., 1995): 9–11, Patsi Bale Cox's notes to *Floyd Tillman* (Columbia FC 39996, 1985), Rich Kienzle, "Floyd Tillman," *Country Music* 167 (May–June, 1994): F–G, Adam Komoroswki, "Floyd Tillman," *Hillbilly Researcher* no. 15: 13–27 and no. 16: 28–30, and John Rumble's notes to *Floyd Tillman* (MCA MCAD 10189, 1991). The Daffan quote is from the notes to *Portraits of Floyd Tillman in Stereo* (Bagatelle LP-92827, 1971). The role that country musicians played in the development of electric instruments still has not been addressed

in the detail it deserves. Eddie Durham, Charlie Christian, Floyd Smith, and T. Bone Walker are normally given credit, particularly in jazz circles, for first exploring the possibilities of the electric guitar. And while the sharing of ideas and licks with black musicians like Christian certainly occurred, many of the white country instrumentalists living in Texas and Oklahoma developed in a similar fashion on their own. Gunther Schuller is one of the few jazz scholars who has recognized this fact. See Schuller, *The Swing Era,* pp. 564–65, including footnotes. For the perspective from the country side, see Coffey, "Steel Colossus," p. 99; Malone, *Country Music USA,* pp. 157–58, 172; Tosches, *Country: The Twisted Roots of Rock 'n' Roll,* p. 180; Townsend, *San Antonio Rose,* pp. 127–28, and Kevin Coffey's notes to *Nite Spot Blues: Hot Western Swing from the Southwest, 1929–1941* (Krazy Kat KKCD 20, 1998).

28. Tosches, "Honky-Tonkin'," p. 156.

29. Willie Nelson with Bud Shrake, *Willie: An Autobiography* (New York: Simon and Schuster, 1988), p. 59.

30. Ronnie Pugh, *Ernest Tubb: The Texas Troubadour,* First Paperback Printing [with corrections] (Durham: Duke University Press, 1998), is the definitive Tubb biography and also includes a complete discography of the Texas Troubadour's forty-five-year recording career.

31. Ibid., p. 66.

32. Prior to the emergence of the radio disc jockey as platter spinner in the late 1940s, the jukebox occupied a place of primary importance with jukebox sales and plays having a strong influence on who and what kind of music was recorded. See Vincent Lynch and Bill Henkin, *Jukebox: The Golden Age* (Berkeley: Lancaster-Miller, 1981), John Morthland, "Jukebox Fever," *Country Music* 6 (May, 1978): 34–36, and Russell Sanjek, *American Popular Music and Its Business: The First Hundred Years,* Vol. 3 (New York: Oxford University Press, 1988), pp. 132–38, 240.

33. Two years after Tubb came to the Opry, he was joined on WSM by another Texan and future member of the Country Music Hall of Fame, Grant Turner. Born in Baird, Texas, in 1912, Turner, who was elected to the Hall of Fame in 1981, is the first radio announcer and disc jockey to be so recognized.

34. Nelson, *Willie Nelson,* p. 59. Pugh, *Ernest Tubb,* p. 113.

35. *Down Beat* 14 (Oct. 8, 1947): 3. The discrimination against country musicians even extended to the American Federation of Musicians. It was not until the early 1940s that many local chapters of the union ended the practice of routinely denying membership to country pickers who could not sight-read sheet music. This is in fact the reason that Bob Wills and members of his Texas Playboys were not initially allowed in the union in Tulsa. For a humorous account of the band's travails with the Tulsa chapter of the union, see Al Stricklin with Jon McConal, *My Years With Bob Wills* (San Antonio: Naylor, 1976), pp. 80–82.

36. Peter Guralnick, *Lost Highway: Journeys & Arrivals of American*

*Musicians* (Boston: Godine, 1979), p. 22. A similar quote is found in Pugh, *Ernest Tubb,* p. 132. See also the sources cited in footnote 16. Of course in recent years, "hillbilly" has been turned on its head with alternative-country groups and even mainstream performers such as Dwight Yoakam and Marty Stuart using the term with a renewed sense of pride. For example see Marty Stuart's comments in *Hillbilly Hollywood: The Origins of Country & Western Style* (New York: Rizzoli, 2000), p. 105.

37. Mike Streissguth, "Cindy Walker: You *Do* Know Her Songs, *Journal of Country Music* 19, no. 1 (1997): 7–9, Robert K. Oermann, "Cindy Walker: The Greatest Living Songwriter of Country Music." *Journal of the American Academy for the Preservation of Old-Time Country Music* 50 (Aug., 1999): 4–6, and John Morthland, "Songwriter," *Texas Monthly,* Dec., 1999, pp. 90–92, 120–23, offer an up-to-date look at Walker's career while Arnold L. Rogers, "Cindy Walker," *Yesterday* 1, no. 6: 8–9, 31, provides a useful listing of many of her compositions. The Walker quote is from Mary A. Bufwack and Robert K. Oermann, *Finding Her Voice: The Saga of Women in Country Music* (New York: Crown, 1993), p. 145. Information on Walker's Decca recording sessions with Texas Jim Lewis comes from *The Decca Hillbilly Discography, 1927–1945,* compiled by Cary Ginell (New York: Greenwood Press, 1989), pp. 205–206. There still seems to be some confusion about the exact chronology of events of Walker's first year in Hollywood. I used Autry, *Back in the Saddle Again, The Decca Hillbilly Discography,* and J. Roger Osterholm, *Bing Crosby: A Bio-Bibliography* (Westport, Conn.: Greenwood Press, 1994) to help sort out the details in my own mind.

38. Information on Walker's Decca recording sessions comes from *The Decca Hillbilly Discography,* pp. 276–77.

39. John Ryan, *The Production of Culture in the Music Industry: The ASCAP-BMI Controversy* (Lanham, Md.: University Press of America, 1985) covers the creation of BMI and the rivalry with ASCAP.

40. Information on the Walker-Autry songs comes from the discography and filmography in Autry, *Back in the Saddle Again.* The album of Walker songs that Tex Ritter recorded is *Bump Tiddil Dee Bum Bum! Tex Ritter Sings the Songs of the Great Country Composer Cindy Walker* (Capitol T-2890, 1968). Another more recent tribute album is Leon Rausch, *Close to You: A 20 Song Salute to the Music of Cindy Walker, Vol. 1* (Southland Records SR-7627, 1998). Information on the Walker songs that Wills either recorded or used in the Russell Hayden westerns comes from Bob Pinson's discography and filmusicography in Townsend, *San Antonio Rose.* Information on the Walker songs that Tubb recorded comes from the discography in Pugh, *Ernest Tubb.*

41. The "tailor-made" quote is from Cindy Walker, interview with John Burnett, National Public Radio, Nov. 7, 1998. The Walker quote is from Deborah Voorhees, "A Cowgirl Roundup," *Dallas Morning News,* Oct. 28, 1998, 7C.

# 4

# Early Texas Bluesmen

## John Lightfoot

The blues was born in the Mississippi Delta in the nineteenth century out of the human misery of slavery. The pain of the South's "peculiar institution" on blacks inspired them to create their particular "how-long-oh-Lord?" type of music that has become so popular in America and around the world. As Rick Koster aptly states in his *Texas Music,* "the blues spontaneously generated in the sweltering fields as a form of therapy as much as for entertainment as to pass the never-ending hours. Evolving from traditional African chants and rhythms, and incorporated into 'call and response' field hollers, early spirituals, and dance music, the blues soon enough became an identifiable and separate artistic entity unto itself."[1]

Following emancipation, while blacks were still subject to horrible poverty and discrimination, they were at least free to travel, and travel they did. Many of them went west to Louisiana and Texas where they established sharecropper communities. Almost all early Texas bluesmen were born in these communities. Virtually all of the early Texas blues lyrics included different aspects of love: good love when your woman is "steadfast, loyal, and true," bad love when your woman "does you wrong," and really bad love when your woman does something so wicked that you have to kill her. Other subjects were poverty, hard work, whiskey, magic, and prison laments. None of the songs were written down, but rather everything was transmitted through the oral tradition. When the boll weevil devastated cotton crops in the 1890s, many rural blacks headed for Dallas and Houston in search of other livelihoods. All of them settled in segregated sections of the cities where black subcultures were formed. These highly populated ghettos provided audiences that enabled Blind Lemon Jefferson to become the first well-known Texas bluesman.

Even though Texas did not invent the blues, the state's blues tradition trails only Mississippi in importance. Besides Jefferson, other early Texas bluesmen who played significant roles were Huddie "Lead Belly" Ledbetter, Mance Lipscomb, and Sam "Lightning" Hopkins. Actually Louisiana had just as good a claim on Lead Belly as Texas did. He was born on the east side of Caddo Lake but spent lots of time in Shreveport. He can be called a Texan because he lived in Texas off and on for many years. Also he went to prison, first near De Kalb, and then later in Sugarland. While Jefferson and Hopkins sang and played primarily blues, Lead Belly and Lipscomb performed all kinds of music. Lipscomb even preferred to be called a songster rather than a bluesman, so a discussion of their music needs to range outside the blues. This chapter will explore the subjects and lyrics of these early Texas bluesmen.

### ❧ Blind Lemon Jefferson ❧

Born in 1897 near Couchman (near Wortham, which is eight miles north of Mexia), Blind Lemon Jefferson was sightless from birth. Folklorist Mack McCormick called him "the keystone—the single most influential figure in early recorded blues. A blind, burly, lustful singer, he never begged with a tin cup, but had dollars stuffed in his pockets by crowds that quickly gathered on street corners at which he would arrive in a touring car driven by a uniformed chauffeur."[2] Pete Welding says that, according to relatives, Jefferson played dances and country suppers as a teenager and moved to Dallas in 1917 where he was successful enough with his music to get married, start a family, buy a car, and hire a chauffeur. He also played back country dances and parties, lumber and levee camp barrelhouses, and brothels.[3] Lead Belly was Jefferson's partner in these gigs for about five years.

Jefferson also traveled extensively, playing in such places as Memphis, the Mississippi Delta area, Alabama, Georgia, the eastern seaboard, and Chicago. According to Welding, the powerful imagery of his

*Blind Lemon Jefferson.*
*Courtesy UT Institute of Texan Cultures*
*at San Antonio*

lyrics matched or exceeded his guitar playing: "on the whole there is a vast amount of superior, moving folk poetry, ranging from almost wholly traditional to highly individualized. Such songs as 'Rabbit Foot Blues,' 'See That My Grave Is Kept Clean,' and 'Matchbox Blues' have been associated with him ever since he recorded them."[4] Jefferson recorded more than eighty songs, all of them for Paramount Records. Because he was a loner, there were few who knew him well. One Paramount secretary told Orrin Keepnews (the producer of the Milestone album from which all lyric quotes are taken) that Jefferson was a "gross, drunken lecher who ate with his fingers and was paid off for record dates in cheap whiskey and prostitutes."[5] Pianist Romeo Nelson remembered him as a warm, cordial neighbor on the south side of Chicago. Others said that he was kind and generous. The details of how and when Jefferson died are also a mystery: "Some accounts allege foul play, while others attribute his death to overexertion, heart failure, freezing to death in the bitter winter cold of Chicago, or some combination of these causes."[6] Estimates on his date of death range from shortly after his last recording session in September, 1929, to mid-1930. He is buried in Wortham Cemetery.

Many of Jefferson's blues songs provide humorous double entendres for sex. "Baker Shop Blues" says, "I'm crazy about my light bread and my pig meat on the side/ (repeat)/ If I had some jelly roll, I'd be satisfied." "That Black Snake Moan" is in a similar vein. A good modern version is on Joe Ely's live album from Europe when he opened for the Clash: "Ohhhhh, black snake crawling in my room/ (repeat)/ Some pretty momma gonna get this black snake soon." "Broke and Hungry" is more about bad women than the title suggests, and there's some sexual double entendre as well: "I feel like jumping through the keyhole in your door/ (repeat)/ If you jump this time baby, you sure won't jump no more."

Jefferson's most famous song, and the one most often covered by bluesmen whom he influenced, is "Matchbox Blues." It is a tune about bad love where women just won't "do right": "Sat there and wonder will a match box hold my clothes/ (repeat)/ Ain't got so many matches, but I got so far to go." It goes on to say: "Girl one time wanted to be my teddy bear/ (repeat)/ Put a string on me, and I'll follow you anywhere." (Elvis Presley fans will remember his early hit record, "Teddy Bear," with very similar lyrics.) Jefferson also manages to sing about sex, "There's a peg leg woman come to town a year ago/ (repeat)/ I rap on her little white love light, I'm selling jelly rolls."

Two "real bad love" songs are "Lonesome House Blues" and "The Growling Baby Blues." In the former, Jefferson sings, "I'm gonna wait for you momma just to wear you on my mind/ (repeat)/ So if I live here in Chicago, murder's going to be my crime." Even worse is the latter in which Jefferson's woman tells him the baby he is rocking is not his own when she grabs the baby to spank it and he tries to make her leave it alone: "I tried my best to stop her, and she said she rules the home/ (repeat)/ Many a man rocks another man's baby, and the fool thinks he's rocking his own."

Jefferson also recorded several prison songs, and even though he never went to prison, one would never know that, because the tunes sound so authentic. In "Prison Cell Blues," he blames his misfortune on a woman named Nell. Were it not for her, he would not be in his "lonesome cell." "Penitentiary Blues" was also covered by Lipscomb and Hopkins. According to the lyrics, Groesbeck, Texas, is not a good place to have your trial: "I hung around Groesbeck working hard to stay out of the rain/ (repeat)/ I never felt that uneasy till I caught that penitentiary-bound train." But the most delightful of the three is "Lockstep Blues." Even when he is dead serious, Jefferson manages to inject humor into the pathos: "I couldn't keep away from wild women, bad liquor, cards, and dice/ (repeat)/ Now that I'm locked up, baby, things ain't so nice." He goes on to sing: "Mean old jailer take away my dancing shoes/ (repeat)/ I can't strut my stuff when I got those lock step blues."

Blues lyrics can sometimes involve other things than love, hard work, poverty, or prison. In "Mosquito Moan," Jefferson says the mosquitoes are so bad that he cannot get from his house to his whiskey still. Jefferson's subjects ranged from serious matters to transparently ribald situations. Koster sums up Jefferson's contributions well: "Blind Lemon Jefferson's songs and innovations had a terrific effect on generations of performers in a variety of ways, and his reputation as an absolute blues giant is inviolate. But his influence during his lifetime was similarly impressive. No less than Robert Johnson, Huddie Ledbetter, Aaron 'T-Bone' Walker, Sam 'Lightning' Hopkins were indebted to him."[7]

## Lead Belly

Huddie "Lead Belly" Ledbetter was born January 15, 1888, on the Louisiana side of Caddo Lake. (The lake's west side is located in Northeast Texas.) He attended school until he was twelve or thirteen, learning to read and write quite well. By black standards of the day, Ledbetter was upper class. He was a hardworking farmer after he quit school.[8] Lead Belly was also a musical child prodigy, learning to play numerous instruments before the age of six.

He went to prison the first time in Texas in 1918 for murdering a black friend, Will Stafford, in a fight over a woman. His court-appointed attorney was not an expert in criminal law, and the son of one of the partners in the law firm, J. Q. Mahaffey, said, "Huddie wouldn't receive a fair trial because at that time a black man in Bowie County was treated as the 'equivalent of a stray dog.'"[9] Race relations in Texas were even worse than usual at this time because of the recent Houston race riot involving black army recruits from the north and native Houston whites. After two years at Shaw State Prison Farm near De Kalb, Huddie was transferred to the Central State Prison Farm in Sugarland, twenty miles west of Houston.[10]

Huddie probably got his nickname in prison. Because he was large, strong, and hard working, the name probably refers to his strength and vocal ability rather than to his real name, Ledbetter: "One day the chaplain of the (Sugarland) prison, the Reverend 'Sin Killer' Griffin, came to him. 'He says to me, you're a hard driving man. Instead of guts, you got lead in your belly. That's who you are, old Lead Belly!'"[11]

Lead Belly learned many of his songs in prison, including "The Midnight Special," a song from the oral tradition. Lead Belly added verses and made it famous in numerous recordings. His version is the one popularized by young folksingers of the 1950s and 1960s.[12] The title refers to a Southern Pacific train that passed the Sugarland prison every night headed west. The song "became a cruel, tantalizing and regular reminder of life beyond the Sugarland fences."[13]

When Governor Pat Neff came to the prison in 1924 to hear the inmates perform, Lead Belly sang an original song pleading for a pardon: "In nineteen hundred and twenty three when the judge taken away my liberty/ (repeat)/ Say my wife come wringing her hands and crying Lord have mercy on that man of mine."[14] Neff liked the song. The pardon was slow in coming, but it finally arrived January 16, 1925. During Lead Belly's first term in prison, the blues became popular nationally, moving from red light districts to vaudeville and records. Blind Lemon Jefferson's records began appearing in 1926. Race records (black music for black audiences) also were released in the 1920s, and Lead Belly heard most of them.[15]

Lead Belly was sent to prison the second time to Louisiana's Angola Prison in 1930 for having a knife fight with a white man named Dick Ellet and others at a Salvation Army concert. The dispute began when Lead Belly drunkenly tried to dance when the band played "Onward Christian Soldiers."[16] Conditions in Angola in 1930 were as close to slavery as anywhere in America. Yet even while behind prison bars, Lead Belly kept playing, singing, and learning his craft. In 1933, John Lomax came to Angola in search of folk songs and folksingers. Lomax taught in Texas but was trained under Harvard folklorists Francis James Child and George Lyman Kittredge.[17] Over the next several years, Lomax and his son Alan recorded more than one hundred songs by Lead Belly for the Library of Congress. Liner notes for the six lengthy albums reissued by Rounder Records are by Kip Lornell, music specialist at the Smithsonian Institution's National Museum of American History and co-author of the best biography of Lead Belly. Lead Belly's most famous song, "Goodnight Irene," was recorded at the first session. Lomax was among the first actually to record songs in the field on portable equipment. Previous collectors had taken dictation and written down the music.[18] In a subsequent session in 1932, Lead Belly recorded "Governor O. K. Allen," pleading again for a pardon. Legend says his plea was successful, but Wolfe and Lornell claim that Lead Belly was routinely released early under the "good time" law.[19]

"Goodnight Irene" leads off *Midnight Special,* volume one of the Rounder reissue series. "Goodnight Irene" is not a blues song; in fact, it is a popular folksong waltz made even more famous in 1950 by the Weavers. Lead Belly is listed as composer, although he probably borrowed it from oral tradition. Lornell cites Lead Belly enthusiast John Reynolds as pointing out that a prototype of "Irene" appeared in print in 1888: "The group that published the song, Haverly's United American European Minstrels, also performed in northwest Louisiana in the late 1880s."[20] "Matchbox Blues" is a Blind Lemon Jefferson song that Lead Belly undoubtedly picked up from Jefferson during the years they played together. "Midnight Special," is Lead Belly's second-most popular song. Lornell says it was recorded as early as 1925 by Sodarisa Miller and in 1927 by Sam Collins. These versions are similar to Lead Belly's but not identical, and he is listed as composer: "If you're ever in Houston, you better walk right/ you better not squabble, and you better not fight or the judge will sentence you penitentiary bound."[21] "Governor O. K. Allen" is his plea for a pardon: "I know my wife gonna jump and shout when the train rolls up and I come stepping out." Lead Belly also covers traditional songs about violent marital disputes. "Frankie and Albert" later became "Frankie and Johnnie." Johnny Cash recorded it in 1959 as "Frankie's Man, Johnny." The song has an interesting reversal in that a woman shoots her man who was doing her wrong. In "Ella Speed," covered by numerous bluesmen, the woman gets shot down for being a rounder.

"Get Up in the Morning" is about life in Angola. It is hard to get up at 3 A.M., go to the fields before light, and cut sugar cane, "But the sun's gonna shine in my back door some day." "You Don't Know My Mind" is about the traditional no-good woman: "Lookee here momma, see what you done done/ you got my money, now you done run." "Take a Whiff on Me" is a cocaine song: "Cocaine for horses, not for men/ doctor says it will kill you but he don't say when." "De Kalb Blues" is a real bad woman blues set in the small town in Northeast Texas: "Buy me a pistol, get me a Gattling gun/ (repeat)/ If I catch you baby, we gonna have some fun." "Careless Love," the old country song, demonstrates that Lead Belly was a songster in addition to being a bluesman.

*Gwine Dig a Hole to Put the Devil In,* volume two of the Rounder Lead Belly series, contains a variety of music types: blues, country, ballads, topical folk songs, and traditional dance tunes. "C. C. Rider" is a well-known blues ballad that has been collected across the South. According to Lornell, it appeared as a race record as early as 1924.[22] Chuck Willis had a big hit with it in 1957. "Governor Pat Neff" was Lead Belly's successful 1924 plea to the Texas governor for a pardon. Neff commuted almost twenty-three years of Ledbetter's murder sentence. "Alberta," is a formula blues song with interesting lyrics: "Take me Alberta, take me down in your rocking chair/ So when the blues overtake me I can rock on away from here." "Old Rattler" is a traditional song found in the repertoires of both black and white performers. For example, Country Music Hall of Famer Grandpa Jones recorded "Old Rattler" in 1947, and he continued to sing it on the Grand Ole Opry and later on *Hee Haw.* It is interesting to compare Lead Belly's version with Jones's. Lead Belly says, "Here, Rattler, here, here," while Grandpa Jones gives it southern dialect: "He-ah, Rattler, he-ah, he-ah." Lornell says "If It Wasn't for Dicky" is not as old as a Child ballad (old English folksong), but it had been around for decades. Dicky is a good milk cow, and the melody sounds English, Scottish, or Irish.[23]

"Queen Mary" is a topical folk song about the maiden voyage of the big English ship. Lead Belly paid $1 to tour the ship, but he lost his pass. He adds a comment on race relations when he says the first black heavyweight champion Jack Johnson tried to buy a ticket on the return voyage, "but the captain says I ain't hauling no coal." According to Lornell, "Momma Did you Bring Any Silver (Gallis Pole)" is Lead Belly's heartfelt version of the British Child ballad "The Maid Freed From the Gallows." Lead Belly makes the prisoner a mother's son in prison, and she needs money to buy his way out: "Mother did you bring me any silver, mother did you bring me any gold?/ What did you bring me dear mother to keep me from the Gallis Pole?" "Bourgeois Blues" is one of Lead Belly's best-known songs. Lornell guesses that Alan Lomax talked Lead Belly into writing it about racism in Washington, D.C.: "I'm gonna tell all the colored people, I want 'em to understand/ 'cause there ain't no place for no colored man." "Green Corn" is a southern country dance tune or folk song like "Old Joe Clark." Lornell says, "The importance of Lead Belly's introduction of these songs to a nonsouthern, white audience cannot be underestimated." Lyrics here don't matter: "Green corn, come along Charley/ green corn, go and tell Polly."[24]

Volume three of the Rounder Lead Belly series, *Let It Shine on Me,* is half gospel songs and half folk songs/blues. All the selections here except "Mr. Hitler" came from a long Friday recording session in August, 1940. Lomax was trying to document Lead Belly's wide variety of material. According to Lornell, the origins of most of his gospel songs are from the 1800s. He learned them as a boy in the Baptist church. It is unclear why Lead Belly had so many topical and protest songs in the 1930s. Many liberals and intellectuals during this period, including Lead Belly's performing buddy Woody Guthrie, were communists or left leaners opposing fascism in Spain and Germany. Lornell speculates, "Perhaps it's a sign of the times or maybe his numerous appearances at Communist fund-raisers and concerts. I would also guess that Alan Lomax helped to raise his consciousness, especially with regard to social matters.[25]

"Backslider, Fare Thee Well" is gospel, followed by a long Lead Belly monologue on hypocrisy of church folk. He says he was twenty when he joined the church, stayed a week, and then became a backslider himself. Lead Belly preferred nonchurch settings where there would probably be more wild women, whiskey, and, most importantly, money to be made. "Down in the Valley to Pray" is another traditional song and well known: "As I went down in the valley to pray, studying about that good old way/ who shall wear that starry crown? Good Lord, show me the way." "Let It Shine on Me" is a gospel song that Lead Belly does three ways: the Baptists do it slow; the Methodists speed it up; the "Holy Ghosts" make it almost rock and roll.

The remainder of the compact disc concerns secular matters. "Howard Hughes" is about aviation of his day and talks about the millionaire's flight: "He said I'm gonna take a little trip up in the air/ he taken a trip all around this world to try to beat the record of the great Lindberg." According to Lornell, "When I Was a Cowboy" reveals Lead Belly's Texas roots and recalls the recordings of Jimmie Rodgers and one of Lead Belly's idols, Gene Autry.[26] The song sounds like a cross between the two styles with a western subject like Autry but a yodel like a not-so-good imitation of Rodgers: "Many years I rambled, drank corn liquor and gambled, but I thought one day I would settle down." His yodel sounds more like the whoops of Sonny Terry and Brownie McGhee. "The Roosevelt Song" illustrates Lead Belly's populist roots: "President Roosevelt went all over the United States trying to get Hitler and Germany to hesitate about that war, about that war." "The Scottsboro Boys" is Lead Belly's analysis of racism in the Deep South. The Scottsboro boys were four blacks unjustly convicted of rape in Alabama:

"Scottsboro boys they can tell you what it's all about/ I'm gonna tell the colored people don't you go down there." "No Good Rider" is a traditional country blues about a worthless woman: "She's a no good rider, she ain't no good, she got drunk this morning, broke up the neighborhood/ She taken me to her house, she called me honey, but she just wanted all my money." "Mr. Hitler" is more populism, a country blues about the dictator: "That's one thing Mr. Hitler did do wrong/ (repeat)/ When he started out driving the Jews from their homes." The chorus says America is going to "tear Hitler down some day."

In the liner notes to volume four, *The Titanic,* Lornell quotes a 1992 issue of *Newsweek* as naming Lead Belly "America's greatest folksinger." He states that this may seem grandiose in light of the legacy left by people like Pete Seeger, Muddy Waters, or Woody Guthrie, but he agrees that it is probably the truth.[27] "Blind Lemon Blues" is borrowed from the bluesman who most influenced Lead Belly, Blind Lemon Jefferson. The two met in 1912 and traveled together for about five years. Lead Belly also acquired his first twelve-string guitar in 1912. The song is a bad woman blues that answers the question of what to do when your woman packs her trunk. The answer is, "Get a half a gallon of whiskey and go on a great big drunk." Lead Belly does numerous jail/prison songs, like "Shreveport Jail." This is appropriate because he spent much of his life incarcerated (and would have spent more had John Lomax not "rescued" him from Angola). "Angola Blues" explains a day in the life of a black inmate: "Got up this morning so doggone soon/ (repeat)/ Couldn't see nothing but the stars and moon." After spending all day cutting sugar cane, Lead Belly tells his woman what he wants her to do if he ever gets out: "There's just one thing baby I want you to do/ (repeat)/ I want you to meet me on Texas Avenue." "Dallas and Fort Worth Blues" is halfway between bad love and real bad love: "First time I met her she was holding out her hand/ (repeat)/ When I give her my money, she give it to her brand new man."

"Mary Don't You Weep" is the well-known, traditional spiritual, patterned after a blues song: "Oh Mary, don't you weep, don't you moan/ (repeat)/ Pharaoh's army got drowned, Oh Mary don't you weep." "I Ain't Bothered a Bit" is a prison work song that never would have been sung where the white guards could hear. It is not a "Yes-sir-Mr.-Boss-Man" number: "Shit in the coffee, shit in the cage/ I hadn't been watching you shit on me, Son I ain't bothered a bit." "Boll Weevil" is the famous funny ballad about the awful pest that devastated southern cotton. No matter how hard the farmer tries, the weevil wins. Lead Belly adds a

final verse not heard on Tex Ritter's better-known recording: "If anybody asks you who composed this song, tell him it was a dark-skinned
nigger with a pair of blue duckins on/ he's looking for a home." "Tight
Like That" sounds like double entendre for sex, but Lead Belly says it
is a dance song (maybe it could be both): "She's tight like that, easy
to bump/ (repeat)/ Taken her to a dance, she danced with another." He
concludes by saying he has had no rest since he "stepped in the bumble
bee's nest." "Sail on Little Girl" is a traditional bad love blues, but it has
an interesting twist. Lead Belly admits in the introductory recitation
that the bad woman is his mistress, not his wife, who is home starving
to death. Consequently he admits that love gone wrong is not always the
woman's fault.

Volume five, *Nobody Knows the Trouble I've Seen,* contains spirituals, blues, work songs, and topical folk songs.[28] "Shorty George" is a
blues song about a prisoner losing his woman to Shorty George, a man
on the outside whom all the prisoners envy: "Shorty George done been
here and gone/ (repeat)/ He taken my woman to a world unknown." The
song goes on to talk about how Shorty George has taken many women
from good men who are in "the pen." "Bring Me Water Silvy" was a hit
record for Harry Belafonte in the 1950s: "Bring me a little water Silvy,
bring me a little water now/ bring me a little water Silvy, every little once
in a while." It is a work song about needing water more frequently working in the fields in July and August. "Ain't Gonna Ring Dem Yellow Woman's Doorbell" is another work song about men working a crosscut saw:
"On a Monday I was arrested, on a Tuesday they locked me up in jail,
on a Wednesday my trial was attested, on a Thursday nobody would
go my bail." Johnny Cash recorded a version of this song in 1959 as
"I Got Stripes," but the above four lines are the only ones that are the
same. Cash's chorus continued, "I got stripes, stripes around my shoul-
ders/ I got chains, chains around my feet."

"Rock Island Line" is a work song about chopping wood (lots of men
with pole axes, some cutting left-handed, some right): "The Rock Island
Line is a mighty good ride/ got to ride it like you find it, get your ticket
at the station on the Rock Island Line." If this sounds familiar, the English folksingers, The Lonnie Donegan Group, had a big hit record with
it in 1956. "The Hindenburg Disaster" is Lead Belly's description of the
horrible dirigible disaster: "Oh the Hindenburg, the Hindenburg/ everybody talking about the Hindenburg." Lead Belly says the disaster occurred because "it got up too high." The next three are all gospel songs
or spirituals. In "Git on Board," Lead Belly tells what he is going to do

with the motherless children: "I'm gonna take 'em by the hand and lead 'em to Jesus." Lead Belly claims "Outshine the Sun" is an original "spiritual/Communist recruiting/organizing" song, but it would be hard to identify any Communism therein. The song sounds just like a spiritual. "Nobody Knows the Trouble I've Seen" is the traditional, well-known religious song. "Nobody knows the trouble I've seen/ nobody knows but Jesus."

The final Rounder compact disc, *Go Down Old Hannah,* tries to complete Lead Belly's repertoire of songs and to plug up any unfilled holes. There are several lengthy monologues in which Lead Belly answers questions posed by John Lomax.[29] "T.B. Blues" is a blues about the dreaded disease. Jimmie Rodgers, who died of tuberculosis in 1933, also wrote and recorded a song with the same title. According to Rodgers's biographer Nolan Porterfield, at the turn of the century ninety percent of American adults had been afflicted by it. As late as 1950, it was the leading cause of death for Americans between the ages of fifteen and thirty-four.[30] Lead Belly then offers an almost thirteen-minute monologue on black square dances, which he calls "sookey jumps." Lead Belly says sookey comes from sooey, the word used to call cattle or hogs, and the word jump indicates that the rhythm was fast paced. He lists several of the more popular tunes like "Shoo Fly," "One Dollar Bill Won't Buy You No Shoes," "Green Corn," "Gwine Dig a Hole to Put the Devil In," and "Tight Like That." Then comes an eight-minute monologue on the blues in which Lead Belly says his grandfather taught him the genre. He also sings an early blues song—not listed in the liner notes—called "Red Cross Store." Therein a woman who has left her husband in 1917 tries to get him to enlist in the army so she can get his enlistment bonus: "I told her no, I don't want to go/ I ain't going down to no Red Cross Store." She even brought their seven-year-old child along to try to win sympathy from the recruiter.

The remainder of the album contains mostly gospel/spirituals with which most people are familiar: "Amazing Grace," "That Old Time Religion," "You Got to Walk This Lonesome Valley," "Swing Low Sweet Chariot," and "Ain't Gonna Study War No More." In a seven-minute Christmas monologue, Lomax asks Lead Belly, "Do you think when the sisters get happy in church, they're pretending?" Lead Belly replies, "They ain't putting on. When they get the feeling of God, they ain't ashamed. My momma was the shoutingest woman you ever seen." "John Henry" is the song about the mythical black hero, "that steel driving man," who could outwork all comers. Lead Belly says he learned

"John Hardy" from his buddy Woody Guthrie. It is about an outlaw who murders someone and has to go to prison. His girlfriend says she would rather see him dead than in jail. The title song "Go Down Old Hannah" is a spiritual, but it is also a work song that laments the plight of blacks: "There's a man lying dead on every turn row."

In the early 1940s, Lead Belly worked with and became friends with a new generation of folksingers like Woody Guthrie, Pete Seeger, Burl Ives, and other newly arrived southerners like Josh White, Sonny Terry, and Brownie McGhee. From this point of his life on, Lead Belly was more a folksinger than a bluesman.[31] Neither type of singer made much money in the music business. According to his income tax return for 1945, Lead Belly grossed $1,183.[32] In December, 1949, six months after Lead Belly's Harlem funeral, "Goodnight Irene" was released by the Weavers (Seeger, et al.), and it became the most popular record of 1950.[33] The song also was recorded by both Ernest Tubb and Frank Sinatra. By October, 1950, the *New York Times* estimated that "Goodnight Irene" could be heard 1,400 times per minute over the 2,583 radio stations, 99 television stations, and approximately 400,000 jukeboxes in the United States.[34] Even though Lead Belly never made much money either as a singer or songwriter, at least his heirs did, and that was because John Lomax scrupulously listed Lead Belly as composer of the song.

## Mance Lipscomb

Mance Lipscomb was born April 9, 1895, near Navasota, where he lived all of his life. He died January 30, 1976, having worked most of his eighty years as a sharecropper on the rich bottomlands along the Brazos River.[35] A little-known fact about Lipscomb is that country star Jimmie Rodgers came through Navasota and asked Mance to go on tour with him. Mance declined, and he remained a diamond in the rough until 1960 when Mack McCormick and Chris Strachwitz "rediscovered" him.[36] In the liner notes to Mance's *Texas Songster* compact disc, Strachwitz says that he was in Houston trying to record Lightning Hopkins but was unsuccessful because Hopkins was leaving town with John Lomax to play a West Coast folk festival. He and McCormick decided to try to locate Tom Moore's farm near Navasota. Moore is the subject of the serious protest blues song covered by both Lipscomb and Hopkins about inhumane treatment of blacks in the first half of the twentieth century. Tom Moore was the father of former state senator Bill Moore, long known as the "Bull of the Brazos" and "A&M's Senator." When they found Tom Moore's office over the bank building in Navasota and asked him if he knew any good black guitar players, he directed them to "Peg Leg" at the railroad station, who directed them to Mance's house. "That night I recorded many songs for the Songster album, and it was Arhoolie's first release in 1960," Strachwitz said. "For his first song, Lipscomb played what he thought white men would want to hear, 'St. Louis Blues,' but then I asked if he knew a song with 'a great deal of personal meaning for Negroes of the Brazos bottoms.' He replied, 'Oh well then, you want to hear the real stuff.' Mance recorded from 8 P.M. until 1 A.M. even though he had to get up for work at 5 A.M."[37]

Lipscomb was more than just a bluesman. He called himself a songster, an apt description for Lipscomb and for Lead Belly. McCormick says the term suggests a musician who usually had a day job and entertained Saturday nights and Sundays at country suppers, beer joints, and open-air dances. Blind Lemon Jefferson was also a songster, but because he recorded only blues records, he is best remembered for those.[38] Black music was predominantly associated with rhythms of work, church, and dance, and the songster was "the community musician who played and sang for the social affairs of his neighbors. In 1960 when he was first recorded, Mance had worked forty-seven years, six days a week, as a sharecropper: 'Saturday night I'd play all night—till 11 Sunday morning—and go right back and play for the white dance Sunday night and then go to the field on Monday.'"[39]

Lipscomb's three best albums are on Arhoolie Records, and the first is *Texas Songster.* "Sugar Babe (It's All Over Now)" is a song about a pimp's prostitute who is not working hard enough, and he is willing to beat her to make her comply: "All I want my baby to do is make five dollars and give me two/ . . . Went downtown and bought me a rope, whup my babe till she was all broke." Numerous Lipscomb tunes are about sex. "Going Down Slow" is a narrative about a man who probably is dying of syphilis. He says he has led a sinful life, asks forgiveness, and outlines his dying requests. "Freddie" is a real bad love song in which Freddie catches his woman in bed with another man and has to shoot her: "You got mad, you got bad, with your gun in your hand." According to McCormick, "Freddie" is one of numerous songs about blacks singing their way out of jail. Indeed, Lead Belly did sing his way out of prison, and Lightning Hopkins and Texas Alexander sang their way off East Texas road gangs. McCormick says, "These stories are probably true for it is an honored Texas tradition to release Negro prisoners who make an eloquent plea. It is easy for a Negro to be sent to prison, and by the same token, it is relatively easy for the individual to gain his release."[40] Lipscomb says "Freddie" was about a real prisoner in the Falls County Jail in Marlin.

Everyone covered "One Thin Dime." Mance learned it from Blind Lemon Jefferson whom he met on Deep Ellum Street in Dallas around 1917.[41] Lead Belly sang it too. Lipscomb says he will save his last dime for his girlfriend. "Shake, Shake Momma" is an original double entendre about sex: "Little bitty woman, hips just like a snake/ Late last night my love come tumbling down." He also offers some interesting automobile/sex symbolism: "Clutch started slipping, car won't even sing/ Losin' compression from my piston rings." McCormick says "Ella Speed" was more popular than any other ballad in Texas except for "Casey Jones," including "Frankie and Albert" (Johnnie). The ballad was written by Bill Martin who shot Ella in Dallas and wrote a song about it.[42] "Bout a Spoonful" is sexual double entendre, more clever and less bawdy than most: "Tell me what you gonna do with your brand new baby bout a spoonful."

Almost every modern bluesman includes "Big Boss Man" in his repertoire. Jimmy Reed had a giant hit record with it in 1961. Lipscomb says it is a field work song: "I got a big boss man, just won't treat me right, works me hard all day long/ I can't sleep at night." He concludes the chorus, "Well you ain't so big, you're just tall, that's all." "Blues in G" is another song about real bad love. When the singer catches his girlfriend with another man, he shoots her. Then when she does not die, he beats her. Then he complains about her throwing him out: "I didn't have no money, my shoes had done worn thin/ (repeat)/ Didn't have a decent pair of pants to go to Sunday school in." How he got from murder and wife beating to Sunday school is typical of Lipscomb's brand of Negro lore. He just mixes it all together, shakes it up, and makes the second half of the song an instrumental. For some reason, everything seems to fit. But not all of his female subjects are bad women. "Knocking Down Windows" is a celebration of the attraction of women. "They're what makes the world go around: Brown skin woman make a preacher lay his Bible down"; likewise, a "jet black woman make a rabbit love a hound."

Volume two of the Texas Songster trilogy, *You Got to Reap Just What You Sow,* was recorded May 2, 1964, at Chris Strachwitz's house in Berkeley, California.[43] The songs range from blues to spirituals and from ballads to pop songs, with emphasis on the blues because Lipscomb believed that they were better received by his audiences: "Texas people didn't know nothing about the blues until they came from Mississippi. My father didn't know blues, but he played waltzes, two-steps, ring plays, schottisches, church songs and breakdowns." "You Got to Reap Just What You Sow" is about a bad woman who "Took all my money, left me cold in hand/ Taken my money and give it to your other man." According to Strachwitz, "Bumble Bee" was composed and made famous by Memphis Minnie in the late 1920s and early 1930s. The lyrics contain an obvious double entendre for sex: "You got the best little stinger of any bumble bee I've ever seen/ Now you stung me this morning, I been looking for you all day long." "Silver City" concerns Lipscomb's normal condition of being hard up for money. He says if he had plenty, all his problems would be solved: "If I had money like leaves grow on trees/ (repeat)/ Get any woman I want, work when I please." "So Different Blues" is a Lipscomb original. He says he is too blue to go to work, and his woman is no good either. But he can still see the humor in his bleak situation: "Ain't never loved by the four women in my life/ (repeat)/ My momma, my sister, my sweetheart, and my wife." "You Rascal You" is a violent song popularized in the late 1920s and early 1930s by Louis Armstrong. It is an attack on a man who made a pass at both his wife and his daughter: "I'm gonna cut your arms off too you rascal you/ (repeat)/ Something else that's attached to you." In "Police Station Blues," Mance says it is hard to get his daddy out of jail because his daddy "done testified." The jailer tells wives of all rounders they better keep their men locked up at home; otherwise he will lock them up in his jail. The last line is the best; maybe it explains why his daddy was in jail: "If the blues was whiskey, I'd stay drunk all the time."

The third volume of the series, *Captain, Captain*, contains twenty-four widely divergent types of tunes, but again the blues predominate.[44] "Captain, Captain" is a work song blues that Lipscomb learned from an ex-convict working in the Navasota area: "Six months ain't long, two years ain't no great long time/ (repeat)/ Got a friend in the penitentiary doing ninety-nine." "I Want to Do Something for You" is a courtship song in which Mance's girlfriend turns down his offer of a diamond ring and a Chevrolet, but accepts a "sedan Ford." "Santa Fe Blues" is a train song not much different from several of Jimmie Rodgers's train song blues. If Lipscomb had yodeled, you could not tell the difference: "If you don't want me baby, why don't you tell me so/ (repeat)/ Hand me down my shoe soles, down the road I'll go." "Frankie and Albert" was covered by everyone. One interesting switch, however, is that the wronged woman has to shoot her cheating man: "Frankie walked down the street, wasn't gone very long/ under Frankie's apron was a Colt 44, that's my man, gonna kill him shore." "Black Rat" is another real bad love song: "You was raised in my kitchen, et up all my bread/ soon as I left home you start to cut up in my bed." The most interesting song on the album is "Tom Moore's Farm," a protest song about bad working conditions: "Reason why people like Mr. Tom Moore so well/ (repeat)/ when you set down to his table, look like some Rice Hotel." By the end, the song tells of physical violence suffered by Moore's farm workers: "Mr. Tom would whup you, dare you not to tell." Lipscomb once sang the song at a party for Bill Moore, but he is said to have toned down some of the harsher lyrics. "Going Back to Georgia" and "Easy Rider Blues" are two more songs about bad women. In the former, Lipscomb says, "I pulled you baby before you got ripe Sugar Babe/ (repeat)/ I pulled you baby before you got ripe, but now I know you ain't my type." In the latter, he sings, "If I had my pistol and you got in some woods/ (repeat)/ I'd shoot you so bad you couldn't do no man no good."

According to Rick Koster, Lipscomb "crisscrossed the United States, appearing before adoring fans and bedazzled musicians at various clubs and blues and folk festivals, but he found a spiritual home in Austin. For almost ten years, Lipscomb was a kind godfather to a citywide family of players" until he died in 1976.[45] To all who knew him, Mance Lipscomb was a kind, gentle, decent man, and his legacy lives in all the bluesmen he influenced.

## ❧ Lightning Hopkins ❧

Sam "Lightning" Hopkins was a successor to early country bluesmen Blind Lemon Jefferson and Texas Alexander. He was born on March 15, 1912, in Centerville, and he died in Houston on January 30, 1982. By the early 1920s, Hopkins had left home to be a bluesman and migrant farm worker. He and his cousin, Texas Alexander, played together on the streets of Houston from the 1920s to the early 1940s, but the two never recorded together. Sam got his nickname Lightning because his first records were made accompanying a pianist named "Thunder" Smith. In the late 1940s, Anne Cullum, promoter and talent scout for Aladdin Records, heard Hopkins and Alexander performing on Dowling Street in Houston. She arranged for them to record on her next trip to California, but, according to Chris Strachwitz, Alexander scared her (he had just gotten out of prison), so she substituted Thunder Smith for him.[46] Hopkins's first regional hit record was "Katie Mae," followed by "Short Haired Woman." Cullum tried to get him to play the Chittlin' Circuit (black clubs for black audiences), but Hopkins preferred staying in Houston. In Houston he recorded for Bill Quinn's Gold Star Records between 1947 and 1950. Strachwitz says, "Hopkins took his inspirations for songs from life as he observed it; intermingled with traditional verses, he planned songs out in his heart. The songs, like all of Lightning's recordings, represent brief audio snapshots of one of the great folk poets to emerge from the Afro-American experience in Texas."[47]

"Short Haired Woman" on the first volume of the Gold Star sessions is a remake of his hit for Aladdin. It is a song about a trifling woman: "I don't want no woman if her hair ain't no longer than mine/ (repeat)/ She ain't no good for nothing but trouble." "Going Home Blues" is a mournful tune that Strachwitz says is "the ultimate autobiographical performance and was probably not released at the time because the lyrics were so self centered. Yet it's an honest picture of Lightning's attitude of self pity."[48] "I was born March fifteen, nineteen hundred and twelve/ (repeat)/ You know ever since that day Lightning hasn't been doing so well." In "Loretta Blues," Hopkins gives us a contest between a bawdy house and religion, which sex, naturally, wins: "Oh Miss Loretta, where did you get all these good looking women from?/ (repeat)/ She said they came in here unexpected, Sam, blowed in by a storm." Lightning often played in Galveston where prostitution was legal until the early 1950s. Mance Lipscomb says he met Hopkins in 1938 at a Galveston house party where Sam was playing.[49] Later in "Loretta Blues," Lightning sings, "Sugar momma, sugar momma, won't you please come back to me/ (repeat)/ Bring me my bright little sugar, ease my misery." In the last verse, Lightning went to church and says he "had praying on my mind," but so were Miss Loretta's girls, and he could not get the prayer right.

No one is sure why Hopkins calls Tom Moore "Tim" in "Tim Moore's Farm." In this version of the protest song, Moore would not let Lightning off work to attend his wife's funeral. In Lipscomb's rendition, Moore beats black workers for not working hard enough. Strachwitz says he heard a rumor that Moore attended a dance in Conroe at which Lightning was playing and told him never to play that song around there again.[50] In "Fast Life Woman," Hopkins preaches on the evils of excessive drinking. Of course, Lightning drank a lot too: "Take it easy, fast life woman, cause you ain't gonna live always/ (repeat)/ If you keep with your fast way of going, whiskey may carry you to your grave." Hopkins covers a wider variety of subjects than the three previously discussed bluesmen, and that is illustrated in "Death Bells" and "Airplane Blues." In the former, he hears "death bells ringing all in my head," and he wonders if his chariot is coming. He says you can run from death, but everyone gets caught. In the latter, Lightning sings, "I got a woman, she's always out of town/ (repeat)/ I'm gonna get me an airplane, fly that woman down." "Unsuccessful Blues," is about being broke, a condition that all bluesmen have had to face: "I went down to my boss man's house, that's where everybody was getting paid/ (repeat)/ you know my wife had already been down there, and taken up all in this world that I made." Strachwitz reports that Bill Quinn once paid Hopkins's wife for one of his recording sessions. In the last verse, Lightning says he would try to get the money from her, "but she's built up kind of like Joe Louis."[51]

The songs on the second volume of the Gold Star sessions are mostly about sex, bad women, or being broke.[52] "Shining Moon" is a Peeping Tom song about good love: "I ease over to her window to see how sweet she snore/ (repeat)/ She make me feel like jumping through the keyhole in her door." "Mercy" is a bad love blues about a woman who fools around: "I don't want no woman if she wants every man in town/ (repeat)/ she ain't good for nothing but to tear your reputation down." "Whiskey Blues" concerns both the joys and problems of alcohol: "If whiskey was a woman, I'll tell you what I'd do/ (repeat)/ I'd get there early in the morning, work all day for you." But Lightning says he cannot drink any more like everybody else because the doctor has told him "it's about to ruin my health." "European Blues" is the funniest song on the album. It is about World War II. From Hopkins's point of view, the more men who are drafted, the more women will be left home alone for him: "My girlfriend got a boyfriend in Europe, you know that fool's already across the sea/ (repeat)/ You know I don't hate it so bad, I know there's a better place for me" (home with all the girlfriends). Lightning in effect volunteers to keep the home fires burning.

Of all the sexual double entendre in this chapter, the lyrics of "What Can It Be" are the least difficult to unravel: "My baby says she got something hid out in the woods for me/ (repeat)/ You know poor Sam begin to wonder, oh Lord, what can it be." She tells him it is "round like an apple, Sam, and it's shaped just like a pear/ (repeat)/ She says you might find it if you search all around me somewhere." Strachwitz says that "Lonesome Home" was one of Hopkins's earliest releases, and it brings him back to the theme of his first hit, "Katie Mae." But the woman in "Lonesome Home" is unfaithful, while Katie Mae is steadfast, loyal, and true.[53] Here Lightning says that he gave the woman everything, but all she ever did was lie in bed and read. He even gives her an electric fan so she will be cool, but "Women act funny when they get another man/ (repeat)/ She won't look right at you, and she's always raising sand." In "No Mail Blues," Lightning sings that it is sad to be broke and looking for a check, and nobody will send you any mail. "My wife is barefooted, said she was hungry too/ (repeat)/ If I don't get my money, I don't know what on earth I'm gonna do." "Old Woman Blues" and "Henny Penny Blues" are both about sex. In the first, Lightning says that older women are less likely to be unfaithful and more likely to put up with his running around. In addition, they have more experience in bed and know better how to make a man happy in the morning. "Henny Penny" contains delightful double entendre about an unfaithful chicken: "Now I don't like chicken, but I owns a big fat hen/ She cackles for me but she lays for the other man." He goes on to say: "I like the way she cackles, her thighs are fat and fine/ I'd like her much better if she'd lay for me some time."

Hopkins's third Arhoolie album, *Texas Blues,* contains tunes on a variety of subjects from gambling, to woman trouble, to slavery, to prison, to novelty songs.[54] "I Once Was a Gambler" is about all the bad things that happen to gamblers; you lose your money, your woman, your home, your friends: "If you'll forgive me, Poor Lightning won't gamble no more/ (repeat)/ She says I can't help you now, sold out to the devil and that's the way you go." "Love Like a Fire Hydrant" sounds like it is going to be a typical Hopkins sexual double entendre song, but Lightning is dead serious. He has big time woman trouble and is hurting bad: "Darlin' your love is like a fire hydrant, you know how to turn it off and on/ (repeat)/ Darlin' when I be looking for you, girl you done turned it off and gone." Lightning presents his views on slavery and the black condition thereafter in "Slavery Time." He instructs blacks how to behave in order to avoid being lynched: "When I was born my people teach me this way/ (repeat)/ Tip your hat to the people, be careful about what you say."

It is hard to determine if "I Would If I Could" is a novelty song about going to the movies to see the famous outlaw Jesse James or a more serious song about envying the white man's power and saying what he would do if he possessed it: "I know they're gonna say I'm crazy, gonna say I'm insane/ (repeat)/ Ain't but one picture I want to see there—old Jesse James." In the chorus he goes on to sing: "I'm gonna tell 'em I would if I could/ (repeat)/ But I just can't shoot that good, but I'm gonna tell 'em old Lightning would if he could." The ambiguity may be richer than at first glance.

According to Strachwitz's liner notes, "Bud Russell Blues" is about the man who was chief transfer agent for the Texas State Prison system from about 1915–44. He picked up prisoners from all over Texas and took them to Huntsville where they were put into work camps along the Brazos River bottoms. Lead Belly mentions Russell in "Midnight Special," and he is one of the most notorious figures in black Texas folklore.[55] Beneath the surface of many Hopkins songs, there is a recurring threat of violence: "Please take care of my wife and child, I may not return to my home life/ (repeat)/ the next time the boss man hits me, I'm gonna give him a big surprise." "Send My Child Home to Me" concerns the universal love of a mother for her son who is off rambling somewhere. Lightning says that he overheard his mother praying: "Good Lord, please send my child home to me/ (repeat)/ I don't know if he's cold or if he's gonna freeze." "Black and Evil" is an interesting philosophical song, maybe a rationalization of weakness, perhaps a refusal to take responsibility for one's actions: "You know I'm black and evil, but the black man didn't make himself/ (repeat)/ You know the same God that made me, that man made everybody else."

*Mojo Hand: The Lighting Hopkins Anthology* is another good collection of Hopkins reissues.[56] It contains songs on many subjects and styles: his first hit record from 1946, hit records from 1951, attempts at crossover hits, songs about ghosts and magic, prison songs, and, of course, songs about bad women. "Katie Mae" was Lightning's first hit record. It is upbeat and happy: "Katie Mae's a good girl, folks say she don't run around at night/ (repeat)/ You know you can bet your last dollar Katie Mae will treat you right." "Play With Your Poodle," a 1947 recording, is straight-ahead rock and roll several years before it was "invented." As one anonymous bluesman put it, "The blues had a baby and they called it rock and roll." The song, covered by Marcia Ball in 1997, employs a playful double entendre: "That little poodle's got a long shaggy tail/ I tried to buy him but he wasn't for sale." The chorus goes: "I want to play with your poodle/ (repeat)/ I mean your little poodle dog." By the end of the song Sam has two old maids together in bed, one playing with the other's poodle. "Give Me Central 209" and "Coffee Blues" both made it to number six on Billboard's Rhythm and Blues list.[57]

Hopkins kept recording through the 1970s, and although some of his more famous tunes like "Mojo Hand" came later, none ever charted. "Lightning Don't Feel Well" was recorded in Houston in 1954 for the Herald label. Bill Haley's "Rock Around the Clock" came out the same year. Rock and roll was about to change the musical landscape, and the old bluesmen were about to be left out in the cold. Lightning says he is sick and has to go to the doctor. Maybe subconsciously it is rock and roll that has made him sick. "Had a Gal Named Sal" is also rock and roll. The song sounds like something Chuck Berry would do. Hopkins is obviously trying for a crossover hit, but it did not work out.

"I Asked the Bossman" is a prison song. Lightning's woman is in prison, and his guitar almost cries: "Release my little Margie, bossman please let her come back to me/ (repeat)/ You know the longer my little Margie's gone poor Lightning suffering in misery." He is tormented in "Black Ghost Blues": "Black ghost stay away from my door/ (repeat)/ You know you worry poor Lightning so much I just can't sleep no more." And when he does get to sleep, he dreams about black ghosts. "Mojo Hand," recorded several times over his career, may be Lightning's most famous song. It has been recorded by numerous other people, including Clarence "Gatemouth" Brown: "I'm going to Louisiana, get me a mojo hand/ (repeat)/ I want to fix that woman so she can't have no other man." The song is about magic spells.

According to Greg Drust, Mack McCormick—a folklorist and Houston disc jockey—"discovered Hopkins in 1959 and helped him join the folk music revival. He fit in well with this group because of his anti-war feelings and his repeated concerns about social and topical subjects. Lightning had been a folkie all along but didn't know it."[58] Drust and Stephen K. Peeples assert that Lightning Hopkins was "a true pioneer of contemporary American music, not only a direct link to the rural blues tradition, but also a key figure in the transition from country to city blues."[59] Hopkins was also Texas' most spontaneous bluesman, who never played a song the same way twice. His influence was extensive upon Aaron "T-Bone" Walker, Clarence "Gatemouth" Brown, and many others. Drust and Peeples contend, "His lyrics reflect sensitivity and tenacity, as well as the influence of booze and women. The intensity of his life and art allows the audience to vicariously experience the pain and joy about which he sang."[60]

Although Texas did not invent the blues, early Texas bluesmen Blind Lemon Jefferson, Lead Belly, Mance Lipscomb, and Lighting Hopkins played immeasurably vital roles in the development of the music. Their successors have been many and include Linden's Aaron "T-Bone" Walker, one of the first guitarists to electrify his instrument; Orange's Clarence "Gatemouth" Brown; Gilmer's Freddie King; Leona's Albert Collins; and Dallas's Stevie Ray Vaughan. The only discouraging word about the blues, and not just in Texas, is that most of its fans and performers now are white. But the color of the participants makes no difference in the quality and popularity of the music. It is a feeling, not a color, and the blues will never die.

## ∾ Notes ∾

1. Rick Koster, *Texas Music* (New York: St. Martin's Press, 1998), p. 143.

2. "Mack McCormick's List of Twenty Major Figures in Texas Blues," *The Book of Texas Lists!!* edited by Anne Dingus (Austin: Texas Monthly Press, 1981), p. 152.

3. Pete Welding, liner notes, *Blind Lemon Jefferson* (Milestone MCD 470222, 1992).

4. Ibid.

5. Ibid.

6. Ibid.

7. Koster, *Texas Music,* p. 144.

8. Charles K. Wolfe and Kip Lornell, *The Life and Legend of Lead Belly* (New York: HarperCollins, 1992), p. 9.

9. Ibid., p. 72.

10. Ibid., p. 79.

11. Ibid., p. 82.

12. Ibid., p. 83.

13. Ibid., p. 84.

14. Ibid., p. 86.

15. Ibid., p. 91.

16. Ibid., pp. 98–99.

17. Ibid., p. 108.

18. Ibid., pp. 114–15.

19. Ibid., pp. 119–20.

20. Kip Lornell, liner notes, *Midnight Special* (Rounder Records CD 1045, 1991).

21. Ibid.

22. Kip Lornell, liner notes, *Gwine Dig a Hole to Put the Devil In* (Rounder Records CD 1045, 1991).

23. Ibid.

24. Ibid.

25. Kip Lornell, liner notes, *Let Shine on Me* (Rounder Records CD 1046, 1991).

26. Ibid.

27. Kip Lornell, liner notes, *The Titanic* (Rounder Records CD 1097, 1994).

28. Kip Lornell, liner notes, *Nobody Know the Trouble I've Seen* (Rounder Records CD 1098, 1994).

29. Kip Lornell, liner notes, *Go Down Old Hannah* (Rounder Records CD 1099, 1994).

30. Nolan Porterfield, *Jimmie Rodgers: The Life and Times of America's Blue Yodeler* (Urbana: University of Illinois Press, 1992), pp. 266–67.

31. Wolfe and Lornell, *The Life and Legend of Lead Belly,* p. 214.

32. Ibid., p. 250.

33. Ibid., p. 257.

34. Ibid.

35. Chris Strachwitz and Mac McCormick, liner notes, *Texas Songster* (Arhoolie CD 306, 1989).

36. Mance Lipscomb, *I Say for Me a Parable: The Oral Autobiography of Mance Lipscomb, Texas Bluesman,* as told to and compiled by Glen Alyn (New York: Norton, 1993), p. 26.

37. Ibid.

38. Ibid.

39. Ibid.

40. Strachwitz and McCormick, liner notes, *Texas Songster.*

41. Lipscomb, *I Say for Me a Parable,* p. 181.

42. Strachwitz and McCormick, liner notes, *Texas Songster.*

43. Chris Strachwitz and Pete Welding, liner notes, *You Got to Reap Just What You Sow* (Arhoolie CD 398, 1993).

44. Chris Strachwitz and Pete Welding, liner notes, *Captain, Captain* (Arhoolie CD 465, 1998).

45. Koster, *Texas Music,* p. 147.

46. Chris Strachwitz, liner notes, *The Gold Star Sessions, Vol. 1* (Arhoolie CD 330, 1990).

47. Ibid.

48. Ibid.

49. Lipscomb, *I Say for Me a Parable,* pp. 224–25.

50. Strachwitz, liner notes, *The Gold Star Sessions, Vol. 1.*

51. Ibid.

52. Chris Strachwitz, liner notes, *The Gold Star Sessions, Vol. 2* (Arhoolie CD 337, 1990).

53. Ibid.

54. Chris Strachwitz, liner notes, *Texas Blues* (Arhoolie CD 302, 1990).

55. Ibid.

56. Greg Drust and Stephen K. Peeples, liner notes, *Mojo Hand: The Lighting Hopkins Anthology* (Rhino Records R4 71226, 1993).

57. Ibid.

58. Ibid.

59. Ibid.

60. Ibid.

# 5

## Roots of
## Classical Music in Texas
*The German Contribution*

## Larry Wolz

"Some future poet will say that of all of the good fairies who came to the birth of the free nation, none was more generous than Teutonia, who brought the refining, elevating, humanizing gift of music."[1] With these words George William Curtis, writing for *Harper's* magazine in 1881, drew attention to the tremendous influence of German immigration to the history of music in the United States. The story of how these wise gifts from the east shaped and influenced American musical culture up to about World War I is one that has yet to be told completely. And probably it never can be told successfully, because the German influence from the middle of the nineteenth century until World War I was so pervasive. Indeed, the classical tradition in American music *was* German during those years. To separate the German people and institutions from the total picture of American music culture during that period would leave, perhaps, only a blank canvas.

Likewise, it would be quite impossible to tell the story of music in Texas without stories of the German immigrants who created and nurtured most of it even from the days of the Republic. The classical tradition of music was diligently perpetuated by German settlers among themselves and eventually shared with their fellow Texans.[2] This process of cultivation created the foundations for the high level of choral, symphonic, and operatic music that the state enjoys today.

Of course, Texas was not unique in reaping great cultural benefit from pioneer immigrants. Raising the level of culture on any frontier depended on these settlers whom historian Louis B. Wright called "the better element." In his book, *Culture on the Moving Frontier,* Wright described this "better element" as "the conservators of traditional conduct, traditional ways of doing things, traditional manners and morals, [who] sought to preserve and perpetuate the ancient inheritance of things of the mind and spirit. In short, they tried to reproduce in the new environment the best of the civilized way of life they had previously known."[3] German settlers in Texas were part of this "better element." American musical institutions as a whole owe much of their earliest existence to these men and women who, when faced with a frontier environment in the realm of classical music, persevered to recreate in their new homes—often by the end of a single generation—what had taken almost one thousand years to evolve in their German homeland.

German communities often isolated themselves from their new Texas neighbors at first. Sometimes the isolation was total, as in the case of Hill Country German settlements like New Braunfels and Fredericksburg. But even in larger established cities such as San Antonio, German immigrants segregated themselves into discrete neighborhoods like the King William district. Much of this clannishness was a concentrated effort to maintain their *Deutschtum* or Germanness. Part of that *Deutschtum* was, certainly, their traditional musical institutions. Although insular at first, the perpetuation of traditions like the *Gesangvereine* or singing societies would bring cultural dividends for all Texans eventually. This essay will present the stories of some of those music pioneers in the Lone Star State and the institutions they founded, many of which still resound on the Texas soundscape.

Although the bulk of German immigration to Texas occurred after Texas attained statehood, German influence on music in Texas began to be apparent even during the days of the Republic. A survey of concert life in the theaters of Houston and Galveston finds one of the most popular entertainers to have been Madame Louise Thieleman, who had immigrated to New Orleans in 1835 and then journeyed to Houston as part of Henri Corri's theatrical troupe.[4] She specialized in singing roles for the company but also gave well-received concerts in the capital city. On December 17, 1839, she entertained with both serious and comic songs in the Senate Hall of the Capitol building. Thieleman often sang an aria from Auber's *Fra Diavolo,* and it was perhaps the first operatic selection heard in the new republic. The singing actress made an impression on no less than the indefatigable Gustav Dresel, for he wrote admiringly of her in his Houston journal: "The theater often produced quite tolerable performances, especially as long as Madame Thieleman figured as prima donna. She possessed a great gift of impersonation and a fine appearance, and she sang to the general satisfaction of the whole public."[5]

The following spring Emil Heerbrugger presented probably the most ambitious musical program heard in Texas to that time. Heerbrugger was described in his advertisement as "one of the best musicians in this country or the United States." Primarily a violinist, he also played guitar and cornet. The program presented on April 22, 1840, at the Capitol was the first in Texas for which a printed program survives.[6]

CONCERT OF INSTRUMENTAL MUSIC AT THE CAPITOL
On Wednesday Evening, April 22, 1840

Part I

1. Overture to Tancredi, 2 Violins and Piano                     Rossini
2. Fantasie, on the French Horn,
   to "What Fairy Like Music"
3. Ipsilanie Waltz and Gallopade,
   de "la Clockette ou diable page"                             Herold
4. Solo—Piano, Introduction,
   Variations & Finale sur un air
5. Solo—Violin
6. Grand Finale from the Operetta,
   "The Siren Girls in Arms"

Part II

7. Overture to Fra Diavalo, 2 Violins and Piano                  Auber
8. Solo, on the French Horn,
   with piano accompaniment
9. New Orleans Waltz and Gallopade,
   2 Violins and Piano
10. Solo—Guitar
11. "Oh Steal not the Ray," 2 Violins and Piano                 Mozart
Finale

*Mrs. Lehman will preside at the Piano Forte*
Concert to commence at 8 o'clock precisely
Tickets, $2.50 each

Thieleman and Heerbrugger were itinerant musicians who soon left the state, but among the flood of German immigrants who made their way to Texas in the next fifty years were musicians who would remain to nurture musical culture from the grass roots of their own German organizations to the flowering of institutions visible to the general populace. These organizations were ancestors to the state's choirs, bands, orchestras, and opera companies.

## The German Mark on Opera in Texas

Though German-language works have never been a dominant feature of the state's operatic fare, the first performances of *any* opera in Texas were given by a German opera troupe at Lone Star Hall in Houston on March 21, 1856. The company, which apparently presented only operatic selections, traveled to Texas from St. Louis and also performed in Galveston during its brief tour of the state. Only one other German opera company visited Houston and Galveston before the 1870s, when the advent of widespread rail transportation would make touring companies more common. That was Marie Friederici's Grand German Opera Troupe under the management of Henry Grau, one of the most prominent impresarios of the nineteenth century. The company performed in Houston (January 15–16, 1869) and Galveston (January 18–21, 1869). Its longer stopover in Galveston is clear evidence of that city's continued cultural dominance over her northern neighbor at the time. Three operas were performed in Houston (*Martha, Fra Diavalo,* and *The Magic Flute),* while six operas in four days were played for Galvestonians (*Martha, Fra Diavalo, Der Freischütz, The Magic Flute, Faust,* and *Il Trovatore).*

The Galveston theater was under lease to Henry Greenwall and his brother. Henry Greenwall (1832–1913) is yet another example of a prominent German immigrant who would shape musical culture in Texas. Greenwall's parents brought him as a child in 1837 to New Orleans, where he grew up in that rich cultural melting pot. He moved to Galveston after the Civil War and began a long career managing the largest theatrical circuit in Texas with theaters in Galveston, Houston, Dallas, Fort Worth, and Waco. Greenwall eventually would own theaters in Arkansas and at New Orleans as well. He became a legend in American theater history in the last decade of the century when he single-handedly opposed the monopoly of theatrical bookings by the Syndicate, a theatrical trust based in New York City, thereby championing the independence of theater managers in the South. Through his theaters ran a steady stream of the best musical entertainers and opera companies of the day. Greenwall and all promoters of opera and concerts in the late nineteenth century depended, of course, on German patronage; the success of their bookings rested on the approbation of these cultured and discriminating citizens.

German or German-led amateur musical organizations and social clubs also helped produce opera for Texans in the nineteenth century.

The German Casino Club of San Antonio built Casino Hall in 1859 for their entertainments and shortly thereafter staged portions of Weber's *Der Freischütz*. This was undoubtedly the first amateur production of German opera in the state of Texas. They also presented a performance of Weber's *Preciosa* for members and their guests on April 10, 1872. Likewise, in San Antonio, the Teutonia Singing Association presented three performances of Lortzing's *Czar und Zimmerman* (July 9–11, 1880). This popular German comic opera had seen, until then, American productions only in Cincinnati and Milwaukee, two other American cities with large German populations.

Later that same year a Professor Katzenberger put together a local production of Flotow's *Martha* featuring Madame Anna Rosetti, a professional soprano who had retired from one of the touring opera companies to settle in San Antonio. Performers for this production of *Martha* were apparently drawn from the city at-large, not just from the German population. German promotion of opera in earlier times had led now to more widespread interest. The San Antonio Opera Club began to figure prominently in the Alamo City's cultural life the following year, and local interest in opera continued to build on the foundation laid by her German citizens.

A similar sequence of events launched opera in Dallas. Another German musician, a Professor Otten, staged a complete performance with orchestra of Flotow's *Martha* at Field's Theatre on February 9, 1875. The Dallas *Herald* headline for the performance's review proclaimed: "THE OPERA. First Performance of One in Dallas." Although led by Professor Otten, the cast was a remarkable mix of German and non-German amateur singers from the community. Again, German impetus led to wider support for opera. Professor Otten would later move to Fort Worth, where his efforts there led to local talent presenting Planquette's *The Chimes of Normandy* on February 15, 1884. Both operas produced by Professor Otten were sung in English translation, yet another sign that German cultural attainments were being assimilated.

### ➳ German Singing Societies ➳

Undoubtedly, the most potent forebears of concert music in Texas were the *Gesangvereine* or singing societies that sprang up all over the state from at least 1850, and grew steadily until the disaster of World

War I. From these multi-faceted singing societies evolved the great choral traditions of the state as well as the beginnings of orchestral music.[7]

Both San Antonio and New Braunfels laid claim to being the site of the first German singing society in the state. Simon Menger claimed he founded the San Antonio *Männergesangverein* in July of 1847, but documentary evidence of the group does not exist before 1851. The *Gesangverein Germania,* however, was positively founded in New Braunfels in 1850. Galveston probably had a German singing society before 1850 also, and other, smaller, short-lived groups could have existed as far back as the 1830s. Austin and Houston formed groups in 1852, and new towns in the Hill Country boasted at least quartet-sized ensembles by the time the singing societies met for their first statewide *Sängerfest* in 1853.

New Braunfels hosted the first Texas *Sängerfest* October 16–17, 1853, as well as most of the rest of the festivals held before the Civil War. Groups from Austin, San Antonio, and Sisterdale traveled to New Braunfels for the meeting, which was almost rained out. Torrential rains the week of the festival had swollen rivers and creeks, many of which were almost impassable. The rains continued as the festival began, making it difficult to reach the *Festhalle,* which had been erected for the occasion. One must stand in awe at the perseverance of these sturdy musical pioneers who traveled on horseback or in ox-drawn wagons for two days along roads that were mere trails, crossed raging rivers in driving rain, risked their lives, and lost some of their possessions (including precious songbooks), all to establish in Texas the choral tradition that had been an integral part of their lives in Germany.

After some rehearsal on Sunday morning (October 16), the concert of the first state *Sängerfest* commenced at 6 P.M. with all the singers, about fifty, joining together in Adolf Marschner's "Vaterlandslied." Each of the groups alternated numbers for the remainder of the program, which closed with the massed group singing Mendelssohn's "Der Jäger Abschied." The full program of this historic event follows:[8]

First Part

|   |   |   |
|---|---|---|
| 1. | Vaterlandslied | Adolf Eduard Marschner |
|    | Massed Choruses |  |
| 2. | Liebesscherz | Folk Song |
|    | Austin Gesangverein |  |
| 3. | Minnelied, Quintet | Julius Otto |
|    | New Braunfels Germania |  |

4. Der Tanz, Waltz                                      Julius Otto
     San Antonio Männergesang-Verein
5. Das treue deutsche Herz                         Julius Otto
     New Braunfels Germania
6. Trinklied                                    Conradin Kreutzer
     Sisterdale Gesangverein

Second Part

1. An die Freundschaft                             August Neithardt
     Massed Choruses
2. Lebewohl                                    Friedrich Silcher
     Austin Gesangverein
3. Gesang der Geister über den Wassern         Bernhard Klein
     text by Goethe
     Sisterdale Gesangverein
4. Schlosserlied                                  Julius Otto
     New Braunfels Germania
5. Was ist des Deutschen Vaterland             Gustav Reichardt
     San Antonio Männergesang-Verein
6. Der Jäger Abschied                          Felix Mendelssohn
     Massed Choruses

In the tradition of the German *Sängerfests,* judges were appointed to award a prize to the best singing group. Most fittingly, the gilded prize lyre was bestowed on the hosts, the New Braunfels Germania. The following day the participants convened a "German meeting" where they discussed general issues relating to the German population, including the teaching of German in the public schools. After an afternoon band concert, the festival closed with the traditional ball and a resolve to convene another *Sängerfest* in San Antonio the following year.

The San Antonio *Sängerfest* (May 13–16, 1854) saw the beginnings of the movement toward a league of singing societies or *Sängerbund.* In the months following this second *Sängerfest,* the Deutsch-Texanischer Sängerbund would be organized officially. Theodore Albrecht, noting the impact this organization and its *Sängerfests* would have on music in Texas, wrote: "The musical progress that the Germans brought to Texas can be seen in virtually every successive Sängerfest from 1853 until the last before World War I, celebrated in 1916 (see figure 1)."[9]

The massed choruses in San Antonio sang in English for the first time (Philip Phile's "Hail Columbia"). This display of American patriotism did not, however, offset the anger and suspicion raised by the "German meeting" held later during the *Sängerfest.* At this meeting the

Figure 1
*Deutsch-Texanischer Sängerfesten*
*1853–1916*

| | |
|---|---|
| 1853 New Braunfels (October 16–17) | 1885 Houston (April 28–May 1) |
| | 1887 San Antonio (April 13–17) |
| 1854 San Antonio (May 13–16) | 1889 Austin (April 23–25) |
| 1855 New Braunfels (May 28–30) | 1891 Galveston (April 25–27) |
| 1856 New Braunfels (October 12–14) | 1892 Dallas (May 10–13) |
| | 1894 Houston (May 8–10) |
| 1858 New Braunfels (October 17–18) | 1896 San Antonio (April 28–30) |
| | 1898 Galveston (April 25–27) |
| 1859 Fredericksburg (May 29–31) | 1900 Austin (May 7–9) |
| 1860 New Braunfels (May 26–30) | 1902 Houston (May 5–7) |
| 1869 New Braunfels (August 22–23) | 1903 New Braunfels (October 4) Fiftieth Anniversary |
| 1870 San Antonio (September 9–11) | 1904 Dallas (April 25–27) |
| | 1906 San Antonio (April 18–21) |
| 1873 New Braunfels (May 10–13) | 1909 Galveston (May 17–19) |
| 1874 San Antonio (October 9–11) | 1911 Austin (May 22–24) |
| 1877 San Antonio (October 12–14) | 1913 Houston (May 5–7) |
| 1879 Austin (April 15–17) | 1914 Dallas (May 12–14) |
| 1881 Galveston (April 18–22) | 1916 San Antonio (May 7–10) |
| 1883 Dallas (May 15–17) | |

group adopted a German platform that included an antislavery plank, setting off heated debate among the non-German population of the state concerning the loyalty of these German immigrants. From this point on, the *Vereins* were looked upon by some as secret subversive societies.

Certainly, the early *Sängerfests* were organized by Germans for Germans primarily; the performers and the audiences were mostly German. Consequently, at the third festival in New Braunfels there were only about one dozen "American visitors" in the audience. In the years after the Civil War, though, the *Sängerfests* would grow in influence beyond the German community.

Instrumental accompaniment, chamber music, vocal soloists, and eventually a mixed choir in New Braunfels would be signs of innovation in the *Sängerfests* leading up to the war. The seventh and last of the *Sängerfests* before the Civil War was again held in New Braunfels and featured the town's new mixed chorus in a selection from Haydn's oratorio *The Creation*. The delegates resolved at this festival to include even more instrumental music at the next *Sängerfest* to be held in Austin, but the war postponed these plans for almost a decade.

## ◁≋ German Bands ≋▷

Especially in the larger cities, the *Gesangverein* groups were often affiliated with some sort of instrumental ensemble, usually a band. The German penchant for civic bands did much to advance the band movement in Texas and throughout the United States. Civic bands had been common in German towns from the earlier nineteenth century, beginning with the civic militia bands that appeared after the Napoleonic era. In the latter half of the century, these bands became much more entertainment-oriented and were often associated with local singing societies. A census of bands in Europe around 1900 found at least 1,560 civic bands active in Germany alone. These bands varied greatly in instrumentation, some based on the older French model of *Harmoniemusik,* where the clarinet was the principal melodic instrument; others, especially after mid-century, were brass bands. In this country, of course, band instrumentation was even more varied, because—particularly in smaller towns—it was dependent on any and every available player and instrument.[10]

Civic bands, whether associated with German singing societies or not, played an important role in the lives of their respective communities. They played for parades and picnics, gave outdoor concerts, and perhaps most importantly in German communities, played for dances. These aspects of German influence on music in Texas bring the classical and popular traditions to intersection. Bands, especially those associated with the singing societies, might perform the works of European masters in one hour to be followed in the next by drinking songs and polkas for dancing. Most of the *Sängerfest* concerts were followed by *Kommers* (literally, supper) featuring lots of food, beer, spirited singing, and dancing accompanied by the German band. German immigrants brought with them to this country all the popular dances of the nineteenth century—the polka, redowa, schottische, and, of course, the waltz. The great "Waltz King" himself, Johann Strauss, Jr., began his career as a bandmaster, playing for dances often sponsored by German singing societies.

German bands were often the only band in the town or region and hired themselves out to play dances beyond the German community as well. In the larger cities, like San Antonio, some bands became quite professional and gave their members almost full-time employment. Carl Beck's Military Band in San Antonio is an excellent example of such a group. Beck, who also conducted the Beethoven Männerchor in that city, was kept busy playing for dances and other social occasions throughout the Alamo City, and he and his band became well known in the community-at-large. His group was quite obviously modeled on the German civic militia bands he had known in his homeland, down to the name and the military-style uniforms. Beck always proudly related the story of his band's playing at the San Antonio train station to welcome Teddy Roosevelt and his Rough Riders, who were en route to Cuba for service in the Spanish-American War in 1898.

Carl Beck (1850–1920), whose role in establishing orchestral music in Texas will be discussed later, is perhaps the perfect example of the important role individual German musicians played as cultural pioneers in Texas. Leaving San Antonio in 1905 after more than twenty years as one of the premier musicians there, he moved to Odessa in far-away West Texas, where he took on the direction of a fourteen-piece town band that he quickly built into regional prominence. Typically, the group played for any civic or social occasion, large or small—their leader's only source of income was these engagements and the teaching of individual lessons. Beck's Odessa band became so well known that it performed as the official band for the 1909 West Texas Fair in Abilene, some 170 miles to the east.

The following year, Beck moved even farther west to Pecos, where he took a similar position as leader of the Pecos Commercial Club Band. The Pecos band is also representative of the importance placed by communities on their bands as barometers of pride and cultural attainment. The *Reeves County Record* of March 24, 1911, announced that the Electric Theatre in Pecos would donate proceeds from one of its coming showings to benefit the Commercial Club Band and in the process commented on Carl Beck's work there: "Professor Carl Beck, director, is untiring in his efforts to give us one of the best bands in the state, and it is up to us to do our part. A band is one of the best boosters a town can have, and the stranger who is in our city on Friday night, when the band gives a free concert, will go back to his native town with words of praise for our city—where something is doing all the time." Carl Beck's work in Odessa and Pecos was replicated in untold numbers of cities and towns throughout the United States in the nineteenth and early twentieth centuries.

The social dimension of these German bands is perpetuated to this day in the polka or "oompah" bands that dot the state in or near communities of German or Czech heritage. The instrumentation of these groups with clarinet, accordion, and drums is representative of later developments in Eastern European folk bands when the fiddle and other

*An early Odessa Band conducted by Professor Carl Beck, ca. 1905–1906.*
*Courtesy Betty Orbeck Collection, Permian Historical Society, UTPB*

melodic instruments were replaced by the accordion, which could single-handedly replace the trouble and expense of a band, especially for dancing. German and Czech immigrants to the United States were probably the first to introduce the modern accordion to American ears. Its utilitarian practicality made it especially attractive to smaller communities where instrumentalists were scarce. Both the accordion and the German dances that it accompanied were early adopted by Mexican Texans in the creation of the distinctive *norteño* or *conjunto* music in the early twentieth century.

## ⧽ The Growth of Orchestral Music ⧽

Instrumental ensembles—from brass bands to orchestras—figured prominently in the *Sängerfests* after the Civil War. These instrumental groups also drew more non-Germans to the concerts and would lead eventually to the establishment of permanent orchestras in major cities throughout the state.

As noted earlier, bands of one kind or another for parades and dances had always been part of the *Sängerfests* since the first in 1853, but in 1874, when San Antonio hosted the eleventh state *Sängerfest,* organizers fielded an orchestra of strings and winds conducted by a Professor Müller to play overtures before each half of the concert program. The orchestra played overtures to Bellini's opera *Norma* and Rossini's *Tancredi.* When San Antonio hosted the next state festival in 1877 the orchestra had grown to thirty-eight pieces. The group not only played several overtures and Haydn's "Toy Symphony," but also accompanied choruses and soloists in larger choral works such as Rossini's *Stabat Mater.* The concert on October 13 drew more than 2,000 listeners, 1,500 inside the festival hall and several hundred outside, listening through the windows.

When Austin hosted the state *Sängerfest* in 1879, organizers imported the New Orleans Theater Orchestra from St. Louis. This orchestra played Beethoven's "Overture to *Egmont*" and von Suppe's "Light Cavalry Overture," among others. Expansion of the Texas *Sängerbund* was evident in this and subsequent festivals, with the advent of groups from Galveston and Dallas as well as the traditional Central Texas contingents.

As the larger cities began to dominate the state organization, however, the smaller groups from the Hill Country felt excluded, their performances often being relegated to nonpublic social events during the *Sängerfests.* Therefore, on Easter Sunday, April 18, 1881, the West Texanischer Gebirgs Sängerbund (West Texas Hill Country Singers League) was organized, officially separate from the state organization. Other regional *Sängerbunds* would emerge, but the original state league of singers would remain the most important for the continued development of concert music in Texas.

Galveston hosted the 1881 state *Sängerfest,* building an immense beachfront pavilion seating 5,000 for the occasion. Galveston also produced an orchestra which accompanied works by the Galveston choruses and played Weber's *Jubel* overture and the first movement of Beethoven's second symphony. For the first time in the history of the festivals, the English-language newspapers gave the event more space than their German-language counterparts. A decade later, programs for the festival concerts would bear further witness to Anglo interest in the concerts—texts printed in both German and English.

The larger the state meetings became, the more organizers had to appeal to citizens beyond the German population to help finance the endeavors. Dallas hosted the state *Sängerfest* in 1883, expanding the event to three public concerts, although instrumental forces for the event were less elaborate than those pioneered in San Antonio. The second half of the third concert was devoted to Frederic Cowen's *The Rose Maiden,* a major choral work in English, an unprecedented event in the history of the state *Sängerbund.* This was again a sign of German assimilation in Dallas—already noted in the first Dallas opera production almost ten years earlier.

The 1885 *Sängerfest* held in Houston introduced the state to a conductor who would build instrumental resources in Texas toward permanent orchestras in the early twentieth century. Carl Beck, who had moved to San Antonio in 1884 to direct the Beethoven Männerchor, was chosen as musical director for the orchestra and used the occasion to program probably the first Wagner heard in Texas, "Overture to *Tannhäuser.*" The orchestra he organized also impressed listeners with Rossini's famous overture to the opera *William Tell.* It was only the beginning of things to come in the realm of orchestral music under Beck's direction (see figure 2).

When San Antonio hosted the 1887 state *Sängerfest,* Beck took advantage of the opportunity to focus attention on instrumental music at the festival. He directed an orchestra of 49 men and the massed male chorus, now grown to 226, along with his own local mixed chorus of 122 and also expanded the programming for the *Sängerfest* to six major concerts, four of them with orchestra. The programs included Beethoven's "Overture to *Fidelio,*" Mozart's "Overture to *Die Zauberflöte,*" Saint-Saëns's "Danse macabre," and for the first time in Texas history the performance of a *complete* symphony, Mendelssohn's Symphony No. 4 ("Italian"). The whole festival ended with choruses and orchestra joining together in Handel's "Hallelujah Chorus" from *Messiah.* Subsequently, Beck would conduct the festival orchestra in 1896 in San Antonio, again demonstrating a superior level of programming.

The high standards set by Beck and his San Antonio orchestra led eventually to the founding of the San Antonio Symphony. Carl Hahn (1874–1929) succeeded Beck as director of the Beethoven Männerchor around 1904. He and Mrs. Eli Hertzberg of the Tuesday Musical Club worked together to form the first group known as the San Antonio Symphony Orchestra. The thirty-eight-piece ensemble gave its first public concert May 18, 1905. The orchestra had a fitful existence until Arthur Claassen (1859–1920) arrived in San Antonio to conduct the Beethoven chorus in 1914. Claassen revived the San Antonio orchestra by

Figure 2
*Orchestral Repertoire of Carl Beck in Texas*

| | |
|---|---|
| Adam | Overture to *Si j'etais roi* |
| Auber | Overture to *La muette de portici* |
| | Overture to *Le Cheval de bronze* |
| Beethoven | Overture to *Fidelio* |
| | Violin Concerto (1st movt.) |
| | Symphony No. 5 (2nd movt.) |
| Boieldieu | Overture to *La dame blanche* |
| Delibes | Selections from *Sylvia* |
| Grieg | Piano Concerto in A minor |
| Herold | Overture to *Zampa* |
| Mascagni | Intermezzo from *Cavalleria Rusticana* |
| Mendelssohn | Symphony No. 4 ("Italian") |
| Meyerbeer | Coronation March from *La Prophete* |
| Mozart | Overture to *Die Zauberflöte* |
| Rossini | Overture to *Semiramide* |
| | Overture to *William Tell* |
| Saint-Saëns | Danse macabre |
| Suppe | Overture to *Poet and Peasant* |
| Thomas | Overture to *Raymond* |
| | Overture to *Mignon* |
| Volkmann | Serenade in F major, Op. 63 |
| Wagner | Bridal Chorus from *Lohengrin* |
| | Overture to *Tannhäuser* |
| | Prelude to *Lohengrin* |
| | Siegfried's Funeral Music from *Die Götterdämerung* |
| Weber | Overture to *Oberon* |
| | "Jubel" Overture |
| | Overture to *Der Freischütz* |
| | Konzerstück in F major |

increasing its size to fifty and renaming it the San Antonio Philharmonic for a time. It would return to being the San Antonio Symphony
Orchestra by 1916, however, as it remains to this day.

Similarly, German leadership in the *Gesangverein* movement in
Dallas organized the first symphony orchestra there. Hans Kreissig
(1856–1929), longtime conductor of the Frohsinn Männerchor, organized a thirty-two-member Dallas Symphony Orchestra in 1900 and remained its leader until 1912, when he was succeeded in both positions
by Carl Venth (1860–1938). Venth attempted to revive the orchestra

whose performances had been rather sporadic since its founding, but his efforts were cut short by lack of financial backing and his eventual move to Fort Worth in 1915. Of course, all German musical efforts were soon curtailed in the wake of World War I.

##  The Ubiquitous German Music Professor

Throughout this essay many of the German musicians discussed have had "professor" attached to their surnames. In fact, for many German musicians working in Texas during the nineteenth century, we know only the surnames following that title. No one knows how the honorific "professor" became associated so specifically with music teachers, but it eventually became universal. Every town of any size had a music "professor," usually German, who directed the town band, directed the church choir and played the organ, gave music lessons on a variety of instruments, or—more likely—most of the above. The ubiquitous German music professor is an icon of nineteenth-century musical culture throughout the United States, and he was perhaps one of the most important propagators of the cultivated tradition in music. The remarkable American-born piano virtuoso, Louis Moreau Gottschalk (1829–69), once remarked that it seemed that all musicians in this country were Germans. These jack-of-all-trades musicians often settled in small towns where they became the arbiters of musical culture and taste for the citizenry. Without their, often thankless, struggle to bring music into the lives of even the smallest communities, the cultivated tradition in music would have been much slower to take hold in the state. We can be thankful for the wanderlust that drove some of these itinerant musicians, many of them extremely gifted, from town to town. Two of these German music professors working in Texas can serve as exemplars of the legion who made the Lone Star State their home.

The first of these the reader has encountered more than once in this essay. Carl Beck, the leader of the Beethoven Männerchor of San Antonio, the orchestral conductor who introduced Texas to Wagner, and one of the most distinguished German musicians in the state by the end of the nineteenth century, abandoned the glory and stability of probably the most cultured city in Texas to become an itinerant music professor in West Texas. Inexplicably, he moved first to Odessa, a town with a population of less than five hundred. Later, following his wanderlust, he moved farther west to Pecos. In both towns he conducted town bands and taught music lessons. In 1914, Beck returned south, this time settling in Kingsville. There, Professor Beck, now sixty-five years old, retired from the life of a bandmaster. Little is known about Beck's Kingsville years, but Alena Collins Smith, whose parents had moved to Kingsville in 1914 from Cincinnati, related this telling memory of Beck during his years there: "There was a Professor Beck, a little heavy-set German who wore a fez, conducted the Presbyterian choir and taught piano lessons in his room at the Kivlin's. I never took lessons from him, but he was reputed to rap his pupils on the knuckles with a ruler if they missed a note."[11]

Beck would have probably remained in Kingsville the rest of his life, but the Beethoven Männerchor of San Antonio, desperate for a conductor after the resignation of Arthur Claassen in 1919, convinced him to return to San Antonio. It was his ignominious task to preside over the waning fortunes of the once-proud musical organization until his own death on October 2, 1920. Because Beck had no family in the United States, his musical family gave him a funeral befitting a pioneer of instrumental music in Texas. A band made up of former associates and pupils accompanied his coffin to City Cemetery No. 4, playing the strains of Chopin's "Funeral March," and the Beethoven Männerchor sang "Still ruht dein Herz" ("Still rest thine heart") over the grave. The wandering minstrel was home.

Another most important German musician in nineteenth-century Texas was Julius Weiss (1840/41–?), who was listed, appropriately enough, as "Professor, Music" in the 1880 census taken at Texarkana, Texas.[12] Weiss emigrated to the United States in the mid-1860s after university and conservatory training in Saxony, settling ultimately in St. Louis. Around 1878, he was engaged by Colonel Robert W. Rodgers to provide musical training for his children. Rodgers was a prominent businessman in Texarkana, and Weiss came to live as a tenant in the Rodgers' large house, teaching music to the six children (violin for the boys and piano for the girls). Professor Weiss left Texarkana in 1884 after the death of his employer. His name appeared in the mid-1890s in the Houston city directory in partnership with W. C. Stansfield, selling pianos, organs, and music on Main Street there. His fortunes declined, however, by the turn of the century when he seems to have been working in a gambling establishment in the city, entertaining the customers with his piano playing. He disappeared from records after 1901.

Julius Weiss was probably the German music professor that Scott Joplin (1868–1919), Texas-born King of Ragtime, remembered so fondly to his wife in his later years. Weiss came into Joplin's life when Joplin's father, Giles, somehow scraped together enough money to buy the Rodgers' old square piano after Weiss had traveled to New Orleans to choose and purchase a new cherry-wood square grand with lyre pedal and mother-of-pearl keyboard for the family. Joplin's mother, Florence, may have done cleaning and washing for the Rodgers family, as she was known to have done for other prominent Texarkana families, giving her an inside track to purchase the older piano. Also, Weiss may have had a hand in encouraging the Rodgers family to sell the piano to the Joplins because he had by this time (1880) probably heard the young boy playing around town. It was also around this time, when Joplin was eleven or twelve years old, that Weiss began to give him the free lessons that would broaden his musical horizons. Along with piano lessons, Weiss also talked with the boy of the great composers, played musical classics for him, and shared, especially, his love of opera. This priceless musical education for the son of former slaves was never forgotten. Joplin's widow remembered in later years that her husband occasionally sent gifts of money to a German musician somewhere, his first teacher, now poor and ill.

Weiss was undoubtedly the inspiration for Scott Joplin's quest to continue his musical education in 1897 at George R. Smith College in Sedalia, Missouri, and to use his ragtime style in conjunction with larger musical forms, like ballet and opera. Joplin became obsessed in the last years of his life with the composition and production of his full-length grand opera, *Treemonisha,* a work that shows every sign of the composer's knowledge of mid-century German operatic forms that Weiss would have taught him. Joplin's subject was the importance of education to the advancement of African Americans in American society.

Here, then, are two itinerant German music professors who shaped the history of music in Texas and beyond. Without the spade work of Carl Beck, the development of the symphony orchestra in Texas surely would have been delayed by decades. And certainly the generosity and tutelage of Julius Weiss raised the sights of a talented black pianist whose music would radically alter the entire course of American popular music. But these are only two of an inestimable number of German musicians who tilled the musical soil of Texas. Multiply by hundreds their number and thousands their pupils to gain but an inkling of the influence these priceless propagators of culture had on musical life in Texas.

The German contribution to the history of music in Texas, then, was one of transplantation, nurturing, and conservation of cultivated classical tradition art music until that time in the late nineteenth century when a majority of Texans began to have the inclination borne of leisure time and monetary capital to support their own musical institutions. German "professors" perpetuated these cultivated traditions, teaching in towns large and small, training new generations of musicians, Anglo and German, who would demand the best in music for their children. From these modest beginnings grew the world-class professional orchestras and opera companies that Texans now enjoy. This is our rich legacy from those sturdy German pioneers.

### ≈ Notes ≈

1. Joseph Horowitz, *Wagner Nights: An American History* (Berkeley: University of California Press, 1994), p. 36.

2. American musicologists generally recognize two separate streams of music in this country from the mid-nineteenth century until about 1920. Writers have used a variety of terms, the most widely known as classical/popular. Other pairs include: art/folk, edifying/entertaining, cosmopolitan/provincial, serious/light, cultivated/vernacular, formal/informal, artistic/functional. An excellent discussion of this dichotomy can be found in Richard Crawford's essay, "Cosmopolitan and Provincial: American Music Historiography," in his book *The American Musical Landscape* (Berkeley: University of California Press, 1993), pp. 3–37. The reader will note throughout the current essay that the German contribution, although predominantly classical, was not limited to only one side of the stream, nor is one stream implied to be more important than the other.

3. Louis B. Wright, *Culture on the Moving Frontier* (New York: Harper & Row, 1955), p. 12.

4. The chronology and other details of concert life presented here were drawn primarily from two sources: Joseph Gallegly's *Footnotes on the Border: The Galveston and Houston Stage Before 1900* (The Hague, Netherlands: Mouton, 1962) and the author's thesis, "A Survey of Concert Life in Texas during the Nineteenth Century" (master's thesis, Texas Christian University, 1976). Both are based largely on newspapers of the time.

5. Max Freund, *Gustav Dresel's Houston Journal: Adventures in North America and Texas, 1837–1841* (Austin: University of Texas Press, 1954), p. 100.

6. Donald Wagner Pugh, "Music in Frontier Houston, 1836–1876" (Ph.D. diss., University of Texas, 1970), pp. 22–23.

7. Any survey of the history of German Singing Societies in Texas is indebted to Theodore Albrecht's "German Singing Societies in Texas" (Ph.D. diss., North Texas State University, 1975).

8. Ibid., pp. 99–101.

9. Ibid., pp. 90–91.

10. The discussion of the band movement is drawn partially from David Whitewell's monumental *The History and Literature of the Wind Band and Wind Ensemble,* 9 vols. (Northridge, Calif.: WINDS, 1984) and Kenneth Kreitner's *Discoursing Sweet Music: Brass Bands and Community Life in Turn-of-the-Century Pennsylvania* (Urbana: University of Illinois Press, 1990).

11. Kleberg Historical Commission, *Kleberg County, Texas* (Austin: Hart Graphics, 1979), p. 700.

12. The account of Julius Weiss is based on Theodore Albrecht's article, "Julius Weiss: Scott Joplin's First Piano Teacher," *College Music Symposium* 19 (fall, 1979): 89–105.

**6**

# Make a Joyful Noise
## *Some Popular Religious Music in Twentieth-Century Texas*

## Kenneth W. Davis

Popular religious music in the first six decades of the twentieth century in Texas flourished not only in rural and urban churches of various denominations; it was also found in singing schools, some sponsored by individual churches or consortiums of churches and in singing conventions almost all of which had at least some affiliation with church groups. With the advent of broadcast radio in the mid-1920s, religious music became readily available in homes across the state.

Although popular church music served the primary purpose of offering praise to God, it functioned also to provide in many instances at least rudimentary musical education for a great many whose exposure to knowledge of music was limited. In some churches, deliberate efforts were made to teach the scales and even some aspects of sight reading of notes, but, for the most part, churchgoers learned to sing by following a leader who with gestures, with lining out of songs, and by his or her own examples taught melodies for the often highly poetic lyrics. In some congregations time was set aside—usually in the summers after major farm work was done—for more formal training, which included exercises in breath control, posture, and the uses of gestures as well as in learning the scales and to read notes. Of particular interest also were schools in which training in Sacred Harp music was taught.

Named for Benjamin White's *The Sacred Harp* (1844), and sometimes called white spirituals, these songs were sung a cappella; the human voice was the sacred harp. Like many examples of popular church music, sacred harp music had its beginnings in the Southern Highlands and the Deep South. As Francis E. Abernethy (*Singin' Texas,* 1983), George Pullen Jackson (*The Story of Sacred Harp: 1844–1944,* 1944), and B. F. White (*The B. F. White Sacred Harp,* 1988), have written, sacred harp singing was based on the seven-note scale.[1] A singing master led his students through songs by first singing the notes before the singing of the songs' words. When songbooks were available, shaped notes (right triangle for fa, circle for sol, square for la, and a diamond for mi) were used. Still used in some congregations, there are singing schools that teach with the use of shaped-note songbooks. In Lubbock, Texas, the Quaker Avenue Church of Christ sponsors each summer a singing school to teach with the use of shaped-note hymnals. According to Dr. Thomas A. Langford, an elder in the church, the use of shaped notes is highly effective for learning to recognize notes and to sing scales properly.[2]

Singing schools such as those held for many years at Lariat, or McMahan, or Live Oak gave students—youth as well as adults—basic training in singing as well as in some elements of music theory. Students learned how to read notes and were drilled in phrasing and voice control. Under the careful tutelage of a singing master they learned to follow the directions of song leaders who made use of hand and arm gestures to direct timing and emphasis. Some singing masters also gave lessons in piano, violin, guitar, and other stringed instruments.

Like many aspects of religion, training in music served functions that went beyond the worship of God. At the end of singing school sessions (sometimes also called "conventions"), recitals were held. Students sang collectively and individually—solos helped prepare musicians to contribute "specials" in the usual Sunday morning services in their home churches. These recitals became social events at which welcomed visiting occurred along with courting among the youth who attended the singing school or who merely were present for the social aspects of the recitals. Some recitals were accompanied by time-honored customs such as dinner on the grounds, usually held on Sundays, and pie suppers, which were more commonly held at night—especially on Wednesday nights. The association of food with religious or quasi-religious events is, of course, part of a surviving folk tradition. The cooking of pies, cakes, and other desserts as well as meats and vegetables provided opportunities for parishioners to demonstrate their culinary skills and gave delight to people who came to recitals not only for the spirited music. Whether the setting was a small rural church in an isolated community, or one in a city, people were glad to have an opportunity to swap stories, comment on politics, and catch up on local news and gossip.[3]

Anecdotes grew out of these gatherings. The late Texas novelist, Jane Gilmore Rushing, supplied an account of how a small church near Pyron, Texas, very nearly split because the singing master moved his arm to form squares rather than the usual triangles when he led the singing. Some members of this particular congregation believed that the use of squares rather than the triangular movements was a heresy: the triangular movements, after all, showed respect to the trinity: God, Jesus, and the Holy Ghost. How this theological dilemma was resolved is a mystery now lost in the mists of time.[4]

The broader functions of singing schools included the kindling of an appreciation for music that led some to seek formal training. Thus, religious music, like the many colleges founded by religious groups, helped enhance culture. The Southwestern Baptist Theological Seminary's School of Music was and is a leader in the formal teaching of popular church music, particularly gospel music that succeeded the Sacred Harp, spiritual, and shaped-note traditions. This denominational school added courses in church music in 1911 and by 1920 had a School of Gospel Music.[5] Now known as the School of Church Music, its history is documented thoroughly in William J. Reynolds's *The Cross and the Lyre: The Story of the School of Church Music: Southwestern Baptist Theological Seminary.* This comprehensive study comments on the rich variety of types of music instruction offered to all students at this well-known seminary and thus points to the school's past and present influence in churches of various denominations across America. Among many valuable historical observations that Reynolds made in his study were those about the School of Music's outreach to church music directors, musicians, and lay people with a program called the Annual Church Music Workshops.[6]

These workshops continue to attract national and international conductors, directors, and musicians whose leadership and teaching skills help make vigorous and inspirational countless music programs in local congregations across America. The sorts of music fostered by Southwestern Baptist Theological Seminary School of Music include vocal and instrumental music from classical as well as popular, sometimes called "gospel" traditions, and stress highly professional as well as spiritual engagement in the offering of praise to the Creator. Lubbock's First Christian Church organist, Dr. Stephen Z. Cook—a graduate of Southwestern Baptist Theological Seminary's School of Music who received his doctor of music arts degree from the University of Indiana—remarked that individuals seeking competent training in any field of church music could find what they need at the Fort Worth school. Other church-related seminaries and universities offer numerous programs to train musicians, conductors, directors, and those who aspire to the title "minister of music."[7]

Prior to the ascendancy of highly formal college, seminary, or university training, however, for most people in Texas learning to sing popular hymns with joy and vigor was the end achievement of singing schools and popular singing conventions. One grouping of such gatherings were called Fifth Sunday Singing Conventions. Outgrowths of Sacred Harp and singing school traditions, these conventions kept alive some of the teaching functions of those schools, but formal training in music was not the primary purpose of the many singing conventions that were common in the first half of the century. These singing conventions were usually interdenominational and rotated meeting places. Almost without exception church sanctuaries were used, but occasionally public school auditoriums became the sites for these Sunday afternoon gatherings, which featured a variety of musical styles.

The format of a typical Fifth Sunday Singing Convention included the formal welcome by the song leader of the host congregation who traditionally led the first song. He or she would often line out the lyrics, a phrase or two at a time, until the entire verse had been chanted; then, that verse would be sung in unison before the procedure was repeated for each successive verse. Following this first song, the host leader would then in careful alphabetical order and with great dignity introduce leaders from other churches who would each lead one song. Then the cycle would be repeated. Song leaders from noninstrumental churches generally began their songs with a mighty whack on a tuning fork to set the pitch for spirited renditions of favorite hymns. Most singing conventions were held, however, in instrumental churches where pianos were the favored instruments. Generally each participating congregation had its own pianist; each pianist had a distinctive style.

After radio became a key factor in the dissemination of popular religious music, the influence of the Stamps-Baxter groups and other popular performers such as the Blackwood Brothers and similar quartets became prominent in the accompaniment provided for participants in singing conventions.[8] No longer did all piano players play the old hymns as they were originally written. Instead, many pianists began to add runs and arpeggios with sometimes-joyous abandon. During World War II, these innovations led some traditionalists to complain that the grand old hymns of the church were being turned into gospel boogie-woogie. The newer styles did appeal to many young people, however.[9]

Broadcast radio's influence on popular religious music in Texas was profound. On most radio stations gospel music programs abounded. One well-known group of singers was Bewley's Chuck Wagon Gang, made up of Anna, Rose, Dad, and Jim Carter. Their renditions of old hymns with guitar and piano accompaniment won favor with many urban and rural Texans. The themes of the songs they broadcast mirror much of the content of Texas church music. Some songs dealt with eschatology or final things: "In the Sweet By and By," "Life's Evening Sun," "Just Over in the Glory Land," and "I'll Fly Away"—all concerned the imminent coming of death and the hope of a better life in Heaven. Another favorite Chuck Wagon Gang song, "In the Garden," was popular with many other radio gospel music performers. This song tells of the joys of walking and talking with Jesus and celebrates his earthly presence. Stamps-Baxter songs were generally less traditional in content and in style of delivery. Perhaps the best-known Stamps-Baxter song, "Give the World a Smile Each Day," explains much of the vast popularity of gospel music. This song's theme argues the importance of being happy, of spreading the good news, and of having a positive attitude.

Much that is memorable in Texas popular religious music is indebted to British as well as to continental traditions, many of which came to the American South and Southwest with Scottish and Irish immigrants who brought with them great love and talent for celebrating their spirituality with vocal as well as instrumental music. Christmas carols, of course, are the most common examples of old world influences on popular religious music in Texas. The ancestry of some popular Christmas songs dates to the Middle Ages. Holly and ivy carols, popular with Sacred Harp singers as well as with shaped-note singers and those who use regular notations, can be traced to the fourteenth century. So-called white spirituals and songs sung by slaves also link popular Texas religious music to ancient traditions. Some spirituals from the days of slavery reflect the haunting melodies of ancient Africa. Two songs in popular church music, "Were You There When They Crucified My Lord," and "Come by Here, Lord," exemplify influences of traditional African melodies as shaped in many instances by slaves in America.[10]

Other songs on the popular music canon are also associated with key seasonal events in the world of the religion. Easter in particular occasions the singing of songs of joyous affirmation. "Up from the Grave," sometimes titled "He Arose," celebrates in spirited fashion Jesus's triumph over death: "up from the grave he arose, with a mighty victory o'er his foes; he arose a victor from the dark domain." In larger urban churches, Easter and Christmas are marked with elaborate cantatas often influenced by classical musical traditions. Such cantatas and other lengthy musical productions done in churches merit full treatment and can only be mentioned here. For most smaller congregations, the song "Take Up Thy Cross and Follow Me" by B. B. McKinney was more familiar than "Joyful, Joyful, We Adore Thee," with a melody based on Beethoven's "Ode to Joy," and with lyrics written in 1907 by Henry van Dyke. Nevertheless, in a number of older hymnals, "Joyful, Joyful" is not alone among the songs that rely on melodies and lyrics from the world of classical music.

True to its heritage from the American South and from Europe, popular church music in Texas includes hymns often associated with funeral services. Such songs offer comfort and consolation to the bereaved. "Behold a Host Arrayed in White," based on Revelation 7:9, has a traditional Norse melody with harmony done in 1877 by famed composer Edvard Grieg. It stresses the new and better life following physical death. "On Jordan's Stormy Banks I Stand" is probably better known than "Behold a Host." Set to a traditional American folk melody, its vigorous chorus affirms the conviction of salvation and the afterlife: "I am bound for the promised land . . ." It seeks to persuade others to join in this journey: "Oh, who will come and go with me?" Popular also in many funeral services is "For All the Saints" inspired by Hebrews 11:13. This song offers the consolations of the life well lived and the assurance of the abiding presence of Jesus Christ. Set to music by Ralph Vaughn Williams in 1906 it remains a favorite hymn.

Not all hymns used in memorial services contain specific themes of consolation or even comfort; instead, in the popular tradition, the songs sung at these memorial services may have been chosen because they happened to be favorites of the deceased. Such personal choices are infinitely varied, of course. They may include the strident "Onward Christian Soldiers," a nineteenth-century popular song from the evangelical movement; "A Mighty Fortress," Martin Luther's stirring words of praise and affirmation; or, in the Stamps-Baxter gospel quartet tradition, "I'll Fly Away," sung sometimes a cappella and with spirited clapping of hands.

Popular church music in Texas is not, of course, limited to either mainline conservative or evangelical protestant groups. Past president of the West Texas Historical Association, Darlene Bellinghausen of Knox City described musical elements in the orders of worship at the Catholic church in Rhineland, Texas. A communicant of this active, vital congregation, Bellinghausen supplied copies of songbooks and worship guides. Prior to Vatican II, choirs and priests did much of the singing in Catholic churches. Now, however, congregational singing is also prominent. Materials that Bellinghausen supplied reveal that popular hymnology transcends denominational boundaries. In *Seasonal Missalette: Worship Resource,* the hymn found in almost all protestant songbooks, "Holy, Holy, Holy," appears (p. 202), as do other popular hymns, including "Christ the Lord Is Risen Today," (p. 209) which is often sung at Easter in various religious groups, and "They Will Know We Are Christians by Our Love" (p. 249), sometimes titled "We Are One in the Spirit." *Glory and Praise,* volumes one and two, collections of worship hymns approved by the Bishop of Phoenix for congregational use contain many songs now included in the popular tradition in contemporary worship. Bellinghausen also supplied copies of hymns used in various parts of the Mass. Among those hymns is "O Lord I Am Not Worthy," sung at the time of Holy Communion. Three other hymns used in Catholic orders of worship include longtime favorites across Christendom: "Just As I Am," "My God and I," and the Irving Berlin classic introduced and made popular by Kate Smith, "God Bless America."[11]

If indeed music mirrors the soul of a people, popular church music reveals that religious belief and a love for musical expression were deeply intertwined in the psyches of Texans prior the advent of twentieth-century high technology. This love for making joyful noises unto the Lord persists in individual congregations and in surviving singing conventions and schools in which can yet be heard the plaintive melodies of Sacred Harp singing, the lively strains of the flourishing body of gospel music, or stately cantatas and oratorios, elaborately staged.

## ❧     Notes     ❧

1. Francis E. Abernethy, *Singin' Texas* (Dallas: E-Hart Press, 1983); George Pullen Jackson, *The Story of the Sacred Harp, 1944–1944: A Book of Religious Folk Song as an American Institution* (Nashville: Vanderbilt University Press,

1944; B. F. White, *The B. F. White Sacred Harp,* revised by W. M. Cooper (Samson, Ala.: Sacred Harp Book Company, 1988).

2. Thomas J. Langford, interview with author, Lubbock, Tex., Oct., 1991.

3. Richard Bauman and Roger D. Abrahams, eds., *And Other Neighborly Names: Social Process and Cultural Images in Texas Folklore* (Austin: University of Texas Press, 1981).

4. Jane Gilmore Rushing, interview with author, Lubbock, Tex., ca. 1965.

5. W. R. Estep, "Southwestern Baptist Theological Seminary," *The New Handbook of Texas,* vol. 5 (Austin: Texas State Historical Association, 1996), p. 1169; *Encyclopedia of Southern Baptists,* 4 vols. (Nashville: Broadman Press, 1958–1982).

6. William J. Reynolds, *The Cross & the Lyre: The Story of the School of Church Music: Southwestern Baptist Theological Seminary* (Fort Worth: School of Church Music, Southwestern Baptist Theological Seminary, 1994), pp. 136 ff.

7. Stephen Z. Cook, interview with author, Lubbock, Tex., June, 2001.

8. James Blackwood is profiled in the Sunday, November 14, 1999, edition of the *Dallas Morning News,* Section 3, 1 ff. Founder in 1934 of the Blackwood Brothers Quartet, James Blackwood was vastly influential in the spread of what came to be called gospel music. He was active in radio broadcasting, in teaching music in the singing school tradition, and in the publication of gospel songbooks as well as in recordings of these songs.

9. Harry L. Perkins, interview with author, Bartlett, Tex., May, 1985. Perkins is a longtime Disciples of Christ elder.

10. Too rich and complex for detailed treatment here, the matter of the influences of spirituals from the African American traditions is one that deserves continued study. Of particular interest to the student of popular church music in Texas and across America is the career of celebrated singer Marian Anderson, whose renditions of songs from the days of slavery in America remain hauntingly majestic and beautiful. The continuing influence of traditional elements of ancient African music is found in the performances of the African Children's Choir, an internationally famous singing group made up of children orphaned because of war and famine. This group of talented young people introduce thousands of people across the world each year to the heritage of African music.

11. Darlene Bellinghausen, interview with author, Throckmorton, Tex., May, 2001.

# 7

# Chicano Music
## *Evolution and Politics to 1950*

### José Angel Gutiérrez

This chapter will broadly trace the development of Chicano music from its origins to the 1950s, specifically highlighting the major borrowings from other genres, the subsequent incorporations of musical styles, instrumentation, personal contributors, and the historical and political highlights in that evolution. Chicanos, namely persons of Mexican ancestry who live in the United States, have a music unique to their experience as a people. Chicanos are the progeny of Mexican nationals who were themselves the children of various native peoples of *Anahuac* (the name given to North America by an indigenous people, *los meshicas,* the Aztecs), the Spanish *conquistadores,* and African slaves. The evolution and politics of Chicano music date to the beginning of human history in the Americas. Music is a part of a people's culture, an integral part, as is their history, art, cuisine, religion, language, and their way of life. Each succeeding generation and civilization builds upon that of the previous one in such areas as musical form, rhythm, instrumentation, composition, arrangement, and utility. Music is always in a process of evolution and change. Music, like language, knowledge, and cuisine, borrows components from other peoples over time. Musicians constantly incorporate and modify "new" melodies, instruments, sounds, arrangements, compositions, and rhythms into a fresh synthesis and sound of their own music.

The original sounds of music stem from nature and its fauna and from humankind. The animal kingdom is replete with the panoply of sounds that emanate from the various species. The music of nature, for example, can be the ocean roar, the wind hurrying through the trees, and a multitude of sounds from its inhabitants. Music is the rustle and flutter of feathers, the purring and growl of cats, the pounding of hoofs, the love calls and the chirping of birds, as well as the sounds of humans, from whistling to humming, soft voices to loud baritones.

### ～ The Indigenous Roots of Chicano Music ～
### *Olmeca Culture*

Olmec, in their language, means dweller in the land of rubber. The origin of the Olmec peoples goes back into antiquity and is pre-Christian by 1,200 years. The Olmec civilization that flourished in the present-day Mexican states of Veracruz and Tabasco predates European civilization by more than two centuries. Olmec people inhabited eastern Mexico on the Gulf Coast, primarily the area toward the Yucatán Peninsula, down to central Honduras and western Costa Rica. Their cultural traditions in this region began at approximately 2000 B.C., which is the earliest American civilization recorded.[1]

Today we can view remnants of the Olmec culture in the many archaeological zones, artifacts, glyphs, and codices that have been found in the region. The Mexican encyclopedia has reproduced murals and figures from the Olmec culture. In one such mural, a group of musicians with instruments is depicted. In another, there is a lone figure blowing on a conch.[2] While looking at these reproductions, the viewer can easily imagine an Olmec woman standing on the shores of what is now known as Cancun, Mexico, looking across the expanse of ocean before her as the sun sets behind her, some two thousand years ago. She would be searching for a glimpse of the men in her clan to be returning with the day's catch. In her hand she holds a large *caracol,* a conch. The conch, made from a seashell with a hollowed tip, is her trumpet. She uses it to signal others to come and assist her tribesmen in unloading the seafood. The sound of the conch was not for entertainment but rather was strictly functional. Her people, both men and women, used the conch blare for communication.

The sound of the conch could signal different things: location, danger, emergency, notice, a ceremonial call, or the beginning of a religious rite. The Olmecs learned over time that different-sized seashells made varying sounds, that the position of the lips on the hollow tip would produce a different pitch, and that the force of the breath into the hollow tip altered the sound. Later, the conch was accompanied by the sound of other instruments. The Olmecs noticed that fallen and rotted logs made sound when hit, stepped on, or beaten. They took the best hard woods from the Yucatán jungle, *el lancandon,* to their villages and hollowed them. They then used these rudimentary drums to complement the sound of the conch. In time, the Olmec learned to take these hollowed-out logs and cut them into smaller pieces, and then to stretch deerskin over the open ends. Thus the American drum was born. The people could easily transport this smaller instrument and the conch with them to a hunt, a ceremony, a fishing trip, or to a religious ritual. They dried gourds and filled them with pebbles to make rattles *(maracas)*. They learned that short sticks of hard wood when beaten together *(ticos)* made a crisp, clear sound. The Olmecs used these basic instruments—the precursors of the trumpet, drum, *maracas,* and *ticos*—to imitate the sounds of nature around them and within themselves, such as their rhythmic heartbeat and breathing. Olmec music began to be associated with religious rites and other ceremonial activity. Next their music began to acquire another function: entertainment.

### Mayan Culture

The Olmec civilization eventually gave way to that of the Mayan people. At least 1,200 years before Europe adopted the Gregorian calendar, the Mayan peoples of the Yucatán had perfected their calendar without the need to incorporate the leap year adjustment that we still make today. Also, about 1,000 years before the Hindu mathematicians employed the concept of zero, the Mayans already had used the concept in the astronomical and computational aspects of their calendar. Mayan civilization based in the Yucatán and Chiapas region of modern-day Mexico reached deep into what we know today as Belize, El Salvador, Guatemala, and Honduras.

This civilization gave way about A.D. 400 to be succeeded by various others, which included the Teotihuacana (A.D. 700), Toltec (A.D. 900–1187), and Aztec (A.D. 1325–1519). Sometime between 1111 and 1168, the Aztec people, *los meshicas,* left their homeland, Aztlan (what is now Utah in the United States), and migrated south in search of their prophetic and permanent home. They founded Tenochtitlan, now Mexico City. The Aztec empire was in place in central Mexico in 1519 when the Spanish first arrived to conquer.[3]

## The Caribbean Connection

A thousand years prior to Columbus's arrival in the Caribbean, several native tribal groups occupied this cluster of islands at different times. The *Ciboney* or *Siboney* people settled what today are the Bahamas and Jamaica. Later, the *Arawak* people occupied the whole of the Caribbean. The *Arawaks* divided into three main groups: *Lucayanos* in the Bahamas; *Tainos* in Cuba, Jamaica, and Haiti/Dominican Republic; and *Boriquen* in Puerto Rico. In time, the Caribs followed the Arawaks and challenged them for hegemony over this cluster of Caribbean islands. There were about 300,000 people living in the Caribbean in 1492 when the Tainos, now mixed with Caribs, discovered Columbus sitting in the bay of what is presently the Dominican Republic. Columbus renamed this island, calling it Española.[4] The Spanish arrival began the annihilation of these indigenous peoples and the importation by the Spanish and Portuguese of African slaves. Over time, the Spanish and Portuguese acquired aspects of culture, including music, from both the Caribbean natives and the slaves from various African tribes.[5]

## The African and Spanish Connection
### The Moors

The Moors were an Islamic people located in northern Africa who began intrusion and ultimate conquest of the southern region of Spain in the eighth century (A.D. 711). A mixed, black, African Arabic people, they remained in Spain until the matrimonial union of Ferdinand and Isabela, the Catholic Kings, made possible the unification of two powerful families. The Catholic Kings were able to expel not only the Moors but also the Jews, from all of Spain by 1491. Moorish influence on Spanish heritage, however, is evident to this day. The Spanish spoken in Texas even now contains many words of Arabic origin, for example: *alcol, algodon, almuada, alfombra, alambre, ojala* (alcohol, cotton, pillow, rug, wire, hopefully). The Spanish architecture, music, food, home furnishings, and dance styles were and continue to be heavily influenced by

Moorish culture. The white arches and red tile roofing material associated with the Spanish style (e.g., southwestern style) are rooted in this Arabian architecture. The Moorish invasion of the Iberian Peninsula in the eighth century influenced the guitar and *Mozarabic* chant used in Catholic religious rituals.[6] The painted mosaic or tiles utilized in home decoration is also Moorish in origin. *Flamenco,* the dance, is a mixture of the classic Spanish guitar music with the melancholy chant accompanied with an intricate foot dance and hand clapping of the various nomadic Arabic peoples.

Moorish influence has remained imbedded in Spanish culture for centuries. Early Spanish ballads recount tales of driving out the Moors from the region. Today, across the Rio Grande from the city of Brownsville, Texas, is the Mexican city of Matamoros, a contemporary testament to the Arabic and Spanish influence and the conflict that still permeates Chicano culture. *Matamoros* means "kill the Moors" in Spanish.

Fernal Perez, utilizing a stringed instrument, a precursor to the guitar, was an official musician in the court of King Ferdinand and Queen Isabela. After performing his official duties, he spent hours in the nearby camps of nomadic Arabic gypsies and blended his music with theirs. Together, they developed flamenco. Classical guitar emanates from Spain. When the royal Catholic couple began the expulsion and extermination of all Moors and Jews from Spain, Perez joined Columbus on his first voyage and left Spain. During this voyage, he entertained the sailors with his songs and music. Later, slave ships carrying the human cargoes employed musicians and drummers to alleviate the misery and monotony of these long journeys across the Atlantic to the Caribbean. Slaves, upon arrival, formed *cabildos,* which were mutual benefit secret societies. Their meetings consistently incorporated music. African drumbeats and Spanish guitar were blended into music native to these Caribbean peoples.

The early Spanish explorers brought their influence with them to the Americas. And later, the slaves whom were brought to the Americas introduced and blended their own African cultures with that of the indigenous and Spanish peoples. Dutch and Portuguese slave traders brought African slaves to the Caribbean in 1518 and sold them to the Spanish. The slaves made music an integral part of life. Every stage of life from birth to death was accompanied by music. The heartbeat of African music was the drum, an African tradition. Drums were made of hollowed-out logs covered at the openings with animal skin. Drummers led processions.[7]

## Spanish Colonization and Influence in North America

Any early map of North America will verify the Spanish land holdings in the Americas. There was an emerging Spanish empire over this vast territory long before there were British colonies, much less a United States of America. The Spanish established themselves throughout the land in the New World.[8] Some eighty years prior to the founding of Jamestown, a temporary Spanish settlement, San Miguel de Guadalupe, existed in that general area. The entire northwestern coast of the United States, from California to Alaska, was navigated and charted by Spanish explorers centuries before Lewis and Clark ever reached that coast. Valdez, the city in Alaska, was named in honor of the Spanish naval minister who commissioned that exploration.

On August 2, 1769, Captain Gaspar de Protola named the Los Angeles River. Fray Junipero Serra, the founder of the California mission system, accompanied him. The *pueblo* (city) got its name from the river: Reina de Los Angeles. In 1771, the San Gabriel Mission was founded. The early religious music at these missions consisted of a mass of *alabados* (praise) at dusk and dawn and a *bendito* (grace) before each meal. Mass often had singing, which was accompanied by instruments such as flutes, violins, and trumpets that the local natives had been taught to play by the missionaries.[9] For the local aristocracy, however, the harp "remained the favorite instrument."[10] Franciscan Narciso Duran, the "father of California church music," developed a basic pedagogy to teach church music to the Indians.[11] Harrison Rogers, who was a member of the Jeremiah Smith expedition of 1826, described the small orchestra at the San Gabriel Mission as "consisting of two violins, one bass violin, a trumpet and a triangle. They made tolerable good music, the most in imitation of whites that [I] ever heard."[12]

### ❧  Flags over Texas  ❧
#### Spain, 1716–1821

The early history of music in Texas is the history of blending indigenous and religious music. The native groups in Texas and across the Southwest also had rudimentary instruments consisting of drums, flutes, rattles, and bones. The native groups used their music in ceremonies and for dancing. In due time, the Spanish conquistadors and religious orders also made their way into Texas. In both Texas and California, missionaries set up in a network of missions while the military accompanying these missionaries established a military outpost called a *presidio.* The missionaries set out to convert the natives to Christianity. Many dramatizations and musical arrangements were utilized to teach, train, and convert the natives, such as the Mexican shepherd's play, *Los Pastores,* sometimes also called *Las Pastorelas* and dance of *Los Matachines.*[13]

Mexican independence from Spain in 1821 brought a new style of music to the region. Independence from Spain resulted in the secularization of the mission system, which in turn led to the rapid disintegration of the mission communities. In its place arose the *hacienda* (ranch) system. These haciendas gave rise to feast days, rodeos, weddings, funerals, and other special occasions that were accented by music. These events were preceded or followed by a type of dance, the *fandango.* Social life centered on the owner family and their music. Celebration was part of hacienda life as well. At rodeos, harvest, births, weddings, holidays, fandangos and *bailes* (dances) became commonplace on each hacienda. Fandangos were informal, and the bailes were formal by invitation. At a wedding, usually a three-day event, music and food flowed freely. The *vals* (waltz), a most popular dance form in Europe, was introduced into Texas at this time. However, the church viewed the vals as indecent.[14]

The church missions, even though they had lost their predominance as the center of social life, also had choirs, ceremonies, and cultural festivities. Examples of these religious dramatizations, musical plays with dancing, still presented today are *los matachines* (dance of good and evil), *las pastorelas* (shepherd's play), *las posadas* (nativity play), and *peregrinaciones* (pilgrimages). The Catholic Church rites—baptism, communion, confirmation, wedding, and even some funeral processions—almost always included music.

## The Texas Republic, 1821–35

When Spain, and then Mexican authorities, opened the door to Anglo immigration into the northern part of Mexico, into Texas-Coahuila, many land-hungry settlers came to East Texas. In exchange for land, these immigrants pledged to be loyal to the Mexican government, to affiliate with the Catholic faith, and not to bring slaves after 1829. Of course, they brought their way of life, which included music. This music blended with the local Spanish Mexican music of the era. Many more Anglos came to Texas without authorization, and they disregarded the exchanged promises made by those who had obtained land grants from the government of Mexico. These illegal Anglo aliens, many of whom were outlaws in their respective home states of Tennessee, Kentucky, the Carolinas, the Virginias, Ohio, and Georgia, not only brought others like them, but also brought African slaves to Texas. At one point in time, African slaves outnumbered Mexicans in the province of Texas-Coahuila. Mexicans not only became a numerical minority but also foreigners in their own homeland.[15] These Anglo squatters and slaves also brought additional variants of music to the region. With the growing antagonism between local Mexicans and incoming Anglos, violent encounters soon took place. Anglos defeated the Mexican military of General and President Antonio Lopez de Santa Anna. Anglo domination of all sectors in society—politics, business, law, culture, labor, religion, and land—began in earnest. In particular, this was true of the cultural hegemony that relegated all things Mexican to second-class status compared to the Anglo way of life, and that included music. Overwhelming numbers of Mexicans residing in Texas after the conquest left for Mexico shortly thereafter. Among those few that remained, a new ethnic group, called Mexican Americans, was born in Texas.

## The United States, 1845–60

Texas joined the Union in 1845 and was the first independent republic to join as a state. The land between the Nueces River and the Rio Grande continued to be disputed territory between the United States and Mexico until the United States invaded Mexico in 1846. General Antonio Lopez de Santa Anna, once again, defended the Mexican territory. In this way, music played a part in his defeat. The upper class in Mexico during this period was disenchanted with Santa Anna. They turned a deaf ear to his pleas for funds with which to buy armaments and provisions for his troops. Instead, the wealthy turned to the newest dance craze to hit Mexico, the *polca* (polka). Huge dances and balls were held featuring the polka. This "protest" was billed as the revolt of the *polcos*.[16]

With Santa Anna's defeat in 1848, Mexico ceded a major portion of the land in the Southwest to the United States. The Treaty of Guadalupe Hidalgo provided for the exchange of land in return for $15 million and certain stipulations to protect the rights of Mexicans and their future offspring. Both the pact and its interpretations have been historically controversial and, from the Mexican viewpoint, have constituted bitter issues for more than a century. When the United States incorporated Texas and the West, Mexicans were firmly entrenched in the South Texas area below the Nueces River, northern New Mexico, southern Colorado, and the Los Angeles area. These years marked the formation of essentially two Mexicos, one south of the Rio Grande and the other within the United States. The Mexican Americans in the United States became both an ethnic group and a numerical minority.

These tumultuous events produced songs, mostly *corridos* (ballads), that memorialized the exploits of this or that battle, this or that hero, or this or that event. The corrido functioned as communicative music, because it told a story of an event, happening, person, or area. Some folklorists even attribute the term *gringo* to verses sung by invading Anglo troops while marching into Mexico. According to folklore, "Green grow the rushes wild . . ." heard by Mexican ears was referred to as the song of *los gringos.*[17]

### ≋ The Spanish American War of 1898 ≋
### *Latinization of Mexican Music*

When Teddy Roosevelt organized his Rough Riders, he went to New Mexico to recruit Spanish-speaking soldiers for the campaign. These *manitos* (New Mexicans) took Mexican music to the Caribbean and brought back Cuban music to the Southwest. Previously, Cuban cigar makers in Florida had been the only source of Cuban music in the United States. Harry Belafonte, as narrator in *Routes of Rhythm,* a video documentary on the origins of Latino music, claims that *Carnaval* in Rio de Janeiro, Brazil, and Santiago, Cuba; *Mardi Gras* in New Orleans; *Calle Ocho* in Miami; and other similar celebrations stem from the annual day of praise for the Spanish king when slaves were allowed to beat their drums and dance in procession in the public streets of the villages and townships. Belafonte describes the origins of Cuban music in this fashion: "Rural Cuban farmers are called *Guajiros.* These rural folk created a musical format of ten verses that rhyme. *Guitar* and *guiro,* an instrument that is a dried gourd with etched ridges that are combed to make a rasping sound, accompany the singer. Later, dried gourds were filled with pebbles and mounted on a handle that when shaken make a rattle. The dried gourd was also encased in a loose net of strung seeds that when shaken or slapped by the free hand made a similar noise. And, a circular wooden frame with movable metallic inserts became the tambourine."[18] These gourds were similar to the *maracas* already in use in pre-Columbian Mesoamerica. Among the popular musical forms that U.S. servicemen brought back from Cuba in the late 1890s was the *danzon* (two-step). This dance became popular in the United States, particularly among middle-class Mexican Americans.[19]

In 1913, the *tango* craze hit the United States. The tango has origins in Cuba. The silent movies of the day incorporated Latin music into the soundtrack. The silent movies gave Javier Cugat his break when Charlie Chaplin used his musical sound in his movies, *City Lights,* for example. Later, Rudolph Valentino also incorporated Latin music into his movies to add to the Hollywood characterization of the "Latin lover." W. C. Handy in the early 1900s picked up the Cuban rhythm on a trip to Havana and incorporated the beat into ragtime blues and began jazz. Louis Armstrong in the 1920s added Cuban sounds to his music. By this time, Thomas Alva Edison's phonograph was widely available. Americans, including those of Mexican ancestry, began to have access to recorded music—even music from Mexico and other Spanish-speaking countries.[20]

## The Mexican Revolution of 1910

Civil War in Mexico brought calamity to the country. Persons had to choose sides, even within families, between the *federales* and various revolutionary factions led by such figures as Francisco "Pancho" Villa, Emiliano Zapata, Venustiano Carranza, Manuel Obregon, and Francisco Madero. The outbreak of war on November 20, 1910, between Mexican factions resulted in revolution. Millions of Mexicans lost their lives in the struggle, which lasted nearly twenty years before normalcy was restored. A million Mexicans sought to avoid that bloodbath and migrated north into what once had been their homeland. During these years, many regional and national political leaders in Mexico sought political asylum and refuge in the United States. Ricardo Flores Magón and Francisco Madero, for example, temporarily lived in St. Louis, Missouri, and San Antonio, Texas, respectively. The majority of noncombatant migrants, however, settled just across the border from Brownsville, Texas, to San Diego, California, and with one thought in mind: Return to Mexico, *mañana.* But tomorrow was long in coming, because the revolution lasted until approximately 1930. While they waited for hostilities to subside, their children were being born in the United States. Before anyone realized it, these million Mexicans were a critical mass of humanity affecting labor, religion, social services, local politics, education, intergroup relations, and music along the border. Mexicans in the United States, once again, were holding Mexican baptisms, communions, weddings, dances, funerals, and other *fiestas,* just as they had in the prior century.

Some refugees never intended to return to Mexico, and many of them began businesses in the United States. Ignacio Lozano, Sr., founded *La Prensa,* a Spanish-language newspaper in San Antonio, Texas, in 1913. He expanded his operation to Los Angeles by 1926. This newspaper contained a section, *"Mundo Artistico and Social"* ("Social and Artistic World"), which featured articles on Mexican talent in music, theatre, dance, and film.[21] Lozano created interest and kept interest alive in Mexican entertainment, of which music was a large part. The Mexican Revolution also produced scores of corridos and other songs that came across the Rio Grande with the people. The most famous of such songs are "La Cucaracha" and "Rancho Grande."

### ∾  Early Recordings of Chicano Music  ∾

During the early twentieth century, between 1904 and 1912, writer and photographer Charles F. Lummis produced a collection of 340 recordings of Mexican folk music. They were originally recorded on wax cylinders but have since been transferred to magnetic tape. Catalogued and housed at the Southwest Museum in Los Angeles, these may be the first sound recordings of Mexican American folk songs in California. Lyrics of fourteen songs from the Lummis collection were published in 1923 in *Spanish Songs of Old California.* Many of these songs were the very same ones sung in Texas and other parts of the Southwest.[22] Lummis "was among the first Anglo observers willing to set aside prejudices against Mexican character and culture and, for the most part, sympathetically record the traditions of a people poorly understood by outsiders."[23]

It was just a matter of time before the phonograph and the radio rendered the wax cylinder obsolete. Recording companies such as Victor, Brunswick, Decca, and Columbia "began to exploit for commercial gain the musical traditions of Mexicans in California and in the Southwest." Spanish-language broadcasts began in the late 1920s. *Sinfonolas* (jukeboxes) were introduced into bars and restaurants, thereby spreading the words, music, and style to larger audiences beyond the artist's residential area.[24] Early genres of this music were the *canción mexicana, corrido, bolero,* and *huapango.* The *trio* and the *mariachi* crossed the border. The mariachi of Concho Andrade and Pablo Becerra made the first U.S. mariachi recording in 1903 in Chicago. Another recording—made in Los Angeles by the mariachi of Jose Garcia from Cocula, Jalisco, Mexico—followed in 1904.[25]

The first commercial recordings of vernacular Mexican music were actually made around 1908 by traveling American firms that recorded in Mexico City. These early recordings include selections by Cuarteto Coculense (who turned out to be the first mariachi to record) and Rosales y Robinson. Mexican singers began to record corridos in Mexico City about that time. "Corrido de Macario," "Juan Soldado," and "El Huerfano," sung by the duo of Abrego and Picazo, are some examples. Trio Gonzalez recorded the first corridos in 1919 in New York, followed by Trio Aguirre del Pino in 1920, and Dueto Acosta in 1923, recording in Los Angeles. The honor of being the first border music singers to perform corridos and songs for phonograph records probably goes to Luis Hernandez and Leonardo Sifuentes, who recorded "El Contrabando del Paso" on April 15, 1928, in El Paso. Within the next year, Pedro Roca and Lupe Martinez of San Antonio became prolific recording artists of not only corridos but other songs as well.

### ≋ Mexican Radio ≋

Mexican radio began with Emilio Azcarraga Viadurreta. He returned to Mexico with an education from St. Edward's University at Austin, Texas, where he also was a football star. He and his four brothers set up a radio station in Mexico City in 1921. The business venture closed by 1924. Mexicans did not own enough radio sets at the time, and the few who did heard only English-language programming. Emilio tried again in March, 1930, in Monterrey with *La T de Monterrey* and a second radio station with 5,000 watts, again in Mexico City, *La Voz de America Latina* (The Voice of Latin America). U.S. radio stations with powerful wattage (e.g., 50,000 watts) were broadcasting into Mexico, and Azcarraga could not compete on those same frequencies. In retaliation, Mexican officials authorized more powerful wattage for stations in Mexico and along the border. Moreover, Mexican records could not be sold in the United States.[26]

The first border radio station was started in the fall of 1930. It was a 10,000-watt station in Reynosa, Mexico, just across from McAllen, Texas. Rosa Dominguez, Mexico's Nightingale, was a regular star on border radio stations. By 1934, there were nine super stations operating along the border. Their aggregate power was 2,432,000 watts while the combined wattage of stations in the United States was only 1,700,000 watts.[27] Azcarraga, in time, became the producer of Mexican movies and built the first television network in Mexico, *Televisa,* which continues to influence Mexican and U.S. Spanish-language television programming.

≈   **War over Waves**   ≈
*Border Radio*

In 1934, the United States Congress passed the Communications Act and created the Federal Communications Commission (FCC) to regulate the U.S. airwaves. Radio was no longer a wide-open, free-for-all market. Rather, large corporations worked closely with federal regulators to maintain order and monopolize the broadcasting industry. So began U.S.-Mexico border radio. Radio entrepreneurs seeking to avoid regulation built their radio stations just across the border in Mexican territory. They agreed to special licensing rules outlined by the Mexican broadcasting authorities. Mexico City officials assigned the border stations call letters that began with XE and granted them extraordinary transmission power for their signal, which could cover the entire United States, and in some cases, most of the world.

Most radio stations in the United States broadcasted over transmitters with only about 1,000 watts of power; border radio stations blasted their voices across America with transmitters of 1,000,000 watts. This was AM radio, whose waves bounce or skip off the atmosphere surrounding the globe in much the same way a pitched rock can skip across a water surface. Listeners in Los Angeles, Seattle, Denver, Chicago, New York, or even Anchorage, Alaska, could tune in to the border stations as easily as those in Dallas, Amarillo, or Brownsville. Over the years, these stations developed an international reputation as their signal became familiar to listeners across the world. Country music, popularly called hillbilly music, received a big boost when it became a staple on Mexican radio stations at a time when many domestic stations would not play what they considered music only for poor, white, working-class people.[28]

### ～  Migration, Deportations, and Repatriations  ～
### *The Years of the Depression*

Popular songs during the 1920s and 1930s often detailed the Mexican experience in the United States. One such hit song, "El lavaplatos," (The Dishwasher), composed by Jesus Osorio, was about a Mexican migrant's travails at finding employment in the United States. "El lavaplatos" was recorded in 1930 by several different performers, including Manuel Camacho on Victor, Los Hermanos Banuelos on Brunswick/ Vocalion, and Chavez y Lugo on Columbia. Another hit during the depression years, "Se acabo el WPA," (The WPA is Over), is typical of the *canción mexicana.* It was composed by Alfredo Marin with some lyrics written by E. Nevarez and recorded by Los Madrugadores and Chicho y Chencho (who were Narciso Farfan and Cresencio Quevas) with Los Hermanos Eliceiri in 1937.[29]

Anacaona, a ten-sister troupe from Cuba, began touring with a U.S. jazz band led by a Cuban, Machito. This group had just begun to make an impact when Dizzy Gillespie appropriated this Cuban sound for his jazz band. Hollywood went Latin, too, in dozens of movies including *You Were Lovelier* and *The Gang's All Here.* Even Walt Disney's Donald Duck cartoons incorporated Latin music and had various characters perform the Mexican Hat Dance. At this same time, Javier Cugat hired a young Cuban immigrant, Desi Arnaz, to play drums and perform the *rumba.* Desi Arnaz was the show, and the audience would join him in a *conga* line. American audiences that were introduced to Mexican and Latin music liked it. New dances such as the *mambo* became the craze. Their tolerance for the music's originators, Mexicans and other Latinos, however, reached new low levels.

The legal status of Mexican Americans residing in the Southwest became an important issue during the trying times of the depression. Both Mexicans and Mexican Americans were made scapegoats for the economic woes of the nation. They were targeted for apprehension and subsequent deportation and repatriations. Literally, hundreds of thousands were deported during the 1930s. Corridos telling tales of persons caught in the web of deportation hysteria were popular. In Texas, musicians rerecorded a song about Gregorio Cortez, who, in an earlier time, had single-handedly outmaneuvered scores of Texas Rangers and other law enforcement officials in eluding capture. Similarly, on May 11, 1930, Juan Reyna was accused of murdering a Los Angeles police officer. Reyna was convicted in November, 1930, and immediately began serving a sentence of one to ten years. The Mexican American population came to his defense and protested vigorously. Five months prior to his parole release date, Reyna reportedly committed suicide. Few Mexican Americans believed that a man so close to freedom would kill himself. At least six corridos were written about him during this period, and these recordings made their way throughout the Southwest. Corridos about Joaquin Murrieta, the legendary California *bandido* in the 1840s, were rerecorded. Los Hermanos Sanchez y Linares in Los Angeles recorded "El corrido de Joaquin Murrieta" in the fall of 1934. Versions of these corridos are still played to this day.[30]

Lalo Guerrero is another typical case of the talented Mexican American musician and composer who had to leave the United States during this time of anti-Mexican hysteria. Lalo was born in 1916 in Tucson, Arizona. His father worked for Pacific Railroad as a boilermaker. His mother, who played the guitar and danced, taught Lalo music. Although he never took music lessons from anyone other than his mother, he became, and remains to this day, a contributing member of the Chicano music scene. His ethnicity prevented him from getting work singing in English like such performers as Bing Crosby. He reverted to Mexican music because he "looked" Mexican—dark, Indian featured, and short. He went to Mexico during the depression and wrote two hits: "Canción Mexicana," recorded by Lucha Reyes; and "Nunca jamas," recorded by Los Panchos and Javier Solis. But in Mexico, Mexicans also discriminated against him for being *pocho* or too Anglo-like.[31]

Beginning in the early 1920s and into the 1930s, radio stations across the Southwest sold airtime to Mexican performers or incorporated Spanish-language music into their format to fill periods that did not command premium advertising dollar rates. Radio stations in the major cities across the Southwest—principally Los Angeles, El Paso, San Antonio, and communities in the lower Rio Grande valley—began such programs.

### ≈   Lydia Mendoza   ≈
### *First Chicana Recording Star*

On February 28, 1928, Lydia Mendoza's father encountered an advertisement while reading *La Prensa,* San Antonio's Spanish-language newspaper. The OKeh Phonograph Corporation of New York City, in town to solicit recording artists for their label, would hold auditions at the Bluebonnet Hotel in San Antonio. The Mendozas took several days to arrive from the Rio Grande valley by car. Lydia mesmerized the OKeh representatives. She was a hit.[32]

The Mendoza family had been playing in the town squares, theaters, and *carpas* (tents) along with other vaudeville acts in small cities across South Texas. The Mexican Revolution had been the main reason for the Mendoza family to leave Monterrey, Mexico, for the United States. The Mendoza family came from San Luis Potosí, Villa de Arriaga, in Mexico. Her grandmother, Teofila, knew how to play the guitar. She taught Lydia's mother, Leonor, to play and sing. Leonor married a musician, Lucio Llamas, around 1908. He died soon after, and Leonor remarried Francisco Mendoza. With the advent of the Mexican Revolution—Francisco narrowly escaping conscription and death—they left for the United States. Plus, the couple had children on the way. Sister Beatriz was born in 1914 in Navasota, Texas, and Lydia, in 1916 in Houston. After a few years in Texas, the Mendozas, like many Mexican migrants, went back to Monterrey. A brother and another sister, Francisco and Francisca, were born there in 1917 and 1920.[33]

The Mendoza family recrossed into the United States in the 1920s. They settled near Dallas, in Ennis, where Lydia picked up an interest in music from her mother and grandmother. She made herself a guitar from a box and rubber bands at age four. Her mother, at that time, would not let Lydia touch her guitar that hung on the wall. Lydia learned the words to songs, like "Mal Hombre" (Bad Man) from a gum wrapper that contained the printed lyrics. While attending a *variedad* (talent show) at the Independencia Theater in Monterrey, Mexico, with her father and sister, Beatriz, the artist sang "Mal Hombre" and "Desgraciadito," both tangos. For the first time, Lydia heard the tune for the lyrics she already knew so well. She memorized the melody and rhythm. At home she began to practice "Mal Hombre."[34] Lydia Mendoza became a recording sensation in her teens. She was the first Chicana recording star to sell thousands of her recordings. The songs she composed, arranged, and sang were not only based on traditional Mexican music; they also exemplified the emerging Chicano sound of music in the other Mexico: Texas and the Southwest. The Mendoza family, Lydia particularly, left a musical legacy of more than twelve hundred recorded songs on commercial phonograph records.[35]

In Los Angeles during the early 1930s, Los Madrugadores were among the most successful Mexican artists performing commercially. Originally the duo consisted of two brothers, Victor and Jesus Sanchez, but they became a trio with the addition of Pedro J. Gonzalez. Gonzalez was also the host of an early morning radio program, *Los Madrugadores*

*Lydia Mendoza, "the poor people's song bird,"*
*plays guitar as she sits in front of a microphone in*
*San Antonio, Texas. From the San Antonio Light*
*Collection published August 3, 1938.*
*Courtesy UT Institute of Texan Cultures*
*at San Antonio*

(those that rise at dawn), on radio station KMPC. The group, Los Madrugadores, performed daily on the show. Later joined by Fernando Linares, they recorded more than two hundred different songs for RCA Victor, Columbia, Vocalion, Decca, Blue Bird, Imperial, and Tricolor.[36]

Pedro Gonzalez became a tragic hero, however. A veteran of the Mexican Revolution, serving as telegraph operator for General Francisco "Pancho" Villa, he had relocated to Los Angeles in the 1920s to begin a career in Spanish radio broadcasting. His program and he, himself, grew more popular. Soon, he began advocating political positions on the air, namely defending the Mexican population being subjected to harassment and deportation by the Immigration and Naturalization Service (INS) and by local police agencies. In 1934, Pedro was accused of raping a woman whom he had fired at the radio station. He was convicted and sentenced to fifty years in prison. After eight months in the penitentiary, the woman recanted and admitted that the INS and city police coerced her. Despite the new evidence, he served six years before he was paroled and deported to Mexico. From Tijuana, Mexico, just across the California border, he remained active with radio station XERU. Pedro finally was allowed to return in 1971 to Los Angeles to be reunited with his family. *Break of Dawn*, a commercial movie of his persecution, was released for popular viewing in the United States in 1998.[37]

Las Hermanas Padilla, Maria and Margarita, a duet, rose to fame in the 1930s and 1940s. They started out singing at church benefits and won a talent contest in Pico Rivera, a suburb of Los Angeles. Their first hit was "La barca de oro" (The Golden Barge). In New York, they were billed as the Mexican Andrews Sisters and performed across the Southwest. Another radio personality was Manuel Acuña. He came from Mexico in the 1930s and was the first promoter of Las Hermanas Padilla. Adelina Garcia, originally from Juarez, across from El Paso, met with initial success in that area and then moved to Phoenix, Arizona, and finally, to Los Angeles in 1939. She made her first recording at age fifteen and recorded many *boleros* that became very popular in the Southwest and Latin America. During the Great Depression and in the 1940s, Garcia found more lucrative venues and a greater popularity in Latin America, especially in Brazil and Mexico. She left the United States to make movies in Spanish but eventually returned to Los Angeles in 1955.[38]

## ⋙ The Bracero Program ⋙
### 1942–64

Initially, this program brought contract Mexican labor to the United States to work in agriculture, railroads, forestry, and fisheries. The program was billed as an emergency wartime measure to supplant absent Anglo labor during World War II. More than four million Mexicans legally were brought to work in the United States during this period. These men were physically located in work areas away from cities and in rural areas with little, if any, contact with other Mexicans and Mexican Americans. They had no services available to them other than shelter, food, and work. None had brought with them radios, guitars, or any other type of musical instrument. They made their own music and improvised for instruments, entertaining themselves with homemade music. Life in the camps provided a source of material for new corridos. Working conditions for these men were deplorable, and many jumped their contract. To critics of this program, the arrangement was a rent-a-slave operation. Naturally, the *braceros* (arms, meaning laborers) when they did flee the farm, forest, railroad, or fish hatchery and did not immediately return to Mexico, found refuge in the growing Mexican American *barrios* (neighborhoods) in the cities of the Southwest and Midwest. Like their predecessors of decades past, who had intended to return to Mexico promptly after the Mexican Revolution, these remained. They also married, had children, found other employment, and even died and were buried in the United States.[39]

The Bracero program introduced and addicted agribusiness interests, among other businesses in the United States, to cheap, exploitable Mexican labor. The braceros became the first wave of Mexicans in the United States without legal documents. Thousands of these braceros augmented the growing Mexican American population in the United States, primarily in the Southwest. They hungered for Mexican music and Spanish-language movies, and they provided a ready market for such entertainment. They also influenced the local music scene by creating a demand for rural music from Mexico, not the orchestral type of music but the country sound, the *norteño,* the corrido, and the *conjunto,* Texas-based, working-class music.

Each Sunday, Wednesday, and Thursday in the mid-1940s, the first nationally syndicated radio show in Spanish, *Cadena de las Americas* (Chain of the Americas), aired from New York to Los Angeles, Brownsville to Chicago. On weekends, the Mexican American population would flock to the theaters that ran Spanish-language movies. There they enjoyed viewing and listening to such screen stars as Pedro Infante; José Alfredo Jiménez, who helped popularize the Mexican *canción ranchera;* and Jorge Negréte, whose hit song, "Ay Jalisco no to rajes," was made into a movie. Their English-speaking counterparts of the time were Gene Autry and Roy Rogers.[40]

Arnáldo Ramírez hosted a popular program, *La Hora del Soldado* (Hour of the Soldier), during World War II. Ramírez used this popularity as radio personality to win the mayoral race in Mission, Texas. He also founded Falcon Records, one of the premier labels for the emerging Chicano sound. Ramírez had been a furniture salesman in McAllen. His company advertised on Mexican radio. On his program, he played music of the norteño style, a button accordion accompanying a German/Czech polka melody—the conjunto sound. He made famous Los Alegres de Teran and Baldemar "The Bebop Kid" Huerta, also known as Freddy Fender.[41]

Lalo Guerrero also returned to the United States when World War II began. He recorded with Imperial Records, played in clubs and bars, and did USO tours for five years out of San Diego. In 1943, Lalo Guerrero composed "Chucos suaves," an Afro-Cuban *guaracha son* that sounds like a mambo. Guerrero finally retired to Palm Springs in 1974 and coached Linda Ronstadt for her songs with mariachi. In 1991, she rerecorded Guerrero's "Canción Mexicana" in her second Spanish-language album, *Mas Canciónes.* Lalo is also famous for "La minifalda de Reynalda," "The Ballad of Pancho Lopez," "No Way, José," and "Las ardillitas," a series of children's songs revved up in speed to sound like squirrels. In 1991, the National Endowment for the Arts presented him the National Heritage Award at age seventy-five.[42]

### ⤳ Zoot Suits ⤳
#### *The Pachuco Era and Swing*

Younger Mexican American audiences subjected to the assimilation process, especially American schooling, turned away from the Mexican musical heritage of their parents and were attracted to the big band sounds and swing. These young Chicanos did not identify with their traditional Mexican ethnicity. They created one of their own, a counter-culture, the *pachuco* era. They dressed in long coats, hats, and peg pants—outfits called zoot suits—and sported spit-shined, Stacy Adams shoes. They slicked their hair back and stood out in any crowd. The Chicanas puffed up their hair into high bouffant styles, wore shorter skirts, and used lots of makeup. They neither liked being Mexican nor Anglo; they just learned to like themselves. "Zoot-suiters," the Anglos called them. During the war, these pachucos were made the target of renewed anti-Mexican attitudes among military personnel and local police agency personnel. Violent clashes occurred between Anglos and zoot-suiters in port cities and in El Paso, San Antonio, and Houston.[43]

These zoot-suiters liked boogie, mambo, lindy hop, rumba, jump blues, swing, and early rock and roll. They were bilingual and bicultural, the bridge between two distinct musical worlds. The first rap song was "Pachuco Boogie" by the Pachuco Boogie Boys (Raul Diaz and Don

Tosti). They sang it in *calo,* the pachuco street slang or dialect.[44] After the 1950s, the mambo began to cross over into English-language music, and listeners began generically calling all Latin music *salsa.* The Diamonds used the beat in "Little Darling," as did Johnny Otis in "Willie and the Hand Jive." Sam Cooke incorporated the beat in some of his music. Bo Diddley and Elvis Presley used the beat in "Louisa May."

The pachuco generation did not listen to the Spanish-language radio with their parents or listen to Mexican music. Instead they listened to English radio and watched television through glass windows of department stores. Television sets had made their appearance on the market in the late 1940s. By 1946, some 7 million Americans owned television sets with more to be purchased in the coming decades. Mexican Americans, by and large, could not afford television sets. But they knew of rock and roll, and they saw how the various dances were done. As a generation, they crossed over into American music. It would be generations before they would return to Chicano music, which youth of the Chicano movement in the late 1960s to 1980 made popular and embraced.[45]

≋    **Wolfman Jack**    ≋

The U.S.-Mexico radio war ended on March 29, 1941, with ratification of the North American Regional Broadcasting Agreement (NARBA), initially signed in 1937 in Havana, Cuba. Emilio Azcarraga got what he wanted: control of Mexican radio; expulsion of U.S.-owned stations broadcasting into Mexico; and, control of most of the frequencies. The United States got rid of the border blasters. Mexico got six clear-channel frequencies, at 730, 800, 900, 1050, 1220, and 1570 kilocycles. U.S. border stations on these six channels were limited to daytime operation of one kilowatt of power.[46] By 1947, however, radio stations along the border were on nighttime airplay again with 50,000 watts of power. As part of the new arrangement with Mexican radio authorities, the new generation of border blasters had to program at least one hour of Spanish-language programming, which was beamed into the U.S. mainland. Chicanos, now numbering millions of the population, were listening during those late-night hours.

By the mid-1950s, there were any number of border radio stations available to American listeners. There was XEFW in Tampico; XEXO in Nuevo Laredo (50,000 watts); XEG in Monterrey (150,000 watts); XEAC, XERB, and XEMO in Baja California; and XELO in Juarez. These stations received mail north of the border. XELO, for example, got mail in Clint, Texas. Monterrey's XEG received its mail in Fort Worth, and XEFW had a postal box in Brownsville. Wolfman Jack, Robert W. Smith from Brooklyn, got his start and stardom out of the Mexican station in Ciudad Acuña, across from San Felipe Del Rio, Texas. He talked hip in English and played rock and roll. This type of music was not being played on English-language stations in the United States. Initially, the U.S. authorities turned a deaf ear to this type of music because it was degenerate. Soon, many Mexican cities had English-language radio stations with similar rock and roll formats and English-speaking religious programs, operating such as Tampico's XEFW; Reynosa's XED and XEAW; Monterrey's XEG and XET; Nuevo Laredo's XENT, XEXO and XED; Piedras Negras's XEPN and XELO; and Ciudad Acuña's XER, XERA, and XERF.[47]

Mexican radio announcers learned their vocation in Mexico and crossed into the United States. They took jobs in U.S.-based radio stations employing a Spanish-language format. They sported facial hair as part of their cultural identity; played traditional Mexican music on their programs; employed an extensive Spanish vocabulary; and, generally, looked upon the local Chicano community, its talent, music, and entertainment with disfavor. They were called the "mustachioed jocks" by English-speaking Chicanos. Mexican disc jockeys, like Jesus Gutiérrez, began at San Antonio's KCOR. Later, he and his wife, Sara Suarez, an Argentinian, founded the first Spanish-language newspaper in Dallas, Texas, *El Sol de Texas*.[48]

## Operation Wetback, Swing, and Rock and Roll

The Mexican ancestry population of the United States had increased phenomenally by the 1950s. The group doubled their numbers again by the 1960s; however, educational attainment for Mexican Americans was exceedingly low, less than an eighth-grade education. Very few Mexican Americans were in professional or technical occupations. Most worked in blue collar or service categories. The migrant laborers, the blue collar and service workers, and braceros turned to the polca and Northern Mexican music with fervor. Conjunto music became working-class music while the middle-class preferred the big band sound of *orquesta*.[49]

Once again, during the Korean War and the subsequent economic downturn after the conflict, Mexican Americans were routinely deported. President Dwight Eisenhower implemented "Operation Wetback."

Persons of Mexican ancestry by the hundreds of thousands, many of whom were U.S. citizens of Mexican ancestry, were deported and repatriated to Mexico during the 1950s. Zoot-suiters, also called pachucos at that time, dressed well. These youth were also targeted for harassment by local police and returning military personnel on the West Coast. Luis Valdez, the renowned Chicano playwright, later in time scripted *Zoot Suit,* the history of violence against pachucos.[50] Again, corridos chronicled the Anglos' inhumanity toward Mexicans during this time.

In San Antonio, the Guadalupe Theatre in the West Side barrio and the downtown International Theatre were catering strictly to a Mexican market. They regularly featured live performances by great Mexican stars. In Los Angeles, the Million Dollar Theatre, founded in 1918 by Sid Grauman, of Hollywood's Grauman Chinese Theatre fame, also began catering to strictly Mexican audiences. Such luminaries as Pedro Infante, Maria Felix, Dolores del Rio, Pedro Armendáriz, José Alfredo Jiméunez, and Augustín Lara were regulars on the circuit. Many artists came from Mexico, but Chicano American artists from the United States were not invited to Mexico. However, a few—including Lalo Guerrero and, later, Vicenta Cardona from El Paso, also known as Vikki Carr—succeeded in getting booked south of the border.[51]

By the mid-1950s, Mexican record companies finally acquired rights to export merchandise to the United States. Fans across the border could now buy records from groups like Perez Prado, Mariachi Vargas de Tecatitlan, and Luis Alcaraz. Ernie Casares, the first Chicano big band musician from Texas, was a member of the Glenn Miller Orchestra. Another that made the big time was Andres Rábago. American audiences knew him as Andy Russell. He started his music career as a drummer with the Stan Kenton Orchestra then began singing bilingually for Kenton. Later, he became a national singing sensation like his contemporaries, Frank Sinatra and Perry Como. During his recording period in the United States, Rábago—also known as Russell—sold more than a million records. Among his eight big hits were "Besame Mucho," "Magic in the Moonlight," "Amor," and "What a Difference a Day Makes." Tommy Dorsey hired him away from Kenton but limited his role to drummer. Frank Sinatra was the lead singer with the Dorsey band at the time. In the early 1950s, Russell relocated to Mexico and continued as a singing star on the movie screen and television. He opened up the record market for Capitol Records into Mexico and Latin America. He played and sang in Cuba every six months. Fidel Castro and Spain's General Francísco Franco were among his fans. He received awards for his music from Mexico and Spain, but not from the United States. He died in Sun City, Arizona, on April 16, 1992, at age seventy-two.[52]

Popular reaction to the music of Russell, Guerrero, or Lydia Mendoza, for example, was not only phenomenal but also pioneering. These artists legitimized Chicano music to greater audiences. While their critics frowned on this genre of music played and heard in *cantinas* (bars) on both sides of the border, the poor Mexican working class loved it. Beginning with the Polcos Revolt during the U.S. invasion of Mexico, the accordion and the polca slowly found their way out of old Mexico, crossing the Rio Grande into the other Mexico in the United States. The accordion and the bass guitar *(bajo sexto)* complemented the music and vocals of Lydia Mendoza. The blending of Mexican accordion and German-Czech polkas in Central Texas resulted in conjunto music. Narciso Martínez, father of conjunto, made the form popular in purely instrumental arrangements. Then, Tony de la Rosa added lyrics.[53]

These musicians, like the Mendoza family of the recent past, traveled to their audiences. Vast numbers of Mexican American laborers were in rural areas. Urban migration had not yet occurred on a large scale. Migration was, first, out of Mexico to South Texas and Southern California, then into the northern states: the agricultural and seasonal migrant stream. The musicians followed the migrants who followed the crops. Chicano music, fan driven, went national. The Chicano sound, also called *Onda* (Wave) music, could be heard in California, the Dakotas, Illinois, Indiana, Minnesota, Montana, Ohio, Oregon, Washington, Wisconsin, Wyoming, and in all other states where Texas migrants traveled in search of work. These road bands promoted their music themselves by selling their recordings at performances. Chicano radio programs began to emerge and give them airplay. The "mustachioed jocks" from Mexico were replaced by young Chicano disc jockeys. These new announcers spoke mostly in English while they played Chicano music in Spanish. This new generation of radio broadcasters devoted airtime and promotion exclusively to Chicano music, virtually eliminating traditional Mexican music from the format during this time.

As a countermusic to the emerging Chicano conjunto format, the Mexican American middle class turned to the big orchestra sound being imitated by such greats as Beto Villa and Isidro Lopez. This high-tone music, *jaiton,* as Manuel Peña calls it, soon incorporated conjunto tones and sounds. The young Chicano rock and roll bands of the 1950s, precluded from crossing over to English music by discrimination and prejudice, turned to blending Chicano music with the big band sound and rock and roll. Out of this new synthesis were born Rudy and the

Reno Bops, who were the first to perform Michael Jackson's trademark foot movements; Sunny Ozuna, whose song, "Talk To Me," made it to *American Bandstand;* and Little Joe and the Latinaires, which later became La Familia. This latter group became the archetype of the Chicano sound, *La Onda* music. Their rendition of "Las Nubes" (The Clouds) in the subsequent decade to the 1960s became the unofficial Chicano national anthem.[54]

## Mexican Attitudes Toward Chicano Music

To this day, and certainly decades ago, a snobbish attitude prevailed in Mexico toward the rural music of the northern regions, *música norteña.* Elite and middle-class Mexicans look down upon their fellow citizens who have left for the United States as being culturally deprived, even though they may envy their possibly improved economic status. Mexicans call Mexican Americans pochos and accuse them of willingly forgetting their culture and language. These same prejudices are extended and include the music coming from the north.

Mexican American singers and musicians have struggled in Mexico, partially due to the fact that the audience for this type of music has emigrated from Mexico to the United States. Today, it is still very difficult for Mexican American artists to compete, even in the United States, with the vast number of Mexican stars who are well publicized via films, Mexican television, and records, and who will play for less money and are easier to handle by promoters. The economic postwar boom era of the 1950s not only brought rock and roll but also norteño and conjunto music. When local recording artists like Lydia Mendoza, the Mendoza sisters, Narciso Martínez, Valerio Longoria, Los Alegres de Teran, Tony de la Rosa, Los Donnenos, Conjunto Bernal, and others began gaining airplay and record sales, they became popular attractions. Their music found its way not only into cantinas but also into large dance halls, and later, to auditoriums and arena shows.

The study of music history of the Mexican people is problematic for various reasons. First, the study of indigenous music, in what is now Mexico, requires the scholar to investigate the documentary record of such great civilizations such as the Olmecs, Mayans, Toltecs, and Aztecs. The written record of musical form, style, medium, composition, and notation of these indigenous peoples is simply lost, if in fact it were ever written and documented by its own artists, ethnomusicologists, or historians. The sound of ancient music was extremely perishable. Only with the technological advances of the twentieth century has the sound of music been preserved on wax cylinders, phonographic records, films, compact discs, and videotapes. Today, we can see in artifacts—glyphs, murals, and paintings on pottery, found recently by archaeologists and anthropologists in these regions—musical instruments depicted, people dancing, and ceremonial activity. We can assume that music was then, as it is today, a vital part of such human activity.

Second, another problem associated with researching the origins of Chicano music is the lack of scholarship on its evolution. Historians have focused primarily on European music's influence on the indigenous, not the other way around. Literature on music in the Americas outlines the influence that Greece, France, Germany, England, and Italy had in the New World. The influence of Spanish music in the New World is hardly mentioned. For example, survey texts on the history of music through the various editions, such as Donald J. Grout and Claude V. Palisca's *A History of Western Music* (New York: W. W. Norton, 1960) and Hugh M. Miller's *History of Music* (New York: Barnes and Noble, 1973) mention the Spanish influence only in passing. Both of these works begin their study of music in the Americas with the Greek influence and that of other European countries, not Spain. Yet, Spain was the precursor in exploration and conquest of this part of the world.

Third, the focus on music in the Americas contains an obvious bias toward the music of the ruling class, the wealthy and the privileged, and not the music of the lower class. Ethnomusicologists have tended to focus on religious music and music played for entertainment of those with disposable leisure time. Only in recent times has regional and working-class music, such as Chicano, folk, gospel and spiritual, jazz, blues, country, and rock, found a scholarly niche in the United States.

≈ **Notes** ≈

1. For an ample discussion of the Olmec people in the original Spanish or the English translation (1969), see Ignacio Bernal, *El Mundo Olmeca* (Mexico, D.F.: Porrua, 1968), p. 1.

2. *Enciclopedia de Mexico* (Mexico, D.F.: Enciclopedia de Mexico, S.A., 1975), no. 2, pp. 353–54; no. 9, pp. 574–75.

3. For a general discussion of the various indigenous civilizations in

Mesoamerica, primarily present-day Mexico, prior to the Spanish conquest, see Alvin M. Josephy, Jr., *The Indian Heritage of America* (New York: Knopf, 1970), pp. 196–217.

4. See the Cecil Jane translation of Columbus's first voyage, *The Journal of Christopher Columbus* (New York: Bonanza Books, 1960) for notations of impressions and observations.

5. William Claypole and John Robottom, "Arawaks and Caribs," *Caribbean Story, Book One: Foundations* (Essex, England: Longman, 1989), pp. 6–13.

6. For the origins and branches of plainsong, among them the Mozarabic chant, see Hugh M. Miller, *The History of Music* (New York: Barnes and Noble Books, 1973), p. 15.

7. See the PBS/KCET Television production by Eugene Rosow and Howard Dratch, *Routes of Rhythm* (Los Angeles: PBS/KCET Television, 1989) for a discussion of the African origin of drums.

8. For a chronological survey of Spanish exploration, conquest and colonization, see Nicolas Kanellos with Cristina Perez, *Chronology of Hispanic-American History from Pre-Columbian Times to the Present* (New York: Gale Research Inc., 1995). It pinpoints and dates such activity in what is now the United States of America. A timeline by years on pp. xxxviii–xi specifically details the settlements in the Eastern and Western seaboard of what is now the United States of America.

9. Steven Loza, *Barrio Rhythm: Mexican Music in Los Angeles* (Urbana: University of Illinois Press, 1998), pp. 3–5.

10. Robert Stevenson, "Los Angeles," *The New Grove Dictionary of American Music* (London: Macmillan, 1986), vol. 3, p. 107.

11. Howard Swan, *Music in the Southwest* (San Marino, Calif.: Huntington Library, 1952), pp. 86–87.

12. Harrison C. Dale, *The Ashley-Smith Expedition and the Discovery of a Central Route to the Pacific,* Rev. ed. (Glendale, Calif.: Arthur C. Clark, 1941), p. 204.

13. For a history and details of performance of this play in San Antonio, Texas, see Richard R. Flores, *Los Pastores: History and Performance in the Mexican Shepherd's Play of South Texas* (Washington and London: Smithsonian Institution Press, 1995).

14. Loza, *Barrio Rhythm*, pp. 5–7. See Manuel H. Peña, *The Mexican American Orquesta* (Austin: University of Texas Press, 1999) for a general history of development of the Mexican American *Orquesta,* and particularly the origins, distinctions, and class bias of *fandangos* and *bailes.*

15. John Sharp, *The Changing Face of Texas* (Austin: Comptroller of Public Accounts, 1992), p. 10.

16. Gloria Matsuka's video documentary, *The U.S.-Mexico War* (Dallas: PBS/KERA, 1998), Tape 2, and Leonardo Pasquel, *Antonio Lopez de Santa Anna* (Mexico: Instituto de Mexicología, 1999), p. 128.

17. According to Charles E. Kinzer, "U.S. Music," *The United States and Mexico at War: Nineteenth-Century Expansionism and Conflict,* edited by Donald S. Frazier (New York: Macmillan Reference USA, 1998), "One folk song of the period, 'Green Grow the Lilacs (cf. 'Green Grows the Laurel'), became so identified with the Irish-American troops that it is sometimes said to have given rise to the term *gringo* among the Mexican populace."

18. *Routes of Rhythm.*

19. Peña, *The Mexican American Orquesta,* p. 132.

20. Guadalupe San Miguel, "The Rise of Recorded Tejano Music in the Post–World War II Years, 1946–1964," *Journal of Ethnic American History* 19, no. 1 (1999): 36.

21. Loza, *Barrio Rhythm,* p. 54.

22. Ibid., p. 17.

23. Michael Heisley, "Sources for the Study of Mexican Music," *California's Musical Wealth: Sources for the Study of California,* edited by Stephen M. Fry ([California]: Southern California Chapter, Music Library Association, 1988), p. 60.

24. Manuel H. Peña, *The Texas-Mexican Conjunto: History of Working-Class Music* (Austin: University of Texas Press, 1989), p. 67 and San Miguel, "The Rise of Recorded Tejano Music in the Post–World War II Years, 1946–1964," p. 26.

25. Efrain De La Cruz, *El Origen Del Mariachi Coculense* (Guadalajara: Secretaria de Educacion Publica, 1966), p. 43.

26. Gene Fowler and Bill Crawford, *Border Radio* (New York: Proscenium Publishers, 1990), pp. 159–51.

27. Ibid., p. 159.

28. For the history and politics of border radio and its role in promoting white, working class music, see Fowler and Crawford, *Border Radio,* pp. 1–7.

29. Loza, *Barrio Rhythm,* pp. 22–26.

30. Ibid., pp. 26–33.

31. Ibid., pp. 158–60.

32. Lydia Mendoza, *Lydia Mendoza: A Family Autobiography,* compiled and introduced by Chris Strachwitz with James Nicolopulos (Houston: Arte Publico Press, 1993), p. vii. For additional insight and biographical information on this pioneer of Chicano music, see Carlos B. Gil, "Lydia Mendoza: Houstonian and First Lady of Mexican American Song," *Houston Review* 3 (1981): 250–60, and Dale Miller, "Lydia Mendoza: The Lark of the Border," *Guitar Player* 22 (Aug., 1988): 38–41.

33. Mendoza, *Lydia Mendoza,* pp. 3–10.

34. Ibid., pp. 11, 18–21.

35. Ibid., p. viii, for the estimate of the musical legacy of Mendoza and her family.

36. Loza, *Barrio Rhythm,* pp. 33–34.

37. Ibid.

38. Ibid., pp. 33–36.

39. See Ernesto Galarza, *Merchants of Labor: The Mexican Bracero Story* (Charlotte, N.C.: McNally and Loftin, 1964), and his subsequent work, *Spiders in the House and Workers in the Field* (Notre Dame, Ind.: University of Notre Dame Press, 1970), for early secondary sources on this foreign policy program that brought millions of Mexican men to work in the United States over a period of nearly two decades, 1947–64. See also Richard B. Craig, *The Bracero Program: Interest Groups and Foreign Policy* (Austin: University of Texas Press, 1971); Henry Pope Anderson, *The Bracero Program in California* (New York: Arno Press, 1976); Kitty Calavita, *Inside the State: The Bracero Program, Immigration, and INS* (New York: Routledge, 1992); and Barbara Driscoll, *The Tracks North: The Railroad Bracero Program of World War II* (Austin: University of Texas Press, Center for Mexican American Studies, 1999).

40. Loza, *Barrio Rhythm,* pp. 56–57, 165–66.

41. Fowler and Crawford, *Border Radio,* pp. 10, 16, 163, 247.

42. Loza, *Barrio Rhythm,* pp. 158, 161–65.

43. Peña, *The Mexican American Orquesta,* p. 173.

44. Loza, *Barrio Rhythm,* pp. 80–81.

45. Ibid., p. 41.

46. Fowler and Crawford, *Border Radio,* p. 167.

47. Ibid., p. 177.

48. Jesus Gutiérrez, interview with author, 1996. Video available in Special Collections Department, General Library, University of Texas—Arlington.

49. See Peña, *The Texas-Mexican Conjunto;* Peña, *The Mexican America Orquesta;* Manuel H. Peña, *Música Tejana* (College Station: Texas A&M University Press, 1999) and San Miguel, "The Rise of Recorded Tejano Music in the Post–World War II Years, 1946–1964," for a debate as to the type of class music represented by *conjunto* and *orquesta.* Peña believes conjunto with its reliance on the accordion is working class based (p. 101) and *orquesta* is preferred by the middle class. San Miguel believes too much emphasis of class is made by Peña. San Miguel believes the orquesta type of band is a Chicano adaptation to their binationality.

50. The commercial video of *Zoot Suit* can be rented at most retail outlets; Luis Valdez, *Zoot Suit and Other Plays* (Houston: Arte Publico Press, 1992) contains the play script.

51. Loza, *Barrio Rhythm,* pp. 65, 85–87.

52. Ibid., pp. 136–65.

53. *Songs of the Homeland,* directed by Hector Galan (Austin: Galan Productions, 1995), and San Miguel, "The Rise of Recorded Tejano Music in the Post–World War II Years, 1946–1964," p. 38.

54. Peña, *Música Tejana,* p. 167.

# 8

## Czech and Polish Music in Texas before World War II

### Carolyn F. Griffith

The noted folklorist Francis Edward Abernethy has observed that early Texas settlers "brought the customs and traditions that had always been a part of them and the ways of life that would later bind them to the Texas soil. But best of all, they brought to Texas great stores of songs that had been given to them before they had crossed the blue water."[1] In *Folk Music in the United States,* Bruno Nettl notes that many scholars identify the music the immigrants brought with them as folk music because it was "characteristic music of a country or ethnic group, whether rural or urban."[2] When they began settling in Texas during the 1840s and 1850s, Czechoslovakian and Polish immigrants also brought along their music, and they maintained and enjoyed their musical traditions as they lived in Texas.

### Polish Music

Group immigration of Poles to the United States began in the mid-1850s and continued through the 1880s. The groups that settled in Panna Maria and Bandera, near San Antonio, were the first and second Polish colonies in America. By the time of the Civil War, there were about 1,500 Poles living in Texas. The next major wave of immigrant groups came after the Civil War. They settled near New Waverly, an early farming community near Huntsville, but rapidly moved on to Cestohowa, Kosciusko, Falls City, Polonia, Brenham, Marlin, Anderson, Bremond, and Chappell Hill. There were also Polish communities in both San Antonio and Houston.[3]

Some Poles may have immigrated to escape discrimination at the hands of the Germans in their country or to escape conscription into the Prussian army.[4] However, most of the immigrants were landowners, artisans, and laborers seeking economic advancement through the ownership of land and businesses. Many of the early settlers in East Texas worked as tenant farmers until they saved enough money to buy their own land. The family provided both the social and economic foundation for Polish immigrants. Poles quickly established their own churches and schools, thereby interacting mostly with each other using their native language. They suffered discrimination in the United States similar to that which they had experienced in their homeland. This fact, combined with the continued use of the Polish language, meant that thorough "Americanization" of the Poles did not take place until after World War II.[5]

Music was an important part of day-to-day living for the Polish people in Texas. Brian Marshall, a young Polish fiddle player living in Tomball, says that these immigrants, who were mostly of peasant stock, had very few possessions, but that "they did bring their Catholic faith, culture, and music."[6] The social life of these settlers "was bound up in the feasts and festivals of the Catholic church,"[7] but in addition to songs from church, historian T. Lindsey Baker points out that "almost every child learned the patriotic songs 'Boxe cos Polske' (God Save Poland) and 'Jeszcze Polska nie zginela' (Poland Is Yet Alive)."[8]

Many people played musical instruments, because self-made music was an important part of their entertainment until World War II. The music was passed down orally from generation to generation. The adults played and practiced musical instruments, and children listened to them during long evening hours with neither radio nor television. They learned to play an instrument by listening to others and by practicing on their own (or borrowed) instruments.[9] As Abernethy notes: "Serious fiddling, though, was reserved for the dances."[10]

Steven Okonski, who was born in Bremond in 1916, tells of his musical heritage. His grandfather, who came from Poland and died when Okonski was very young, played the clarinet. Okonski's father played the fiddle, and his mother played the guitar. Okonski started playing the fiddle in about 1925. He learned by both watching and listening to his father and other family members play the fiddle and guitar. Okonski's brother played the guitar.[11]

Ed Marshall, another Polish fiddler, was born in the early 1900s in Bremond. According to his grandson, Brian Marshall, he moved to Houston when he was eighteen and worked for Hughes Tool. During evenings and weekends, Marshall played the fiddle with a band. He taught some of his sons to play the fiddle; others did not learn. These two families were typical of Polish families who played musical instruments to entertain themselves, their family members, and friends.[12]

Few children had formal music lessons outside the home, although some enrolled in band, orchestra, or choir lessons in school. Some of these students may have learned to read music, but most of them played by ear. Marshall remembers everyone teaching everyone else. There were no professional lessons, and because few people read music, most of the music played during these times was not written down. The music was transmitted primarily by musicians listening to, and playing with, each other.[13]

A typical band was composed of one or two fiddle players and a bowed bass player. Occasionally there might have been a clarinet player at Chappell Hill weddings. Clarinets were expensive, however, so they were not common.[14] Okonski says that guitar players sometimes accompanied the fiddle and cello players, but because there was some animosity between Poles and Czechs, the Poles did not want to play an accordion like the Czechs.[15] Marshall concurs: "I'm sure the accordion was a Czech influence as the accordion was not accepted as a Polish instrument at the time of the Texas migration." He believes that "the fiddle was the truest of the Polish instruments for the pre–World War II time period."[16] T. Lindsey Baker agrees that the Poles favored fiddles: "The most popular secular instruments were violins, and some of the Silesians, like Charlie Haiduk of Bandera, became such proficient fiddlers that they were in great demand by the Americans."[17]

Marshall describes two distinct styles of Polish fiddle music in Texas. In the Washington County style (Brenham–Chappell Hill area), the players had a rhythmic sawing style that created strong pulsing sounds. Because of the distinct rhythmic sound almost like a drum beat, the audience stomps the floor to keep time. The bow never stops moving, and the Washington County style results in a song with a steady beat. There are no breaks in the sounds of the song. As Marshall puts it, "the fiddle players burn up the bows."[18]

*John Muszynski and the White Eagles,*
*Bremond, Texas, early 1940s.*
*Top row, left to right: George Pietrowski,*
*Alec Pietrowski, and John Muszynski.*
*Bottom row, left to right: Fred Kempenski,*
*Fruman Muszynski, and Leonard Muszynski.*
*Courtesy Brian Marshall (Marszalek)*

The Robertson County style produces a more melodic song without such distinct rhythms. The fiddler uses smooth, flowing strokes in unison with interspersed melodic notes. Marshall maintains that the music in the Bremond area, home of the largest Polish settlement in Texas, has not changed even to today in instrumentation and sound because of the distance and segregation of Texas musicians from the northern states.[19]

While there are few references in history books about Polish music traditions, James McGuire, writing in *The Polish Texans,* details life in Thurber, a coal-mining town eighty miles west of Fort Worth. The Poles comprised the second-largest ethnic group in the mining boomtown in the late 1880s. They brought their traditions with them to the town. Wedding celebrations were held in the local dance halls. One Polish wedding tradition raised money to give to the bride to spend. Using a plate from a stack of cheap dinner plates, a man threw a silver coin with sufficient force to break the plate for the privilege of dancing with the bride. They usually used silver dollars, and the man had to use a different coin each time until he broke the plate.[20] After the wedding ceremony at the parish church, the family and their guests went to a community hall or a private home. In the home they pushed back the furniture or removed it to make room for dancing and "following dinner, music by local musicians began filling the air, and dancing and eating continued well into the night."[21]

Nettl notes that "much folk music of ethnic groups retains its original function. Wedding songs are still performed at weddings."[22] Marshall describes one of the wedding dances, the Trepina, a bridal dance with specific melodies and symbolic ceremonies. During the Trepina, the bridal attendants danced and surrounded the bride, trying to keep the groom away (up to a point). If the groom were able to get through the girls, he then tried to get the wreath off the bride's head. The band played another part of the Trepina music during this dancing ceremony. When the groom got the wreath off, the bride officially became an "Old Baba" (old woman), and then the band burst forth with a song about the "Old Baba." Another part of the Trepina occurred when the men paid for the privilege of dancing with the bride. For the rest of the evening, the band played a variety of polkas, waltzes, and schottisches.[23]

Weddings lasted two to three days, beginning on Friday afternoon. Prior to the wedding, the families arranged for a druzba (a master of ceremonies). On the afternoon of the wedding, the druzba, the groom, and his family went to the home of the bride and her family. The druzba read the przymowa, a sad story that told the bride of all the responsibilities she was about to assume. It had much symbolism. For instance, her buckets of tears symbolized the buckets of water she would have to carry. At the end of the przymowa, the druzba, said, "OK, the sadness is over; now let's play and be festive." At that instant, the band began playing as the families and the new couple walked out to waiting wagons. The band continued to play all the way into town to the church where everyone attended the traditional late-afternoon high mass. Afterward they returned to the bride's home for the reception with their waiting guests. The musicians left the church first in order to be back at the bride's home when the couple and families arrived. The bride's family built a wooden platform for dancing. Upon their arrival, the bride and groom got out of the wagon and raced to see who would be first to the wedding cake. The one who won the race would be the boss in the marriage. After this symbolic ceremony, the bride, the groom, and the bride's mother served their guests. Her mother served a pinch of salt to the guests as they entered. They were to eat the salt as a symbol of purity. The song being played as they greeted their guests was the "Polish Wedding Polka." The band played into the night and for the next day and night. Players rotated in and out, with some players being better than others. Late at night people thought they were better than they probably were! Some guests, especially the women, would play the harmonica with the band.[24]

Marshall also mentions the Kolenda, another Polish musical custom. At Christmas a group of carolers would gather on Christmas Eve at someone's home. Some of the people dressed in costume. Three were dressed as the three wise men. There also was one fellow dressed in a robe looking like the devil ("torun"). He carried a cow skull placed high on a stick, so the observers only saw the cow skull without knowing how it was moving through the night. These "dressed up" folks, along with the people playing instruments and others, all walked down the country roads singing carols. They stopped at their neighbor's home and sang songs, hoping for a bite to eat and, especially, a drink. There were fiddle players and half-size bass (cello) players in the group, and by late evening, as others joined in hopes of having fun and getting drinks, there would be as many as twenty-five to thirty people. This group then proceeded to midnight mass on Christmas Eve, most often drunk, or at least half-drunk, after all the stops they had made.[25] Baker confirms that Christmas carols were frequently sung during the Yuletide season into the twentieth century.[26]

The house dance was another Polish music tradition. Dances were held in homes because most people could not afford to rent a community hall. Also, halls were not common in Polish communities. The host family moved the furniture out of the living room onto the porch or to the barn. Folks came for sausages and beer and music. The band played until the wee hours of the morning. Guests frequently stayed all night, sleeping on the floor in the home where the furniture had been removed. Marshall says that his grandmother remembers having seventy-five people at her house at one house dance. The house dances were held during the nonplanting, nonharvesting seasons when it was too cold to work. House dances were not held during Lent in observance of that religious season.[27]

According to Marshall, there were no organized bands prior to World War II, just groups getting together to play with friends or at a house dance. As Abernethy points out, "there was no other social function that was looked forward to with as much excitement as a dance with a good fiddler or two."[28] When folks got together, those who had instruments brought them, and they played as the band for the evening. It was not uncommon for women to play instruments and be part of a band for the evening. It was, however, more common for them to fill in when the men needed a rest.[29]

The music at the house parties prior to World War II was generally Polish dance music. Occasionally the house band included a country song or a Czech polka, but, for the most part, the musicians played waltzes, polkas, and schottisches throughout the evening.[30] Some songs called for specific steps, and there were many variations. For instance, there was the "Dupnik," which was a waltz with specific steps and music. The couple bowed to each other, with the fellow bowing and the girl curtsying. Next they turned around and bumped each other on the behind, and then they turned the rest of the way around and began to waltz again. This sequence was repeated over and over. Polkas and schottisches also had many step and tune variations.[31]

Nettl mentions two characteristics of folk music that help explain the type of music the Polish musicians played: "Instrumental music is often favored over vocal in communities with two or more ethnic groups who do not speak the same language."[32] The Polish immigrants often settled near Czech and German immigrants. They also had English-speaking neighbors. None of these groups fluently spoke the language of the other groups, but they could enjoy the instrumental music all evening. Nettl's second characteristic is "that some types of folk music, especially those associated with functions that remain in practice, such as dancing, survive for several generations."[33] Interviews with Okonski, Marshall, and Adam Mazewski show that the Polish music tradition in the early part of the twentieth century fit these patterns. These men remember that the bands played instrumental music for listening and dancing. There were no vocal accompanists, except at the Kolenda.[34]

Immigrants often formed "semiofficial music organizations" to help them adapt to the new country. On a positive note, these organizations served both to integrate and to unify members of the ethnic groups. However, they also help keep the immigrants separate from others in the new community. The members shared a common ethnic identity but probably had no reason to get to know each other before immigrating.[35] The Polish National Alliance was one such organization that provided a social gathering place that kept the Polish people together and preserved their traditions. The PNA provided a community hall in predominantly Polish communities. The first PNA chapter in Texas, St. Joseph's Society, was established in Bremond in 1889.[36] The PNA organization built the Polish Hall in Houston in 1918, and the large Polish community of Houston has supported the PNA throughout the years. Mazewski recalls that the hall held as many as seven hundred people for weddings and weekly dances.[37]

Clearly, music was a vital part of life for the Polish community in Texas; however, the Poles did not market their heritage to others. Marshall maintains that they did not consider "formal recordings of their music a necessity."[38] Texas Poles simply played and enjoyed the music themselves, passing it on orally to the next generation.

### ❧ Czech Music ❧

There were significantly more Czech than Polish immigrants in Texas. Although only about 700 Czechs were in Texas prior to the Civil War, by 1919 the number of foreign-born Czechs in Texas was 15,074. By 1940 there were 62,680 Texans who spoke Czech at home during childhood. An abundance of good, relatively inexpensive farmland led Czechs to settle primarily in the Blackland Prairie area of Central Texas in Austin County. They moved from there to Fayette, Lavaca, and Washington Counties, with Fayette County serving as the center of Czech population in Texas. They also moved out into a larger belt of the Blackland Prairie, northeast of the original settlements, into Burleson, Brazos, Williamson, Bell, McLennan, Hill, Ellis, and Kaufman Counties. There were also concentrations of Czechs in Wharton, Fort Bend, and Victoria Counties on the coastal bend.[39]

Like the Poles, Czechs had been persecuted in their homeland, and they, too, formed close communities after arriving in Texas. They organized around the community church and established fraternal and mutual protection organizations that served as the social and cultural centers of the communities.[40] The *Katolicka Jednota Texaska,* the Czech Catholic Union of Texas, was formed in 1889, and the *Slovanska Podporujici Jednota Statu Texas,* the Slavic Benevolent Order of the State of Texas, was founded in 1897. Both organizations "built meeting halls which evolved into places primarily for dancing. Dancing had long been the central social activity of the Czech people, and the immigrants adhered firmly to that tradition."[41] Musicologist Victor Greene reports: "One estimate was that as many as one hundred such halls were built in the nearly half-century after the late 1800s."[42]

There were several factors in the preservation of Czech music in Texas. One old Czech expression is *Kazdy Check je musikant,* which means "Every Czech is a musician."[43] Estelle Hudson and Henry Maresh even go so far as to say that because the Czech alphabet has sixty sounds or tones like the piano, a "Czech is easily adapted to the making of any known sound."[44] The musical inclinations of the Czechs served as a cohesive force in the Texas Czech culture.

Greene believes that one reason Czech music expanded and endured during the early part of the twentieth century can be attributed to "the relatively slow assimilation process, a reflection of the Czechs' isolation in rural communities with little contact with the culture of the Anglo-American majority."[45] Clinton Machann concurs: "Up to the time of World War I, it had been possible for large numbers of Texas-born Czech to live their lives without ever having fully mastered the English language."[46] Longtime Texas music educator Lota Spell points out that the Czech immigrants continued to live in Texas and that new immigrants continued to arrive. By 1936, there were some 300,000 Czechs in fifty-four settlements in Texas.[47] The substantial increase in population was another reason that Czech music remained viable.

Spell also identifies other factors that helped to preserve Czech music in Texas: "Musical organizations were early established; bands formed; and good music maintained in the churches." In addition, "Czech folk-songs and folk-dances are popularized today by numerous musical organizations which devote themselves specifically to the cultivation of the music of their fatherland."[48] Hudson and Maresh claim thirty thousand Czech folk songs exist. In 1933 in Houston, the Slavia Club was organized to keep the songs alive in Texas.[49]

Other factors also were involved. First, the Czechs built lodge halls and pavilions "to accommodate the group's passion for polkas, waltzes, and the like." Various expositions held in the state during the Great Depression also helped preserve the Czech folk dance in Texas. Greene says, "As elsewhere in the nation, displays of various forms of ethnic culture were quite common at these fairs, and ethnic music and song were performed at the San Antonio Bicentennial of 1931 and the Texas Centennial of 1936."[50] Hudson and Maresh report that a Dallas-area Czech group organized during the 1930s to present six days of programs—including folk songs sung in Czech and dances with dancers in native costume—at the Dallas Fair.[51] All of these factors together created continued use and effective preservation of Czech music in Texas.

Clinton Machann and James Mendl, authors of *Krasna Amerika: A Study of Texas Czechs, 1851–1939*, describe musical ensembles common in Czech communities in Texas. The bands may have been called "brass," "military," "picnic," or "German" bands. For example, "A typical 'brass' band would consist of two or more clarinets and/or saxophones, two or more trumpets and/or cornets, and an accordion and possibly even a dulcimer up front; a trombone, baritone, alto, and/or French horn in the second row; drums, bass horn and possibly a piano in the rear."[52]

During daytime public concerts, bands would play an assortment of military marches, overtures, polkas, and waltzes. However, for dances in the evening, they would drop some of the brass instruments and call themselves an orchestra rather than a band.[53] Machann and Mendl observe that "for the most part the orchestra would stick to the standard repertory of 'old-time favorite' polkas and waltzes, most of which were arrangements of the Czech folk songs."[54] These arrangements could even be "identified with the region of Moravia or Bohemia from which they came."[55] Czech orchestra music was accepted among both Czech and non-Czech audiences, and, as a result, the number of Bohemian musical ensembles grew rapidly. Greene reports, "as many as one hundred Czech bands were active at the start of the depression, around 1930."[56] Carolyn Meiners has identified thirty-four bands and orchestras by name in Fayette County alone.[57]

In *We're Czechs*, Robert Skrabanek recalls one of his fondest memories dating from the early 1930s in Snook when he played with other Czech youngsters in a dance orchestra. Parents arranged for the school band director from Caldwell to give them lessons. At age ten, Skrabanek began playing his brother's abandoned trombone. Eventually, several students got together and began performing at community gatherings, including church programs. They played hymns as well as Czech polkas and waltzes. The group took the name "The Polka Ambassadors" and performed throughout the Central Texas area, including New Tabor, Taylor, Frydek, and Sealy, until the late 1930s.[58]

One specialized orchestra was the Tamburash Orchestra, founded by Josef Drozda in Houston in 1932. According to Helen Valcik Schnell, her father, Steven Schnell, was the behind-the-scenes force that helped begin the orchestra. The orchestra was directed by Mato Gjuranovic, a painter and musician who lived in Galveston and came to Houston to teach music. At ten years of age, Helen Valcik was the youngest member of the orchestra. She played the equivalent of first violin, and her brother played second violin. Helen says that the orchestra was a string orchestra that mimicked the sounds of a regular orchestra. They performed in places such as Hermann Memorial Auditorium, Studewood Hall, and the Scottish Rite Temple during the 1930s. Unfortunately, the orchestra ceased to exist by 1940.[59]

Hudson and Maresh provide further details about the Czech Tamburash Orchestra, which at the time was the only genuine Czech orchestra in the United States. The orchestra, which had the sound range of a piano, played both folk songs and the music of classical Czech composers Dvorak and Smetana. There were six types of stringed instruments in the orchestra, including the tamburash, which comes from the lute family.[60] The orchestra played "beautiful old waltz songs, traditional marches, plaintive melodies and lilting polka numbers, inherently a part of the Czech people."[61]

Further following the musical traditions from the homeland, the Czechs brought their penchant for singing to this country. Many Czechs carried small, leather-bound, wallet-like song sheets with them for ready reference when visiting friends. Family gatherings, neighborly visits, and fraternal lodge meetings were always occasions for singing. On Saturday night there was likely to be a dance featuring orchestral arrangements of folk songs, and then on Sunday, Czech hymns were sung, including Czech Brethren Christmas hymns "Narodil se Kristus Pan" (1522) and "Syn Bozi se nam narodil" (1636).[62]

Czechs were also fond of choral ensembles. Machann and Mendl claim that "choral clubs for the singing of folk songs existed at one time or another in most of the Texas Czech communities."[63] During the 1920s and 1930s in Fayetteville, for example, Czechs organized singing groups under the guidance of Professor Charles Cmajdalka, the organist of St. John's Catholic Church. The group sang both church and secular music. The hymns were sung either in Latin or Czech. A group of these singers performed at the dedication of the monument at the San Jacinto Battleground, April 21, 1936.[64]

House parties were common among Czechs and "were held for any small excuse, but a birthday was the best reason." If the weather were warm, the dance might be held outdoors on a wooden platform built specifically for dancing. During cooler weather, the dance would be held indoors where the furniture would be moved from either the largest bedroom or the living room. An accordion, a fiddle, and a guitar were the usual instruments played together for the house dance. The family put cornmeal on the floor of the dancing room to make the gliding dance steps move smoothly. While many family members danced, the older men might set up tables for dominoes or cards. Around 10 P.M., cakes, kolaches, cookies, and sandwiches were brought out, and everybody ate. Dancing continued before the festivities finally ended with everyone retiring to their own homes.[65]

As the community halls were finished, the dances moved from homes to these halls, and "large-scale community dances began to be a more frequent Saturday night event."[66] Meiners claims that this was an era of "dances being held in almost every dance hall every weekend."[67] During the 1930s, public dances were a major form of entertainment. The dance halls, including SPJST halls at Snook and New Tabor, favored orchestras made up of Czech musicians. According to Skrabanek, "Snook was one of the more popular places, where they normally sold 100 to 125 tickets per dance. Only males paid, and the charge was fifty cents; women got in free."[68] A. J. Blaha gives a sense of how important the dances were in communities: "Dances were and yet are an activity entered into by all members of Czech and Moravian families. In the early days of Hranice, it was one and almost the only social affair where the young and old could meet to dance, talk, and visit, and maybe drink a little beer. The dance steps were many and varied."[69]

A variety of music was played at the dances. Repertoires could "include not only the more familiar Czech *besedas,* polkas, waltzes, and schottisches but also similar selections from the Polish and German traditions and modern dance selections as well."[70] The besedas, somewhat like American square dancing in that it required groups of four couples, were comprised of dances from the 1700s and 1800s originating in various provinces of Bohemia, Moravia, Slovakia, Silesia, Carpathis, and Ruthania.[71] Everyone enjoyed the polka, which was a fast two-step that immigrants brought from Europe. As Blaha recounts, "some couples dance the polka with their individual steps or motions, but for most it was a fast and lively swing around the dance hall or platform. Age or weight make no difference—you either have or had the rhythm or you don't!"[72] The "Pepiky" ("Little Joe") is another popular dance step where "the couple twirls to the tune in one direction and in time with the music, reverses the rotation of the twirl, all the while advancing around the dance floor."[73]

Dancing moved from the house to the outdoor platform to the community hall and, finally, to commercial ballrooms in large cities, although it is unclear exactly when privately owned commercial ballrooms similar to those in the North began to appear in southern cities. Bill Mraz operated one extremely successful dance palace in Houston. Mraz and his family formed their own ethnic family band and also hosted a number of outside musical groups at their dance hall.[74] Commercial ballrooms and community halls depended on Czech bands to provide music for their dances, and several Czech bands rose to prominence playing in Texas before World War II.

The Baca Family Band was founded by Frank J. Baca, Sr., in 1882 in Fayetteville. All thirteen children played in the family band. According to Cleo Baca, the dulcimer that their uncle, Ignac Krenek, built provided the distinctive sound of their band. It was made like a flat, triangle-shaped box with metal wires strung across the top, and it was played by striking the wires with a wooden mallet.[75] For Baca, "this was the beginning of the 'Baca Beat' in the USA. This 'beat' was so different from anything else played that it separated the Baca Band from any other band."[76] The Bacas played throughout the state, and by 1906 Frank J. Baca, Sr., planned to take his band on a national tour, but he did not live long enough to see it happen. Joe Baca, the eldest son, kept the band going after his father's death.[77]

The Baca Band was well known beyond the confines of Fayette County. Antonin Dvorak, the grandson of the famous Czechoslovakian composer, immigrated to the United States, landing at Galveston on a Monday in 1912. He was in Fayetteville on the following Wednesday playing in Joe O. Baca's band.[78] The band retained its image and direction from the Baca family even though non–family member musicians from Fayette County kept the band going.[79] From 1926 to 1927 the Baca Orchestra played regularly on radio station KPRC in Houston. The band made its first recordings for OKeh in 1930 and later recorded for Columbia in 1931 and Brunswick in 1935. Baca's Original Band and Orchestra, under the direction of John R. Baca, became known as the "Polka Kings of Texas."[80] Another of the brothers, L. B. Baca, moved to Rowena, northeast of San Angelo, during the 1930s and established the "Baca-Ripple Orchestra."[81] Greene describes the Bacas as a "family unit with a history of transcending several generations, through a half-century marked by transition from the earlier marching-concert band to the more modern dancing, commercial type."[82]

There were two other notable Czech bands during the 1930s. The Gold Chain Bohemians, who were later known as Adolph and the Boys, developed a widespread heterogeneous following after they performed on the radio. Julius Pavlas and his group won a musical contest to represent Universal Mills of Fort Worth on the Texas Quality Network. They first broadcast live at 8:15 A.M. on November 3, 1935, from a studio in Schulenburg. The broadcast was carried on radio stations in Dallas, Houston, San Antonio, and Fort Worth. The band played a variety of music including Bohemian polkas and waltzes as well as European salon music, winning statewide audiences. Adolph and the Boys relied heavily on strings, especially bass and violins, and they did not use the traditional accordion. They traveled and continued their broadcasts for nineteen months, until May, 1937. Their "whirlwind stardom ended abruptly" at the end of the decade, however, because they could not agree on a contract with their radio sponsors.[83]

Like the Baca bands, Adolph and the Boys, and so many other ethnic ensembles, the Patek Band of Shiner was a family band that continually enlarged its audience by ballroom, radio, and recording work. The father, John, had been a bandleader in Europe in the 1890s just prior to emigrating. The family settled in Shiner and had six sons. Patek established his family band in 1920 and began playing in large cities like Fort Worth, Houston, and Corpus Christi at both private and public venues. The Pateks featured an electric guitar, which was commonly a part of many ethnic bands in Texas, but the group still sang songs in the original Czech.[84]

During the 1920s, the outdoor weekend band concerts with their folk songs were joined by radio "polka shows," the most popular radio entertainment for the Czech community.[85] Skrabanek remembers listening to Czech polka music on the radio, which the family finally got in 1929: "Mama and Papa were especially happy when they got a 'Czech Music Hour' program being broadcast from Temple, Houston, or even as far away as Nebraska at night. The announcers handled all commercials in Czech and played Czech records, mostly polkas and waltzes."[86]

Folk-country music began to change in the 1920s with the beginnings of mass-produced music on radio and records.[87] By the 1930s, "with dozens of Czech polka dances across the state each week and numerous polka shows on the radio, Czech ethnic folk music was in its golden age."[88] All of this, combined with "the growth of the record industry, made the new old-time or international music and dance a permanent cultural feature of Texas society."[89] Unfortunately, the onset of World War II, which disrupted the relative isolation and tranquility of the Texas Czech communities, broke up many of the Czech bands in Texas.[90] But because of the great numbers of Czech people in Texas and their interest in their heritage, Czech music continued to play an important role in the entertainment world and in heritage groups in Texas.

## ∽ Notes ∽

1. Francis Edward Abernethy, "Texas Folk and Modern Country Music," *Texas Country: The Changing Rural Scene,* edited by Glen E. Lich and Dona B. Reeves-Marquardt (College Station: Texas A&M University Press, 1986), p. 139.

2. Bruno Nettl, *Folk Music in the United States,* Third ed., revised by Helen Meyers (Detroit: Wayne State University Press, 1976), p. 130.

3. T. Lindsey Baker, *The Polish Texans* (San Antonio: The University of Texas Institute of Texan Cultures, 1982), pp. 20–22.

4. Ibid., pp. 12–14.

5. Jan L. Perkowski and Jan Maria Wozniak, "Poles," *The New Handbook of Texas* (Austin: Texas State Historical Association, 1996), vol. 5, p. 255.

6. Brian Marshall, "For the Record," unpublished essay, 1997, p. 1.

7. Perkowski and Wozniak, "Poles," p. 254.

8. T. Lindsey Baker, *The First Polish Americans: Silesian Settlements in Texas* (College Station: Texas A&M University Press, 1979), p. 134.

9. Marshall, "For the Record," p. 1.

10. Abernethy, "Texas Folk and Modern Country Music," p. 152.

11. Steve Okonski, telephone interview with author, Nov. 16, 1997.

12. Ibid.

13. Brian Marshall, telephone interview with author, Nov. 3, 1997.

14. Ibid.

15. Okonski, interview.

16. Marshall, interview.

17. Baker, *The First Polish Americans,* p. 134.

18. Marshall, "For the Record," p. 1.

19. Ibid.

20. James P. McGuire, *The Polish Texans* (San Antonio: University of Texas Institute of Texan Cultures, 1972), p. 27.

21. Baker, *The First Polish Americans,* p. 20.

22. Nettl, *Folk Music in the United States,* p. 131.

23. Marshall, interview.

24. Ibid.

25. Ibid.

26. Baker, *The First Polish Texans,* p. 134.

27. Marshall, interview.

28. Abernethy, "Texas Folk and Modern Country Music," p. 152.

29. Marshall, interview.

30. Okonski, interview.

31. Marshall, interview.

32. Nettl, *Folk Music in the United States,* p. 134.

33. Ibid., p. 135.

34. Okonski, interview; Marshall, interview; Adam Mazewski, telephone interview with author, Nov. 16, 1997.

35. Nettl, *Folk Music in the United States,* p. 127.

36. Perkowski and Wozniak, "Poles," p. 255.

37. Mazewski, interview.

38. Marshall, "For the Record," p. 1.

39. Clinton Machann, "Czechs," *The New Handbook of Texas,* vol. 2, p. 465.

40. Roger Kolar, "Early Czech Dance Halls in Texas," *The Czechs in Texas: A Three-Day Multidisciplinary Symposium,* edited by Clinton Machann (College Station: Texas A&M University School of Liberal Arts, 1979), p. 122.

41. Ibid., p. 124.

42. Victor Greene, *A Passion for Polka: Old-Time Ethnic Music in America* (Berkeley: University of California Press, 1992), p. 142.

43. Clinton Machann and James W. Mendl, *Krasna Amerika: A Study of Texas Czechs, 1851–1839* (Austin: Eakin Press, 1983), p. 3.

44. Estelle Hudson and Henry R. Maresh, *Czech Pioneers of the Southwest* (Dallas: Southwest, 1934), p. 318.

45. Greene, *A Passion for Polka,* p. 141.

46. Clinton Machann, "Country Western Music and the 'Now' Sound in Texas-Czech Polka Music," *JEMF Quarterly* 19 (1983): 3.

47. Lota M. Spell, *Music in Texas: A Survey of One Aspect of Cultural Progress* (Austin: n.p., 1936), p. 58.

48. Ibid.

49. Hudson and Maresh, *Czech Pioneers of the Southwest,* p. 319.

50. Greene, *A Passion for Polka,* pp. 142–43.

51. Hudson and Maresh, *Czech Pioneers of the Southwest,* p. 341.

52. Machann and Mendl, *Krasna Amerika,* p. 160.

53. Ibid., p. 5.

54. Ibid., p. 160.

55. Ibid., p. 157.

56. Greene, *A Passion for Polka,* p. 143.

57. Carolyn Meiners, "Musical Groups in Fayette County," *Fayette County, Texas Heritage* (n.p.: Curtis Media, 1996), p. 478.

58. Robert Skrabanek, *We're Czechs* (College Station: Texas A&M University Press, 1988), pp. 126–31.

59. Helen Valcik Schnell, telephone interview with author, Nov. 8, 1997.

60. Hudson and Maresh, *Czech Pioneers of the Southwest,* pp. 316–18.

61. Ibid., p. 318.

62. Machann and Mendl, *Krasna Amerika,* p. 154.

63. Ibid., p. 161.

64. Helen E. Miksu, "Moravian/Czech Folk Dancing and Singing in Fayette County," *Fayette County, Texas Heritage,* p. 483.

65. A. J. Blaha, "Czech-Moravian 'Foxfire' of Hranice," *History of Lee County, Texas,* edited by Mrs. James C. Killen (Quanah, Tex.: Nortex, 1974), p. 208.

66. Machann and Mendl, *Krasna Amerika,* p. 162.

67. Meiners, "Musical Groups in Fayette County," p. 479.

68. Skrabanek, *We're Czechs,* p. 128.

69. Blaha, "Czech-Moravian 'Foxfire' of Hranice," p. 207.

70. Greene, *A Passion for Polka,* p. 142.

71. Mikus, "Moravian/Czech Folk Dancing and Singing in Fayette County," p. 483; Machann and Mendl, *Krasna Amerika,* pp. 162–63.

72. Blaha, "Czech-Moravian 'Foxfire' of Hranice," p. 207.

73. Ibid., p. 208.

74. Greene, *A Passion for Polka,* p. 142.

75. Cleo Baca, *Baca's Musical History, 1860–1968* (La Grange, Tex.: La Grange Journal, 1968), p. 23.

76. Ibid., p. 10.

77. Ibid., p. 13.

78. Ibid., p. 26.

79. Machann and Mendl, *Krasna Amerika,* p. 159.

80. Rose Rohde, "Baca Band," *Fayette County, Texas Heritage,* p. 474.

81. Baca, *Baca's Musical History, 1860–1968,* p. 45.

82. Greene, *A Passion for Polka,* p. 124.

83. Ibid., p. 145.

84. Ibid., pp. 144–46.

85. Machann and Mendl, *Krasna Amerika,* p. 155.

86. Skrabanek, *We're Czechs,* pp. 81–82.

87. Abernethy, "Texas Folk and Modern Country Music," p. 160.

88. Machann and Mendl, *Krasna Amerika,* p. 164.

89. Greene, *A Passion for Polka,* p. 143.

90. Machann and Mendl, *Krasna Amerika,* p. 164.

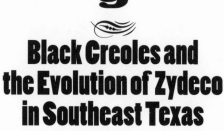

# 9

# Black Creoles and the Evolution of Zydeco in Southeast Texas

## The Beginnings to 1950

## Roger Wood

In the last two decades of the twentieth century, popular music has discovered and occasionally appropriated a distinctly spicy sound now universally recognized as zydeco. This still-evolving black Creole musical form has emerged from obscure origins—on the prairies and bayous of southwestern Louisiana and in the industrial cities of Southeast Texas—to establish itself on the pop cultural landscape of America. Its signature accordion-led melodies, plaintive vocals in French and English, and highly syncopated, rubboard-based rhythms have enhanced soundtracks of feature films, television commercials, and mainstream recordings. Zydeco compact discs and audiocassettes are now regularly stocked in their own category in music stores around the globe. And zydeco superstars have taken center stage at major public events viewed by millions on television.[1]

Like the blues many decades before it, zydeco has evolved from a folk idiom of certain impoverished and isolated African Americans to become a commercially viable musical genre, complete with its own festivals, crossover hits, living legends, and emerging stars. Moreover, as Lorenzo Thomas points out, it has "contributed to the musical vocabulary of 'rock 'n' roll' which, in the late twentieth century, is nothing less than the popular music of the world."[2] For the most part, zydeco has defined itself in an age of ever-pervasive media influence and rural-to-urban mo-

bility, an era in which once-isolated enclaves have had access to popular musical modes, absorbing and syncretizing them with elements from
the folk tradition. Thus, modern zydeco tunes often can sound at once
exotic and familiar to first-time listeners—part of the basis for the music's broad appeal to people beyond its primary ethnic group of origin.

But while casual observers and devoted fans alike readily recognize
the zydeco sound today, popular consciousness generally misconstrues
it to have originated and developed solely in Louisiana. On the con-
trary, the roots of contemporary zydeco grow deep both west and east
of the Sabine River—extending approximately one hundred miles from
this naturally formed state boundary line in both directions. And though
the oldest of the roots—the Creole musical forms known as *juré* and
*la-la*—clearly sprouted first in Louisiana, those forms subsequently
found some of their most essential nutrients and significant cultivation
on urban Texas soil, resulting in the eventual flowering forth of zydeco.
As John Minton has convincingly argued, despite widespread miscon-
ception, zydeco most accurately refers to "a post-war popular music
that first made its mark in Texas cities such as Port Arthur, Beaumont,
Galveston, and Houston" before spreading *back* to the Creole homeland in Louisiana—and eventually to the world.[3] In short, this vibrant
art form is a doubly syncretized musical import-export from the Lone
Star State.

The general public cannot be blamed for miscomprehending zydeco to be a purely Louisiana phenomenon, given the propagation of that
notion in various entertainment media, as well as the state of Louisiana's
successful (and valid) marketing of itself as a cultural tourism destina-
tion with a rich French heritage. Many outsiders discovered the music
in the 1980s—around the same time that traditional Creole and Cajun
cooking emerged as a national culinary craze, concomitant with a
period in which in-state events (such as the New Orleans Jazz and Heritage Festival) grew significantly in size and number, introducing thousands of visitors to zydeco in the process. Moreover, a frequent theme
in zydeco songs—as in many other popular forms, such as blues, blue-
grass, country, and Tejano—is the celebration of an idealized folk past
in some bucolic ancestral home (from which the singer has often been
displaced). The homeland traditionally referenced in most such songs
is, of course, Louisiana—where black Creole culture remains proudly
based to this day.[4] So it is no surprise that the key role of Southeast
Texas—as the hothouse for the actual blossoming of the modern zydeco
sound—has rarely been recognized for what it is.

Yet, as this chapter will show, it was in Texas, especially in Houston, that Creole immigrants and their descendants first fused old Louisiana French music traditions with blues and urban rhythm and blues to create the new sound. And it was in Texas that the two essential instruments for zydeco music—the accordion and the rubboard *(le frottoir)*—were formally adapted in crucial ways to accommodate and make possible that new sound. Recordings using variations of the word *zydeco* first appeared in Houston in the late 1940s. And it was in the Bayou City also that the now-standard orthography and the pronunciation of the term were initially established. In fact, as Michael Tisserand has noted, "Although Houston is often overlooked in zydeco history, the city's relationship to the music can roughly be compared to Chicago's impact on the blues."[5]

This analogy is particularly insightful, for just as postwar Chicago became the proverbial birthplace of modern blues, postwar Houston proved to be the incubator in which the contemporary Creole music called zydeco came into being. From the 1920s through the 1950s, both cities were primary destinations for specific groups of rural African American immigrants in search of jobs and improved living conditions. During this era of increasing urbanization throughout America, thousands of blacks left farms in the Mississippi River region of the Deep South, heading specifically for the place Robert Johnson immortalized as "Sweet Home Chicago." As has been well documented elsewhere, many of these people took with them the acoustic folk musical idiom known as Delta blues, which soon assimilated other influences and metamorphosed into modern electric blues, the progenitor of rock and roll. In a parallel way, during this same time period, members of a unique ethnic group of African Americans—black Creoles from southwestern Louisiana—migrated to Houston, the nearby home of the suddenly booming petrochemical industry. As they created and settled in enclaves such as the city's Frenchtown district, they introduced to Texas an acoustic folk musical idiom known mainly as la-la, which soon absorbed other influences and evolved into modern zydeco, the progenitor of that syncopated, accordion-based sound that seemed to burst suddenly into media consciousness in the 1980s.

As modern musical phenomena, both blues and zydeco first occurred following African American migrations from specific rural regions to specific industrial cities. Thus, any understanding of the notion of the true "home" for either of these two types of music (and certainly for others as well) is complicated by the reality of ethno-cultural mobility. Where did the blues come into being? In Chicago? In the Delta? In Africa? Where did zydeco come into being? In Houston? In the part of Louisiana known as Acadia? In other French colonies? In Africa? The answer to all of these questions might be yes, depending upon how one defines "being." The facts of movement and syncretism often belie the myth of some idealized cultural purity with timeless roots planted firmly in one particular place. And especially for any people correctly defined as Creoles, understanding the culture—as a means of under-standing the music—necessitates an appreciation of mobility, con-frontation, assimilation, and change.

What are the implications of the term Creole, and who exactly are the black people referred to here by this label? Initially, this word was adopted in reference to descendants of French settlers in the Caribbean and in post-1699 colonial Louisiana. As Barry Jean Ancelet explains, "Those born in the colony called themselves Creoles, a word meaning 'home-grown, not imported,' to distinguish themselves from immi-grants."[6] In Louisiana, this primary definition of Creoles originally de-noted members of a privileged class of Caucasian natives based in *le Quartier Français* of old New Orleans and on plantations throughout the region, and this usage of the term persists to some extent today in reference to the socially elite descendants of the old French aristocracy.

But by the later decades of the eighteenth century, miscegenation was occurring as some of these original Creoles procreated with African slaves to produce offspring recognized as *noir*—black Creoles, an iden-tity distinct from that of other Francophones in South Louisiana (such as those of Caucasian European ancestry, including the ethnic group known as Cajuns). These new Creoles were of mixed race, and their cul-ture represented a vital confluence of heritages, both African and French. Prior to the Civil War, the vast majority of them remained en-slaved on French plantations. However, certain others (known as *les gens de couleur libres:* the free colored people) became part of the so-cioeconomic establishment, working as professionals and owning their own businesses—and, in some cases, even their own plantations and slaves.[7] Further convoluting the common understanding of the term, in the decades since emancipation, many black Creoles have intermarried with people of other races, resulting in an even wider range of skin tones, physical characteristics, linguistic traits, and family histories among descendants. In short, the term *black Creoles* historically refers not to a monolithic class of people but to a variety of syncretic human possibilities, both cultural and genetic.

The black Creoles who migrated to Texas from Louisiana—and eventually created the music known as zydeco—mainly have in common a direct or indirect lineage to the old French African slave class. Nuances of genetic identity and social class notwithstanding, these people are primarily distinguished from other descendants of African slaves along the Gulf Coast by the fact of their French heritage—and its various linguistic, culinary, religious, and musical implications. But in contrast to groups such as their close neighbors the Cajuns (i.e., the descendants of Acadians who immigrated from Canada in the late eighteenth century, and with whom black Creoles share many cultural characteristics), these Creoles have an ancestral connection to Africa. This African American heritage differentiates them significantly from other French-speaking peoples in the region—and ultimately sets black Creole music apart from other French-based folk forms originating in the New World.

It is clearly established that large numbers of these black Creoles came to Texas after 1920, but some such people may well have lived west of the Sabine River many decades earlier. We know, for instance, that "wealthy aristocratic Creole planters from Louisiana arrived in Liberty County with their slaves in 1845," though the certainty of mixed-race progeny resulting from that Southeast Texas presence is merely a possibility.[8] (However, the small community of Raywood, located just a few miles east of the town of Liberty, retains to this day a significant black Creole presence.) We also know that in the half-century following the Civil War, the general black population in Houston alone "increased from 3,691 in 1870, to 23,929 in 1910," and that many of these "arrived from rural areas in Texas and Louisiana," suggesting the chance that some black Creoles may have been among those numbers, especially in the first decade of the twentieth century.[9]

The initial major wave of Louisiana-to-Texas immigration was triggered by the discovery of oil in the legendary Spindletop gusher near Beaumont in 1901. As Tisserand notes in his comprehensive history of zydeco, Spindletop gave birth to "the modern petroleum age" and thereby initiated an interstate relocation that would ultimately change American music: "Starting almost immediately, and peaking through the years of World War II, black Creoles migrated to Texas in search of jobs, bringing along their accordions and French songs."[10] Many of them found work, money, and some measure of improved social freedom in the so-called Golden Triangle area of Beaumont, Port Arthur, and Orange—all located on the coastal plains close to the Louisiana border. In addition to jobs in the oil fields, they labored in the shipbuilding yards, chemical plants, rice farms, and shrimp-fishing fleets of the region.

However, large numbers of black Creoles were drawn a bit farther to the west to the quickly established center of the burgeoning petro-chemical industry, Houston. Starting around 1919 these new arrivals began to concentrate their residency in the area of the city known as Fifth Ward. Located east-northeast of downtown on land that had been mostly unpopulated prior to the Civil War, this area had first been settled by freed slaves. It had become the Fifth Ward in 1866 when the city increased its boundaries beyond the four original wards to raise tax revenue and provide aldermen representation for the outlying residents.[11] Within Fifth Ward, the Creoles settled mainly in a neighborhood that became known as Frenchtown. By 1922 when it was formally incorporated, Frenchtown contained approximately five hundred residents in an area that Minton defines as "a dozen or so city blocks," noting also that "as Creole migration increased, especially after the great Mississippi River flood of 1927, the district expanded accordingly, eventually including three times its original area."[12]

Not far from Frenchtown, black Creole men secured employment at various industries along the Houston Ship Channel, as well as at the nearby Southern Pacific Railroad yards. Anderson Moss was among these early immigrants, arriving in Frenchtown in 1928. As he recalls, "Louisiana people took over this town," adding that because of their reputation for hard work, "All you had to do was say you was from Louisiana, and they would hire you right there."[13] Although they worked side-by-side with other African Americans, throughout the 1920s and 1930s the residents of Frenchtown generally maintained their own distinctive cultural identity within the larger black community,[14] facilitated in doing so by their common Creole heritage with its uniquely accented patois, distinctive cuisine, religious foundation in Catholicism, and the unusual music they first called la-la.

La-la was the most common name of the unamplified, accordion-based black Creole musical form that would eventually undergo a crucial transformation in Frenchtown, and elsewhere in southeast Texas, to evolve into modern zydeco. Analogous to the way the word zydeco functions today, la-la can be used as a noun referring variously to either a type of music, a dance step, or a social event at which the music and dancing occur—or as a verb signifying the action of making that music or dancing to it. As longtime Frenchtown resident Clarence Gallien once told historian Alan Govenar, "they didn't call it zydeco at that time

*Zydeco players performing at The Silver Slipper in
Houston's historic "Frenchtown" neighborhood, 1997.
Photographed by James Fraher*

[pre-1950s], it was la-la. They used to give different la-la at the house or at a little cafe. La-la was a house dance when thirty, forty, fifty people get together and have a good time. Any time anybody plays the accordion, we call it a la-la, a country la-la."[15]

The major phase of la-la seems to correspond not only with urban migration but also with a period in which many Creole musicians in Texas and Louisiana began to shift away from playing the old-timey, single-row accordion, which had been utilized from the advent of the instrument through the early 1930s, and instead adopted the more versatile double-row and triple-row models, which offered expanded musical possibilities more amenable to an eventual syncretism with blues. In the 1930s and 1940s black Creole accordionists playing what they called la-la also began to perform more frequently in combinations with other types of instrumental accompaniment, such as percussion (in various forms) and guitars, as opposed to the traditional solo presentation or fiddle accompaniment common in an earlier era.

In fact, pre-dating la-la, the earliest related form of black Creole music in South Louisiana involved a type of ritualized singing with little, if any, instrumental support. Known as *juré* (pronounced joo-RAY) from the French verb *jurer,* "to testify," it was a type of gospel chant that sometimes accompanied a special dance. In such cases it is understood to have been "a localized form of the African American 'ring shout,' consisting of a counterclockwise procession accompanied by antiphonal singing and the shuffling, stamping, and clapping of the dancers, occasionally supplemented by simple percussion such as the ubiquitous metal-on-jawbone scraper or its descendant, the washboard."[16] However, other researchers assert that performance of juré by black Creole Catholics in New Orleans was completely a cappella and "most common during Lent, when instruments and dancing were taboo."[17]

Noted zydeco musician Canray Fontenot defines juré as pre-instrumental, improvisational music built originally on nothing more than hand-clapped rhythms—and created mainly for entertainment and dancing. "They used to have that where they didn't have no musicians," he recalls, adding, "but them old people would sit down, clap their hands, and make up a song. And they would dance on that, them people."[18] It is easy to imagine that such folks might eventually supplement their hand clapping with the spontaneous incorporation of any object readily available on which they could tap, scrape, and pound in rhythm. Because the typical venue for socializing and musical performances involving poor black Creoles of this era was the house party, kitchen utensils such as spoons, bottle openers, and washboards became increasingly common supplements as juré-based traditions began to evolve beyond their religious origins to inspire the more secularized form known as la-la. But many older black Creoles did not forget where the music began. None other than the late "King of Zydeco," former Houston resident Clifton Chenier, located the origin of his music's characteristic syncopation in the church-inspired juré: "The beat came from the religion people," he once bluntly asserted in an interview, as he sharply clapped his hands in time.[19]

Thus, juré is the post-African source for the highly syncopated, polyrhythmic foundation common today in the black Creole music of Louisiana and Southeast Texas—a signature trait distinguishing the sound from that of the neighboring white Cajuns, for instance. While the rhythms now are generated by manipulation of metal instruments, they began much more simply. Utilizing the most basic of sonic devices, the voice and the hand clap, the primary role of juré in the evolution of zydeco is analogous to that of a cappella "Negro spirituals" in the early formation of the secular music called blues. But the development from the instrumentally limited juré to zydeco would not have been possible without la-la, the crucial link between the seed and the flower in black Creole music of the upper Gulf Coast.

Whereas the turn-of-the-century style called juré formally explored the creative potential of plaintive vocalizing over a musical substructure of intense syncopation, the early-to-mid-twentieth-century style known mainly as la-la marked not only a shift from religious to secular emphasis, but it also eventually initiated other distinctly necessary phases in the metamorphosis towards zydeco. Foremost, this music (referred to variously among black Creoles as "French music," "French la-la," as well as just "la-la") had introduced the diatonic one-row accordion as lead instrument. Though this most basic push-pull version of accordion would largely be replaced by more musically diverse models (including eventually the chromatic piano-key type), from its first emergence la-la celebrated the accordion as the primary soundpiece of black Creole music. In the early years, it was often the sole instrument backing the human voice, as well as played solo or accompanied by a fiddle. In this respect, la-la was undoubtedly influenced by Cajun music, in which both accordion and fiddle were already established as alternating lead instruments. However, fiddle playing in black Creole music is now of minor significance (and nonexistent in the more popular contemporary zydeco bands) compared to its continued featured role in Cajun culture.

Singer and accordionist Amédé Ardoin is generally recognized as the most influential figure in the early development of both Creole and Cajun music, two distinct styles that nonetheless have much in common—especially in the years between the two world wars, when the recording of southern folk music first became possible. Born in 1898 in Eunice, Louisiana, this small black Creole man had absorbed the elements of Cajun music so completely that many people who heard his seminal recordings—made between 1929 and 1934, including one crucially important session in Texas—did not know he was actually a Creole. Chris Strachwitz, the founder of Arhoolie Records (a key label in documenting zydeco since the early 1960s), recalls his surprise at learning Ardoin's racial identity: "It wasn't until Clifton Chenier told me that 'Amédé Ardoin was the first colored to make French records' that I realized Amédé was of African-American background. To my ears, the recordings of Amédé Ardoin did not sound all that different from Cajun accordionists I had heard on records."[20] Confusing the matter further, many of Ardoin's recorded performances featured accompaniment by legendary Cajun fiddler Dennis McGee in a biracial collaboration that was—and has to this day remained—fairly rare in the history of black Creole music. Moreover, Ardoin sang in a tense, high-pitched voice with a strong, pleading tone in the manner of the classic Cajun singers (as opposed to the open-throated technique more common in African American vocalizing). His instrument was the traditional single-row diatonic accordion, and his music was based mainly on the popular Cajun waltzes, one-steps, and two-steps. So on first impression Ardoin's special significance as the patriarch of modern black Creole music might be difficult to grasp. But key indicators of his primary role in that music discretely appear on his recordings, and most obviously so during his one session in Texas.

In downtown San Antonio on August 8, 1934, a small group of recording engineers gathered various folk performers, including Amédé Ardoin, in two rooms of the Texas Hotel to make some records.[21] Despite his stylistic affinity with the white French music of rural Louisiana, the six tunes Ardoin documented that day (for the Bluebird/Victor company) included some distinct differences foreshadowing the future of black Creole music. Perhaps most importantly, the titles of two tracks pointed toward the just-emerging synthesis of traditional Cajun sounds and the primary secular music of African America: "Les Blues de Voyage" ("Travel Blues") and "Les Blues de Crowley" ("Crowley Blues," named after a town near Ardoin's birthplace in Louisiana). The latter, in particular, is particularly potent in its highly emotive vocal performance, consonant with the rough style of early country blues—but sung in French by an accordion player, and thus anticipating zydeco. Among the thirty-four titles that compose his entire recorded repertoire, Ardoin made specific reference to "blues" only four times, and one-half of those references occurred during this single session in San Antonio—a fact that symbolically hints at the role Texas would play in the intermingling of la-la and blues for decades to come.

In addition to this emphasis on blues, the Texas Hotel session marked another significant development. Although Ardoin had generally established a reputation for playing in a syncopated style more consistent with his Creole legacy than with straight Cajun music, none of his catalogue of thirty-four recordings included any percussion instrument accompaniment, still a rarity in white French folk music at this time (with the exception of the iron triangle used in some Cajun bands).

Thus, it is especially noteworthy that the six Texas tracks were the first, and only, to highlight on record the organic rhythms of Ardoin's foot tapping, the most fundamental of all percussive effects. As Jared Snyder observes, "Eli Oberstein, who was in charge of the recordings, chose not to damp the sound of Ardoin's foot tapping in time to the music. Foot tapping was a critical part of the performance and was something normally eliminated by recording on carpeted floor."[22] Oberstein's decision resulted in a sound more faithful to what would surely have been heard at an old-style house dance—where foot tapping was often not only present but, in a sense, "amplified" by the practice of having the musician stand upon a strong wooden table placed in one corner of a room, a platform that functioned both as an elevating bandstand and as a resonating surface for foot-based percussion.[23] Although Ardoin's clearly discernible foot tapping on the recordings was relatively subtle compared to subsequently developed percussion effects in black Creole music, it suggested—even if only by chance—the increasingly significant role that rhythmic accents would play in the development of la-la.

In the years following Ardoin's Texas recordings, la-la would formalize the sophisticated musical adaptation of metal percussion devices (such as spoon scraped on washboard) as the defining source of heavy syncopation at the house dances (and eventually on the first zydeco recordings), no longer depending mainly on hand clapping or foot tapping to create the beat. Here black Creole la-la diverged remarkably from traditional, European-inspired Cajun music, which was generally far less rhythmically complex and played at a regular, measured tempo. La-la, on the other hand, increasingly came to highlight an "Afro-Caribbean rhythmic framework" in which accents often shifted to various beats.[24] The role of the rubboard or washboard, known among Creoles as *le frottoir* (pronounced fra-TWA) from the French verb *frotter,* "to rub," became ever more pronounced, laying the trademark "chanka-chank" foundation over which a featured accordionist would perform. And the repertoire of this accordion-washboard collaboration began to expand beyond the old-style French songs to encompass blues, especially as the accordionists started to experiment with the wider-ranging musical capabilities of more technologically advanced instrument types.

Early la-la music thus represents a confluence of Creole and Cajun musical traditions, best documented by the Amédé Ardoin recordings, especially those made in Texas. But at black Creole house dances throughout the upper Gulf Coast region, the old-style acoustic la-la personified by Ardoin began to change even more in the late 1940s as ever larger numbers of Creoles settled in Texas cities and witnessed first-hand the vibrant new sounds of electric blues and the polished crafts-manship of rhythm and blues.

As the black Creole immigrants to cities such as Houston experi-enced increasing financial and material advancement thanks to regular paychecks from the jobs they came to find, it became more and more common for them to socialize with, and be influenced by, non-Creoles beyond enclaves such as Frenchtown. They met and mixed with the general African American population at work and in entertainment venues such as Fifth Ward's famous Bronze Peacock nightclub or Third Ward's swanky Eldorado Ballroom. In the midst of Frenchtown itself, they crowded into the Creole-owned Johnson's Lounge to dance to big band music and see the floor shows. Although they still kept la-la cul-ture alive at private house parties, they discovered that big city night clubs offered an exciting new experience fueled by swing, blues, and jazz. And they absorbed an even wider range of popular music via the medium of sound recordings on jukeboxes and broadcast radio. Unlike friends and relatives they had left behind in relative isolation back in rural southwestern Louisiana, many of the newly urbanized Creoles did not cling to the musical traditions of juré and old-style la-la as much as they began to expand their tastes beyond this root music—and, in some cases, to adapt it into something new, inspired by the dominant musi-cal trends of the day.

African American music writer Nelson George has provocatively observed that "black music is in constant flight from the status quo."[25] While this sweeping generalization is subject to debate in any given case, it suggests several layers of realities influencing the more progres-sive players in urban Texas la-la culture of the late 1940s, of which Clifton Chenier is the most widely recognized example. By the postwar era, thousands of black Creoles working in the state's southeastern in-dustrial cities had already fled the socioeconomic status quo of their slave-descendant ancestors back on the farms. They had moved on mainly in an effort to modernize and thus improve their living condi-tions, but they had concurrently and enthusiastically begun to mod-ernize their preferences in music too. Yet if they periodically fled the status quo of their Creole heritage, they never abandoned it, or its mu-sic. Like their linguistic idiom, their religion, and their distinctive food, la-la composed a major element of their collective sense of self. But, un-til 1949, it was a musical experience mainly shared only with other black Creoles, not performed for the general public in nightclubs or ballrooms around the city. By the time it made its presence known in the clubs, people would refer to it as zydeco.

So the essential metamorphosis of la-la music into contemporary zydeco did not occur suddenly in the urban environment. In fact, it is fair to assume that through the 1940s much of the black Creole music in Texas cities remained primarily acoustic and folk-based (i.e., casual in its performance at specific social functions, utilizing mainly a traditional repertoire transmitted from master to apprentice, often within the family).[26] But the notion of a backward-looking, French-based repertoire was increasingly being challenged by the ubiquitous sounds of popular black culture.

For instance, Anderson Moss, one of Frenchtown's leading Louisiana-born accordion masters from the 1950s into the 1990s, really began learning and playing his instrument decades after moving to Houston in 1928. Significantly, the first two songs he says he mastered came not from the Creole or Cajun tradition rooted back in rural Louisiana but from contemporary Texas blues in the form of hit records produced in California: "Driftin' Blues" and "Stormy Monday." The former had been written and first released in 1945 by the pianist and vocalist Charles Brown, originally from Texas City; the latter had been composed and first recorded in 1947 by the seminal electric blues guitarist and singer Aaron "T-Bone" Walker, originally from Dallas. Neither these artists nor these songs conveyed characteristics associated with the French Louisiana music tradition, or even with the rural blues tradition for that matter. Instead, both Brown and Walker personified an urbane, jazzy style of blues. Yet Moss says that after learning such numbers as these hits by Brown and Walker, he soon found jobs in small cafes throughout Fifth Ward playing them on the accordion for predominantly Creole audiences.[27]

This new form of music, though it was played by a black Creole on an accordion, probably did not sound much like the old Cajun-influenced style called la-la, a label that increasingly suggested an antique mode to some of the urbanized residents of Frenchtown. In the years following World War II, as their repertoire absorbed more songs from the top blues artists of the day, and as the accordionists and washboard players eventually began to perform alongside other instruments common in typical blues and jazz combos, variations of the word now spelled z-y-d-e-c-o came to signify this distinctively syncretized music (as well as the events at which it was played, and the dance steps performed there), in lieu of the term *la-la*. As black Creole guitarist Ashton

Savoy, a longtime Houston resident, explains, "They used to call that 'French la la.' 'Well, we going around to listen at the French la la tonight,' you know. But when they started putting them horns and saxophones and all that stuff in there, well then they started playing the blues, they started mixing that stuff up then, you know. Well, that's when they started calling it 'zydeco' then."[28]

The origins of the word zydeco have been traced to a lyric that surfaced first in various Creole folk songs in early-twentieth-century Louisiana and has recurred ever since: *les haricots sont pas salé.*[29] The name zydeco derives from the first two words in this expression. Following the logic of French pronunciation, with the elision of the *Z*-sounding terminal *s* in the definite article *les,* combined with the vowel sound following the silent *h* in the noun *haricots* (in which the terminal *t* is also silent), the phrase *les haricots* sounds something like *le zarico* (with the final syllable stressed) in standard dialect. Among the various attempts at making an English spelling correspond to the Creole pronunciation, *z-y-d-e-c-o* would eventually win out, thanks to the efforts of Houston folklorist Robert Burton "Mack" McCormick, who formally established the now-standard orthography in his transcription of lyrics for a two-volume 1959 record album called *A Treasury of Field Recordings.* This compilation included various types of folk music documented around Houston, but the key performance—as far as the future of zydeco was concerned—was by a Creole who had immigrated to the city in the 1940s, Dudley Alexander. He played a bilingual version of Big Joe Williams's 1930s-era classic blues "Baby, Please Don't Go" on concertina (a type of small accordion), accompanied by washboard and fiddle. In addition to the lyrics, Alexander added a spoken-word introduction, in a mix of French and English, in which the word McCormick transcribed as *zydeco* occurs.[30]

Translated roughly as "the snapbeans are not salted," the entire utterance *les haricots sont pas salé* operated originally as a common metaphor for hard times—signifying a poverty so severe that there was no money to buy salt (or salt meat) to season the homegrown vegetables. In this sense, zydeco is a word, like *blues* before it, that carries connotations of personal suffering based in socioeconomic deprivation.[31] But just as blues offered some articulation of—and concomitant creative release from—that hardship, so did this music called zydeco. And, in both cases, even when that impoverished milieu of a hard rural lifestyle had been left behind by black city dwellers, the old term was evoked to describe the fundamental music of the culture the migrants had brought with them. Not only did the word zydeco hearken back to the old line about the snapbeans, but McCormick and others noted that people dancing to the music often engaged in a hand gesture reminiscent of the act of breaking open the vegetable pods, "holding closed wrists in front of the torso and then circling or flicking them in a motion that alludes to someone snapping beans."[32]

McCormick had initially settled on the word zydeco to describe both the dancing and the distinctive music that he observed among black Creoles in Houston's Fifth Ward—not as a replacement for the older term la-la but as a way of differentiating this now doubly syncretized urban style from the traditional music rooted back in rural Louisiana. As Tisserand observes, the Houston folklorist had intended only for the term "to apply to the local alloy of Texas blues and French Creole music and he was horrified when the word was sucked backed across the Louisiana border," noting also that McCormick declared, "When I'm talking about zydeco, I'm talking about the music of Frenchtown."[33]

Not only was the term zydeco first formally established on Texas soil as a multivalent reference to a new type of music, a dance step, and an event, but the first two recordings to use variations on the term in this sense, as opposed to the original French sense referring to a bean, were produced not in Louisiana but also in Houston in the late 1940s. Significantly also, these records were made not by artists playing the accordion or in the traditional Creole style. Instead, the first was issued, possibly as early as 1947, by the very personification of Texas blues, Sam "Lightning" Hopkins, and the second appeared in a 1949 recording by rhythm and blues performer Clarence "Bon Ton" Garlow.

In the Hopkins song, which Gold Star Records producer Bill Quinn bewilderedly titled "Zolo Go," the singer offered a rare performance on electric organ, forsaking the guitar for which he is most famous, in an effort to approximate the sound of an accordion—a sound he knew first-hand from his cousin (by marriage), occasional music partner and eventual zydeco superstar Clifton Chenier. Though structurally the song was a standard eight-bar blues, it began with Hopkins declaring, "I'm going to zolo go [actually pronounced more like *zydeco*] for a little while for you folks. You know, the young and old likes that," and the last lines described a woman asserting the need to go "zolo go" as an escape from hard times.[34] As Chris Strachwitz explains, the Gold Star recordings Hopkins made in the late 1940s were mainly limited in distribution to jukeboxes around Southeast Texas, where most African Americans (transplanted Creoles and non-Creoles alike) would easily recognize the sound and the word to which Hopkins alluded on this track.[35]

Clarence Garlow, unlike Hopkins, was of Creole heritage, having been born in Welsh, Louisiana, in 1911. But at age five he moved with his family to the Texas city of Beaumont and spent much of his subsequent life traveling and working between the two neighboring states. As Govenar has documented, Garlow started out playing fiddle and traditional Creole music, but "when he heard the 'amplified sound' of T-Bone Walker, his attitude changed. He wanted to play electric guitar."[36] This inspiration soon culminated with him fronting his own band playing rhythm and blues in clubs around Houston and landing a record deal with the local Macy's label, for which he recorded his signature hit entitled "Bon Ton Roula" in 1949. This song pulsed with a rumba-style percussion and opened with the spoken exclamation *"Eh toi!"*—an interjection common in Creole-Cajun music culture. Though the instrumentation included drums, saxophone, piano, electric guitar, and bass—not exactly characteristic of the traditional Creole ensemble—the singer identified himself as a "Frenchman" giving advice about how to enjoy oneself in a "Creole town," with subsequent reference to "crawfish," "Louisiana," and "French la-la." But the key moment occurred near the end when he advised people to go to the "zydeco" [indeterminate orthography] to have fun.[37]

The Hopkins and Garlow recordings clearly demonstrate that in the late 1940s the concept of zydeco, however it might have been pronounced or spelled, was current among blacks in Southeast Texas—and not as a reference to a vegetable. As blues and rhythm and blues artists such as these two men used the term, it was something of a novelty, but it indicated the level of interchange already underway between black Creole musical culture and popular urban modes. However, at the time these records were produced, it was still practically impossible in the nightclubs around Houston to find the real music—whether it was dubbed la-la or zydeco—played with accordion and washboard and performed by black Creoles. Such presentations remained limited mainly to the house party phenomenon. But by the tail end of the decade, on Christmas Eve of 1949, that situation suddenly changed.

The key event in the movement of black Creole music into the public venues of Houston seems to have occurred by chance. During the same postwar period when popular blues artists such as Hopkins and Garlow were beginning to notice black Creole music and to appropriate elements from it, a rebirth of French la-la was simultaneously occurring, stimulated regularly by new arrivals from Louisiana and rural East Texas. As has been extensively documented by Minton, one of the most respected masters of the old la-la accordion tradition was Willie Green, who had moved to Houston as far back as the 1920s, and who became "the first Houston Creole to perform French music in a public venue" by playing an impromptu Christmas Eve gig at Irene's Café in 1949.[38] From that date until his death in the late 1960s, Green would reign as the king of the la-la sound (his instrumentation usually limited to one or two accordions accompanied by a washboard) at Irene's Café—and at other venues that had soon followed its lead in featuring this music for the entertainment of paying customers. While Green's repertoire included Cajun-Creole classics such as "Jole Blon," it also incorporated blues tunes such as "Baby, Please Don't Go," and as a result was increasingly referred to as zydeco. Yet Green's music retained the stripped-down, primal sound of the old house party la-la, as opposed to the more instrumentally diverse, amplified sound of the progressive zydeco bands that would emerge in the 1950s, inspired by the success of Clifton Chenier.[39]

The fact that Green often played with a second accordion led him naturally into a master-apprentice type relationship with a younger player named L. C. Donatto, who had moved to Houston from Louisiana around 1944. In an interview with Minton, Donatto recounts the sequence of events leading up to that first breakthrough performance at Irene's Café, explaining that he and Green were "just riding around in a car . . . driving and playing that thing and drinking and having fun," when they stopped at a stranger's front yard because a man out front with a guitar hollered at them, "Y'all come on the porch and play." As they obliged his request, accompanied by an unknown washboard player, they spontaneously attracted a huge crowd, including eventually the proprietress of a nearby cafe, Irene. As Donatto tells it, "she heard that, and she come on 'round there, her and her husband, and seen all them people, said, 'Well, why don't y'all come to the café?' And we started from that day. Started from that, and Count Basie or Benny Goodman couldn't draw no bigger crowd than that. And we were the first one played, that's right, zydeco in Houston."[40]

The success of this first appearance and subsequent bookings at Irene's Café benefited not only Green and Donatto, but also other Frenchtown accordionists such as the aforementioned Anderson Moss and his best friend, an important post-1950 figure, named Lonnie Mitchell. Born around 1925 in the Creole community of Raywood near

Liberty, Texas, Alfonse Lonnie Mitchell was first inspired to play the accordion around age twelve, after witnessing the genius of a respected old-timer called Joe Jesse at a house party performance. After moving to Houston (in a year he has given variously as 1946, 1947, and 1950) Mitchell eventually resumed his accordion playing and shared the stage with Willie Green. But Mitchell's big break came when the owner of Johnson's Lounge in Frenchtown decided to cease booking the big bands that had been popular in the 1940s and instead to feature live Creole accordion music, following the success of the venture at Irene's Café. Mitchell's tenure at Johnson's Lounge—which would later be leased for five years by the musician himself and called Mitchell's Lounge follow- ing the death of Charley Johnson, and which would then be rechristened the Continental Zydeco Ballroom when the lease reverted to Johnson's heir, Doris McClendon—lasted from approximately 1951 until Mitchell's own death in 1995. Over this period of close to four and a half decades, the large red-and-white painted structure at 3101 Collingsworth (known consecutively as Johnson's, Mitchell's, and the Continental) established itself as "Houston's premier Creole nightspot," and Lonnie Mitchell was the dominant presence there, sometimes performing as often as six nights per week and influencing several generations of Houston zydeco musicians and fans in the process.[41] Of additional significance, and un- like his friend and elder Willie Green, Mitchell did not limit his accom- paniment to the washboard, as was common in the old la-la tradition. As he once reflected in an article Minton published in the *Journal of Folk- lore Research,* "It makes it sound better, you know, a guitar and drums, to me. I don't know if I could play now with just a washboard. But you know, when you got a guitar and drums and all that, it just, I don't know, give more pep to the music."[42]

One of the black Creoles who came to Texas in the late 1940s and became part of the 1950s Frenchtown scene at Johnson's Lounge was Lonnie Mitchell's good friend Clifton Chenier, the man most respon- sible for eventually taking Texas-bred zydeco—that potent fusion of electric blues with the la-la sounds of accordion and washboard— *back* to Louisiana, and eventually to the world. Born in Opelousas, Louisiana, in 1925, Chenier had moved in 1947 first to Port Arthur, Texas, where he worked at the Gulf Oil Refinery by day and played mu- sic with his older brother Cleveland—performing for tips at quitting time outside the factory gates and in the evenings at area clubs and ice- houses. Eventually they would form the Red Hot Sizzling Band that played along the Gulf Coast, traveling back and forth between Texas and

Louisiana, from the late 1940s into the early 1950s. As he visited and performed in big cities such as Houston, Chenier's self-presentation evolved from that of a country-bred Creole to an urban persona distinctly more fashionably hip. On trips back to Opelousas, his old friends noticed the difference at a glance. As Wilbert Guillory once told an interviewer, "He came back from Texas, he was a changed man. He had all kinds of colored clothes, and he had his conked hair. Gold teeth, talked nice, talked proper," an opinion seconded by Louisiana radio disc jockey Frank Marlbrough, who observed, "He brought in a new style, that's what I think it was. Texas was always ahead in fashion."[43]

But the changes triggered by Clifton Chenier's Texas experience during the late 1940s and early 1950s would not be limited to his personal appearance; the changes would also influence his music—and eventually make him the undisputed father of the post-1950 modern zydeco sound. Chenier's role is enormous, for example, in affecting the primary instruments used in the rise of zydeco to a popular form.

As a child of a single-row, push-button diatonic accordion player back in Opelousas, he had been raised amidst the essence of the old-style sound and technique. But for whatever reasons (and as Tisserand notes, the historical facts on this matter are "not clear"), Chenier chose to play the large, piano-key chromatic model throughout his adult life, presumably before and certainly after his move to Texas—and there is some evidence, including Chenier's own testimony to Cajun-Creole historian Ann Allen Savoy, as well as to Texas music documentarian Alan Govenar, that he really started playing the accordion only after arriving in Southeast Texas.[44] This preference for the relatively newfangled version of the instrument would prove fortuitous once Chenier relocated west of the Sabine River and began to expand his repertoire beyond the rural Creole tradition of his father's generation, experimenting with his accordion's capacity to play blues and rhythm and blues. Given the ability to make music in any key, including flats and sharps, the piano-style chromatic model would prove infinitely better suited to performance of any song he wanted to attempt, especially when he played with other instruments (such as the saxophones, organs, and guitars that he would later incorporate in his various bands). Whereas the single-row diatonic models were locked in a fixed pattern of intervals and could play only in one key, obviously limiting their versatility, Chenier's choice of the chromatic accordion liberated him to explore whatever musical synthesis he could imagine between the popular blues tunes he encountered in Texas and the more traditional Creole sounds he recalled from back home. Moreover, the piano-style chromatic instrument would make the same note whether it was pushed or pulled, unlike the various previously developed diatonic options.

In Texas, Chenier also discovered "famed accordion builder John Gabbenelli, who had recently moved to Houston from Italy," and who would repair and modify old "junk" piano-key accordions for the young musician, making it easier for him to afford and master the instrument.[45] And Clifton Chenier did just that, influencing zydeco musicians and the genre's fundamental sound for decades to come.

The Chenier brothers' initial tenure in the Lone Star State would also mark a major innovation in the traditional la-la percussion instrument, the washboard. Just as Clifton would update and diversify the sonic possibilities of the zydeco accordion by using a different model, he and his brother Cleveland would revolutionize the basic form, playing style, and resultant musical effects of the washboard. In short, they *invented* the modern zydeco frottoir. Instead of continuing to rely on the humble household utensil that had long been adapted for rhythmic accompaniment in black Creole music, they designed a truly unique musical instrument. In doing so, they directly affected practically every zydeco band to come after them. Although Cleveland had started out, like most Creole percussionists before him, holding a traditional, rectangular-shaped small metal washboard and scratching its surface with a spoon, in the late 1940s his brother came up with a radical new idea, which he recalled in a videotaped interview with Chris Strachwitz: "They used to tie a string around it [the washboard], you know, and play it around the neck. So I went on to a white fellow down there at the Gulf Refinery [in Port Arthur]. I told him, I said, 'You got some tin?' He say, 'Yeah.' So I got down on the ground, in the sand, and I drawed that rubboard. And I said, 'Can you make one like that? You know, with a collar plate?' He say, 'Sure, I can make one like that.' And he made one."[46] The result was a type of curving, single-piece corrugated metal vest worn over the shoulders of the player and covering the whole front of his torso, all the way down to the waist.

This innovation provided a much wider and longer surface for percussive improvisation and freed the player to dance and move with the music, because he no longer had to hold the washboard with one hand or awkwardly manipulate the smaller flat-surfaced traditional model as it hung from a string around the neck. Moreover, this sophisticated new design expanded the musical possibilities for zydeco percussion, for, as Strachwitz points out, "The amount of air the player leaves in back of the instrument (by either standing up straight or bending forward) determines the brightness of the sound."[47] Cleveland Chenier effectively exploited this technique and also explored other sonic theories by changing the type and number of hand-held tools with which he struck the metal surface. He eventually traded in the traditional one or two spoons that others had relied on as the washboard equivalent of drumsticks. Instead he adopted a musical approach based on gripping six church-key bottle openers in each hand as he performed, expanding the polyrhythmic effects and creating a richer percussion foundation for his brother's accordion playing. Given these innovations, the frottoir vest, which is now a fixture in practically every zydeco band playing today (as well as in some Cajun bands), is arguably one of the few non-electronic musical instruments to be created in modern times in the United States of America, and by Chenier's own account, it first came into being in Southeast Texas.

The rest is music history. Energized by the lively possibilities of the chromatic piano key accordion and the newly conceived washboard vest, Clifton Chenier's music, more so than any other player's, changed the course of zydeco in the latter half of the twentieth century. From the time of his first sessions in the 1950s and almost until his death in 1987, he recorded in Louisiana, California, and Texas and toured the world—introducing his uniquely realized syncretism of blues, rhythm and blues, and Creole music to fans of all races and profoundly influencing the direction the music called zydeco would take in the last two decades of the century. As Chris Strachwitz, the producer of Chenier's most significant recordings, has written, "Clifton's success gave all the other Zydeco musicians the impetus to put more blues or rock and roll (as they called it) into Creole Zydeco music, especially in the Houston area."[48]

Chenier is also credited with spreading the word, literally: zydeco. Although Mack McCormick formally documented the term and the spelling, most historians agree that Chenier is the individual most responsible for popularizing it. He had first recorded a song for Specialty Records as far back as 1955 entitled "Zodico Stomp," but it was Chenier's breakthrough 1964 session for Arhoolie, recorded at Houston's Gold Star studio by Chris Strachwitz, that gave the world the classic song called "Zydeco Sont Pas Salé," in which the producer followed McCormick's lead, abandoning the French phrase *les haricots* for the potent new word. As Houston promoter Clarence Gallien once explained, "The name changed from la-la to zydeco when Clifton made the record. Clifton is the man who got credit for changing the name."[49]

And while Chenier's impact on the propagation of the word, as on popular music itself, has ultimately been global, he participated in changing the Houston scene in at least one other crucial way that brought the signature music of his ethnic heritage back to its cultural roots. Like many other black Creoles, Clarence Gallien had come to Houston in the early 1940s, where he promptly opened a nightclub featuring live music and dancing. After first affiliating with Our Mother of Mercy Roman Catholic Church in Frenchtown, he later moved his membership to St. Francis of Assisi, where the congregation was exploring ideas for a fund-raising activity. When Gallien suggested promoting a dance for the church's primarily Creole parishioners, the priest approved—and within weeks Clifton Chenier was drawing huge crowds on Saturday nights to "zydeco" at the church hall. As noted by Robert Damora, Gallien had been friends with Chenier back in Louisiana where they "had worked together cutting sugarcane," and their church dance concept rapidly became "so successful in preaching the gospel of zydeco that too many churches began to compete for bands and audiences."[50] Eventually the Catholic diocese worked out a cooperative plan whereby the major black Creole churches in the area would take turns sponsoring the Saturday night zydeco dances, rotating them on a regular basis with updates announced weekly in the *Catholic Herald.* This development did not only benefit the church coffers but also Chenier's local popularity. As Strachwitz has acknowledged, these church-based gatherings appealed to old-timers and youngsters alike, so "entire families would attend and the Zydeco once again became a communal celebration having come full circle from the old community 'house dances.'"[51]

Thus, Clifton Chenier epitomizes the paradox of zydeco, a musical cultural phenomenon that simultaneously has moved away from and back to its roots. Having helped transform the music of old-timey rural Louisiana la-la culture into something bold and new in the cities of Southeast Texas, Chenier also took part in re-establishing the communal spirit of the Acadian homeland among black Creoles who had migrated to Houston. Today Chenier, like Gallien, is gone, but the church dances continue as fixtures in the social life of many Creole Catholics living around Houston. And the zydeco played at the dances today— featuring nationally recognized stars such as Beau Jocque, as well as up-and-comers such as Step Rideau—reflects a continual evolution, an ongoing syncretism of elements from the original Louisiana folk tradition and its subsequent Texas transformation with an amalgam of other media-inspired influences.

And despite the fact that popular consciousness will likely persist in imagining zydeco to be a uniquely rural-Louisiana-based sound, the people most directly responsible for making the music what it is today recognize the importance of urban Texas as the locus for some of the genre's most significant historical development. For instance, the Zydeco Hall of Fame recently established by black Creoles, like the National Zydeco Society itself, is based not in some backwoods Louisiana parish but in Houston.[52] And Southeast Texas remains a creative center of zydeco culture, which is fitting—it being the place where la-la and modern blues initially fused to form the new sound, where the defining word itself first formally appeared on record and in print, where the genre's signature instruments were adapted in crucially progressive ways, and where black Creoles as a people continue to thrive today.

## ⪼ Notes ⪻

1. Among the many examples of zydeco's mid-1980s breakthrough into popular culture are Paul Simon's zydeco-inclusive, best-selling album *Graceland,* which won the 1986 Grammy for Album of the Year; rock star Eric Clapton's 1987–88 affiliation (in the recording studio and on tour) with Stanley Dural, the artist known as "Buckwheat Zydeco"; the soundtrack to the 1987 box office hit film *The Big Easy* directed by Jim McBride; and numerous television advertising campaigns (especially in the 1990s) for major corporations from Toyota to the makers of Reese's Peanut Butter Cups. A musical performance by Stanley "Buckwheat Zydeco" Dural was featured also at the globally televised closing ceremonies of the Summer Games of the twenty-sixth Olympiad in Atlanta, Georgia, in 1996.

2. Lorenzo Thomas, "From Gumbo To Grammys: The Development of Zydeco Music in Houston, *Juneteenth Texas: Essays in African-American Folklore,* edited by Francis E. Abernethy, Patrick B. Mullen, and Alan B. Govenar (Denton: University of North Texas Press, 1996), p. 139.

3. John Minton, "Houston Creoles and Zydeco: The Emergence of an African-American Urban Popular Style," *American Music* 14, no. 4 (winter, 1996): 487.

4. Ibid., see p. 505: "Both as a musical and linguistic idiom, zydeco is distantly tied to a culture approximating the ideal 'folk society.' In reality, though, as both a musical genre and a generic term, zydeco was coined by urban wage earners, more specifically by professional musicians not in rural Louisiana—the 'back home' of the zydeco ethos—but in urban Texas."

5. Michael Tisserand, "Zydeco Beat," *Living Blues* 131 (Jan.–Feb., 1997): 74.

6. Barry Jean Ancelet, "Cajuns and Creoles," *Encyclopedia of Southern Culture* (New York: Anchor Books, 1991), vol. 2, p. 38.

7. Ibid., p. 40.

8. Diana J. Kleiner, "Liberty County," *The Handbook of Texas Online,* 1999 ed., s.v.

9. Howard Beeth and Cary D. Wintz, eds., *Black Dixie: Afro-Texan History and Culture in Houston* (College Station: Texas A&M University Press, 1992), p. 88.

10. Michael Tisserand, *The Kingdom of Zydeco* (New York: Arcade, 1998), p. 15.

11. Bob Tutt, "Houston's Historic Wards Work to Reverse Fortunes," *Houston Chronicle,* Aug. 4, 1996, p. 37A.

12. Minton, "Houston Creoles and Zydeco," p. 492.

13. Quoted in Tisserand, *The Kingdom of Zydeco,* p. 76.

14. Beeth and Wintz, eds., *Black Dixie,* p. 89.

15. Alan Govenar, *Meeting the Blues: The Rise of the Texas Sound* (New York: Da Capo Press, 1995), p. 151.

16. Minton, "Houston Creoles and Zydeco," p. 490.

17. Grace Lichtenstein and Laura Dankner, *Musical Gumbo: The Music of New Orleans* (New York: Norton, 1993), p. 220.

18. Quoted in Tisserand, *The Kingdom of Zydeco,* p. 14.

19. Quoted in Govenar, *Meeting the Blues,* p. 155.

20. Chris Strachwitz, booklet for *Zydeco: Volume, The Early Years, 1949–62* (Arhoolie CD 307, 1989), p. 5.

21. Jared Snyder, "Amédé's Recordings," booklet for *Amédé Ardoin: The Roots of Zydeco* (Arhoolie CD 7007, 1995), pp. 12–13.

22. Ibid., p. 13.

23. Ibid.

24. Nicholas R. Spitzer, "Zydeco," *Encyclopedia of Southern Culture,* vol. 3, p. 348.

25. Nelson George, *The Death of Rhythm and Blues* (New York: Plume, 1988), pp. 107–108.

26. Thomas, "From Gumbo to Grammys," p. 146.

27. Moss identifies these two titles as the first songs he learned, and the key to his early popularity among Houston Creoles, in Tisserand, *The Kingdom of Zydeco,* p. 77.

28. Quoted in Minton, "Houston Creoles and Zydeco," p. 503.

29. While numerous scholars have documented the etymology of the word *zydeco,* perhaps the definitive discussion of the issue occurs in Tisserand's opening chapter (entitled "What's in a Name?") in *The Kingdom of Zydeco,* pp. 9–21.

30. This album was released on the label called 77 Records in England. For more on McCormick's role in creating the now-common spelling, see Tisserand, *The Kingdom of Zydeco,* pp. 17–20.

31. Like alternate pronunciations, alternate spellings have persisted over

the years on signs promoting black Creole musical events in South Louisiana and Southeast Texas, including *zodico, zordico, zologo,* and many others; see Spitzer, "Zydeco," p. 347. And for more on a possible West African cognate and the etymology of the word, see Barry Jean Ancelet, "Zydeco/Zarico: Beans, Blues, and Beyond," *Black Music Research Journal* 8 (1988): 33–49.

32. Govenar, *Meeting the Blues,* p. 141.

33. Tisserand, *The Kingdom of Zydeco,* p. 20.

34. This song, originally recorded on 78 RPM disc, is now available on compact disc: Lightning Hopkins, *The Gold Star Sessions, vol. 1* (Arhoolie CD 330, 1990).

35. Chris Strachwitz, interview with author, Jonesboro, Ark., Apr. 16, 1998.

36. Govenar, *Meeting the Blues,* p. 151.

37. This song, originally recorded on 78 RPM disc, is now available on compact disc: *Zydeco: Volume One, The Early Years, 1949–62* (Arhoolie CD 307, 1989).

38. Minton, "Houston Creoles and Zydeco," p. 496.

39. Field recordings of four songs, including the two titles mentioned here, performed by Willie Green at Irene's Café in 1961 are included on the compact disc *Zydeco: Volume One, The Early Years, 1949–62.*

40. Minton, "Houston Creoles and Zydeco," p. 496.

41. Ibid., p. 497.

42. John Minton, "Creole Community and 'Mass' Communication: Houston Zydeco as a Mediated Tradition," *Journal of Folklore Research* 32, no. 1 (1995): 1–19.

43. Quoted in Tisserand, *The Kingdom of Zydeco,* pp. 95, 97.

44. Ibid., p. 497. Minton cites the Savoy reference in "Houston Creoles and Zydeco," pp. 506–507. In an interview with Chenier, Govenar quotes him as saying, "I learned to play in Lake Charles and in Texas, Houston mostly. I never picked up an accordion until 1947," p. 155.

45. Tisserand, *The Kingdom of Zydeco,* pp. 102–103.

46. This interview is documented in the videocassette *Clifton Chenier: The King of Zydeco,* directed by Chris Strachwitz (Arhoolie, ARV 401, 1987).

47. Strachwitz, booklet for *Zydeco,* p. 7.

48. Ibid., p. 10.

49. Quoted in Govenar, *Meeting the Blues,* p. 151.

50. Robert Damora, "Houston Zydeco: From Churches to Clubs," *Living Blues* 116 (Aug., 1994): 44–47.

51. Strachwitz, booklet for *Zydeco,* p. 10.

52. Roger Wood, "Zydeco Hall of Fame Inaugurated," *Living Blues* 142 (Nov.–Dec., 1998): 12.

# Contributors

The late **Lawrence Clayton** was dean of liberal arts at Hardin-Simmons University. His many publications focused largely on the life and literature of the American West—especially on the contemporary cowboy and ranch life—and include *Benjamin Capps and the South Plains: A Literary Relationship, Watkins Reynolds Matthews: A Biography,* and *Contemporary Ranches of Texas.*

**Kenneth W. Davis** is professor emeritus of English at Texas Tech University and a past president of the Texas Folklore Society, the American Studies Association of Texas, and the Texas Southwest Popular Culture Association. He has authored or edited four books, including one with Lawrence Clayton—*Horsing Around: Contemporary Humor.*

**Carolyn F. Griffith** lives on a ranch near Abilene and is adjunct instructor of English at Abilene Christian University. She assisted in editing *Texas Cowboys: Memories of the Early Days* and has presented papers at the Mosaic of Texas Culture and meetings of the Texas Southwest Popular Culture Association and the West Texas Historical Association.

**José Ángel Gutiérrez** is associate professor of political science at the University of Texas at Arlington. One of the principal organizers of the Raza Unida Party, he is founder and former director of the Center for Mexican American Studies and the author of *The Making of a Chicano Militant: Lessons from Crystal.*

**Gary Hartman** is assistant professor of history at Southwest Texas State University. He is also director of the Center for Texas Music History. His research and publishing interests include examining how music reflects the development and interaction of ethnic communities throughout the Southwest.

The late **John Lightfoot** was 2001–2002 president of the Texas Folklore Society. Among his published articles was "Take Me Out to the Ballgame," which appeared in *2001: A Texas Folklore Odyssey.* He retired from the English Department at Brazosport College where he was also public relations director from 1977–92.

**Dave Oliphant** is the coordinator of the freshman seminars program at the University of Texas at Austin and the author of *Texan Jazz* and *The Early Swing Era.* In addition, he has published several collections of his poetry, the most recent being *Memories of Texas Towns & Cities.*

**Joe W. Specht** is director of the Jay-Rollins Library at McMurry University. A former co-host of his own radio show, *Burning Memories: The Texas Tradition,* he has contributed entries to *The Country Music Encyclopedia* and published articles in *Old Time Music* and the *Journal of Texas Music History.*

**Larry Wolz** is professor of music history at Hardin-Simmons University and research curator for the Van der Stucken Collection at the Pioneer Memorial Library in Fredericksburg. He has published articles in a variety of journals and magazines and has contributed entries to the *New Handbook of Texas* and the *Handbook of Texas Music.*

**Roger Wood** teaches in the English Department of Central College, Houston Community College System. He has written features on regional music history for various periodicals, most regularly *Living Blues* and *Houston Press*. A contributor to *The Da Capo Jazz and Blues Lover's Guide to the U.S.* (Third edition), he is also the author of *Down in Houston: Bayou City Blues.*

# Index

Abernethy, Francis E., 139, 175–76
Abrahams, Roger D., 29n.20
Abrego and Picazo, 157
"Act Naturally," 27
Acuna, Manuel, 163
Adams, Leland H. "Freshman," 45
Adams, Stacy, 165
Adolph and the Boys, 188
Adolphus Hotel (Dallas), 52
African Children's Choir, 145n.10
"Ain't Gonna Ring Dem Yellow Woman's
    Doorbell," 105
"Ain't Gonna Study War No More," 106
"Airplane Blues," 113
Alabama-Coushatta, 5, 6
*Alabama-Coushatta Indians, The,* 28
Aladdin Laddies, 76
Aladdin Records, 111, 112
"Alberta," 102
Alcaraz, Luis, 168
Alegres de Teran, Los, 165, 170
Alexander, Dudley, 205
Alexander, Texas, 108, 111
Allen, Mack, 70
Allen, Rex, 25
"Amazing Grace," 106
*American Bandstand,* 170
American Federation of Musicians, 81,
    93n.35
American Record Corporation, 71, 74, 75
American Society of Composers, 86
"Amor," 168
Anacona, 159
*Anahuac,* 146
Ancelet, Barry Jean, 195
Anderson, Marian, 145n.10
Andrade, Concho, 157

"Angola Blues," 104
Angola Prison, 15, 100, 101, 104
Annual Church Music Workshops, 140
*Arawak,* 149
"Ardillitas, Las," 165
Ardoin, Amede, 200, 201, 202
Arhoolie Records, 15, 108, 114, 200, 212
"Arkansas Traveler," 67, 68
Armendariz, Pedro, 168
Armstrong, Louis, 16, 17, 40, 41, 42, 44,
    48, 54, 55, 57, 110, 155
Arnaz, Desi, 159
Arnold, Eddy, 78
Arnspiger, Herman, 76
Arodin, Sidney, 47
Asleep at the Wheel, 26
"At the Clambakek Carnival," 62n.35
"At the Jazz Band Ball," 46
Austin, Moses, 12
Autry, Orvon Gene, 4, 24, 25, 71–73, 75,
    80, 84, 86, 87n.1, 90n.12, 103, 164
"Avalon," 51
"Ay Jalisco no to rajes," 164
Aztec, 146, 148, 149, 170

*B. F. White Sacred Harp, The,* 139
"Baby, Look at You," 49
"Baby, Please Don't Go," 205, 208
Baca Band, 20, 187, 188
"Baca Beat," 187
Baca Orchestra, 187
Baca, Cleo, 187
Baca, Frank, 20, 187
Baca, Joe, 187
Baca, John R., 187, 188
Baca, L. B., 187
Baca-Ripple Orchestra, 187

"Back in the Saddle Again," 72

"Backslider, Fare Thee Well," 103

Bad Boys, 39

Bailey, Cotton, 39

"Baker Shop Blues," 98

Baker, T. Lindsay, 176, 177

"Ball and Chain," 16

Ball, Marcia, 115

"Ballad of Gregorio Cortez, The," 9

"Ballad of Pancho Lopez, The," 165

Band O' Sunshine, 45, 47

"Barca de oro, La (The Golden Barge),"
   163

Barnes, Fae. *See* Jones, Maggie

Basie, Count, 18, 47, 49, 50, 52, 53, 54,
   55, 56, 58, 208

"Basin Street Blues," 48

Bauman, Richard, 29

Baxter, Phil, 61n.31

Beatles, 14, 27

Becerra, Pablo, 157

Bechet, Sidney, 38, 59n.2

Beck, Carl, 127–28, 129, 131, 133,
   134, 135

Beethoven Männerchor, 127, 131,
   133, 134

Beethoven, Ludwig van, 130, 143

"Behold a Host Arrayed in White," 143

Belafonte, Harry, 154

Bellinghausen, Darlene, 144

Bellini, Vincenzo, 130

Beneke, Tex, 18, 57

Berlin, Irving, 144

Bernal, Eloy, 12

Bernal, Paulino, 12

Berry, Chuck, 16, 116

"Besame Mucho," 168

Besserer, William, 59n.6

Biederbecke, Bix, 41, 45, 46, 47, 48,
   61n.29

Big Bopper, 27

"Big Boss Man," 109

*Big Easy, The,* 214n.1

"Black and Evil," 115

"Black Ghost Blues," 116

"Black Rat," 111

"Black Snake Moan," 98

Black, Clint, 26

Blackwood, James, 145n.8

Blackwood Brothers, 141

Blaha, A. J., 186

Blakey, Art, 55

"Blue and Sentimental," 63n.59

"Blue Canadian Rockies," 86

"Blue Devil Blues," 44

"Blue Lou," 62n.35

Blue Moon Chasers, 48

Blue Ridge Playboys, 80

Bluebird Records, 76, 162, 201

Bluebonnet Hotel (San Antonio), 160

"Blues de Crowley, Les (Crowley Blues),"
   201

"Blues de Voyage, Les (Travel Blues)," 201

"Blues in B," 52

"Blues in G," 109

Boatright, Mody C., 29

"Boll Weevil," 104

"Bon Ton Roula," 207

Bonner, M. J., 69, 89n.6

*Boriquen,* 149

"Born to Lose," 81

"Bourgeois Blues," 15, 102

"Bout a Spoonful," 109

Bowman, Euday L., 57

"Boxe cos Polske (God Save Poland)," 176

Boyd, Bill, 77

Bracero program, 11, 163–64

Bray, Lew, 47

Brazos Valley Boys, 26

*Break of Dawn,* 163

"Bring Me Water Silvy," 105

Broadcast Music Incorporated (BMI), 86

"Broke and Hungry," 98

Bronze Peacock Nightclub (Houston), 203

Brooks, Alva, 42

Brooks, Lawson, 42

Brown, Barty, 76

Brown, Charles, 204

Brown, Clarence "Gatemouth," 16, 116

Brown, Derwood, 76

Brown, James, 16

Brown, Willie Milton, 25, 50, 76–77,
   91n.21

Bruner, Cliff, 77, 80

Brunswick Records, 156, 159, 187
Bryant, Clora, 65n.82
"Bubbles in My Beer," 81, 86
Buckwheat Zydeco, 214n.1
"Bud Russell Blues," 114
"Bumble Bee," 110
Byrd, Charlie, 18

"C. C. Rider," 102
Caceres, Emilio, 58
Caceres, Ernie, 58
*Cadena de las Americas* (Chain of the Americas), 164
*Calle Ocho,* 154
Calloway, Cab, 16, 42, 48, 54, 58, 62n.35
Calvert, Robert A., 28
Camacho, Manuel, 159
"Cancion Mexicana," 160
"Can't Yo Heah Me Callin," 69
Capitol Records, 75, 81, 168
*Captain, Captain,* 110
"Captain, Captain," 110
"Caramel Caravan," 58
Cardona, Vicenta. *See* Carr, Vicki
"Careless Love," 101
Carmichael, Hoagy, 61n.31
*Carnaval,* 154
Carr, Vikki, 168
Carter Family, 70
Carter, Anna, 142
Carter, Benny, 48, 58, 62n.35
Carter, Cecile Elkins, 28
Carter, Dad, 142
Carter, Jim, 142
Carter, John, 57
Carter, Rose, 142
Casa Loma Orchestra, 52
Casares, Ernie, 168
"Casey Jones," 109
Cash, Johnny, 101, 105
Casiano, Jesus, 10
Casino Hall (San Antonio), 123
Castro, Fidel, 168
Central State Prison Farm (Sugarland), 99
Chaplin, Charlie, 155
Charles, Ray, 63n.62
Chavez y Lugo, 159

Chenier, Cleveland, 22, 209, 211, 212
Chenier, Clifton, 22, 199, 200, 203, 206, 208, 209–13
Chenoweth, W. B., 68
Cherokee Cowboys, 26
"Cherokee Maiden," 86
Chicho y Checho, 159
Child, Francis James, 100
Choates, Harry, 23
Chopin, Frederic, 134
"Christ the Lord Is Risen Today," 144
Christian, Charlie, 4, 16, 17, 18, 50, 51, 52, 56, 62n.44, 63n.55, 92n.27
Chuck Wagon Gang, 142
"Chucos suaves," 165
Church, Earl, 39
*Ciboney,* 149
*City Lights,* 155
Claassen, Arthur, 131, 134
Clapp Band, 47–48
Clapp, Sunny, 45, 47, 61n.31
Clapton, Eric, 214n.1
Clarke, Kenny, 55
Clay, James, 64n.72
Cliburn, Van, 4
Cmajdalka, Charles, 185
Cobb, Arnett, 18, 53, 54, 55
"Coffee Blues," 115
Coker, Henry, 55
Cole, Nat King, 56
Coleman, Ornette, 4, 18, 57
Collins, Albert, 116
Collins, Sam, 101
Coltrane, John, 54
Columbia Pictures, 86
Columbia Recording Company, 69, 77, 81, 156, 159, 162, 187
Columbus, Christopher, 149, 150
"Come by Here, Lord," 142
"Come Easy, Go Easy Love," 48, 61n.29, 61n.31
Commercial Club Band, 128
Como, Perry, 168
Conjunto Bernal, El, 12, 170
Continental Zydeco Ballroom (Houston), 209
"Contrabando del Paso, El" 157

Cook, Stephen Z., 141
Cooke, Sam, 13, 166
Cooley, Spade, 78, 91n.22
Corley, George, 56
Corley, John, 56, 64n.75
Corley, Wilford, 56
Corri, Henri, 120
"Corrido de Joaquin Murrieta, El" 160
"Corrido de Macario," 157
"Corrine, Corrina," 23
Cortez, Gregorio, 9, 29, 159
"Cotton Fields At Home," 15
"Cotton-Eyed Joe," 20
Country Music Hall of Fame, 66, 67, 70,
    71, 73, 76, 82, 87, 87n.1, 90n.12,
    93n.33, 102
*Cowboy Songs and Other Frontier Bal-
    lads,* 73, 74, 75
*Cowboy Tom's Roundup,* 73
"Cowboy's Christmas Ball, The," 74
Cowen, Frederic, 131
Coy, Gene, 38, 39, 48, 53
"Crawdad Blues," 41
"Crazy Arms," 26
*Creation, The,* 126
Crocker, David, 61n.31
Crosby, Bing, 18, 71, 77, 80, 81, 84, 160
Cuarteto Coculense, 157
Cugat, Javier, 155, 159
Cullum, Anne, 111, 112
*Culture on the Moving Frontier,* 120
Curtis, George William 119
*Czar und Zimmerman,* 123
Czech Catholic Union of Texas, 183
Czech Tamburash Orchestra, 185

Daffan, Ted, 80, 81
Dalhart, Vernon, 24, 69–71, 87n.1
"Dallas and Fort Worth Blues," 104
Dallas Band, 42
Dallas Conservatory of Music, 69
Dallas Orchestra of Alphones Trent, 50
Dallas Symphony Orchestra, 132
Damora, Robert, 213
Dameron, Tad, 54
"Daniel's Blues," 44, 47
"Danse macabre," 131
Davis, Jimmie, 80

Davis, Miles, 18, 54, 55
Davis, Wild Bill, 55
"De Kalb Blues," 101
De la Rosa, Tony, 12, 169, 170
De Leon, Arnoldo, 28
"Death Bells," 113
"Death of Floyd Collins, The," 70
Decca Records, 74, 75, 76, 80, 81, 82, 84,
    85, 156, 162
Del Rio, Dolores, 168
Denver, John, 27
"Desgraciadito," 161
*Deutschtum,* 120
Dexter, Al, 79
Diamonds, The, 166
Diaz, Raul, 165
Diddley, Bo, 166
Dobie, J. Frank, 73
"Doggin' Around," 63n.59
Dominguez, Rosa, 158
Donahue, Tom, 46
Donatto, L. C., 208
Donegan, Lonnie, 105
Donnenos, Los, 170
"Don't Talk to Me About Men," 85
Dorham, Kenny, 43, 55–56
Dorsey Band, 168
Dorsey, Jimmy, 18
Dorsey, Tommy, 168
Douglas, Clifford "Boots," 42, 56
"Down in the Valley to Pray," 103
"Down on Biscayne Bay," 47
"Down Where the Bluebonnets Grow,"
    61n.31
"Dreamland Blues, Part 1 and 2," 53
"Driftin Blues," 204
Drozda, Josef, 185
Drust, Greg, 116
Dueto Acosta, 157
Duncan, Tommy, 77
Dunn, Bob, 50, 51, 76, 80
"Dupnik," 181
Dural, Stanley. *See* Buckwheat Zydeco
Duran, Franciscan Narciso, 151
Durham, Allen, 41
Durham, Eddie, 18, 41, 44, 50, 51, 52, 56,
    62n.45, 63n.55, 92n.27
"Dusty Skies," 86

Dvorak, Antonin, 185, 187
Dylan, Bob, 14

"Easy Rider Blues," 111
Eckstine, Billy, 49, 55
Edison Recording Company, 69, 70
Edison, Thomas Alva, 155
Eisenhower, Dwight, 167
Eldorado Ballroom (Houston), 54, 203
Electric Theatre (Pecos), 128
"Elephant Wobble," 41
"Ella Speed," 101, 109
Ellet, Dick, 100
Ellington, Duke, 40, 47, 52, 58
Ellis, Herb, 18
Ely, Joe, 98
"End O'Main," 39
"Entertainer, The," 17
Ervin, Booker, 58, 65n.81
"European Blues," 113
Evans, Dale, 25
Evans, Gil, 49
Evans, Herschel, 41, 52, 53, 54, 56, 63n.59
Everett, Dianna, 28

Falcon Records, 12, 164
Familia, La. *See* Hernandez, Little Joe
Farfan, Narciso, 159
Farr, Hugh, 87n.1, 90n.12
Farr, Karl, 87n.1, 90n.12
"Fast Life Woman," 112
*Faust,* 122
Felder, Wilton, 55
Felix, Maria, 168
Fender, Freddy, 30n.26, 165
*Festhalle,* 124
Fifth Sunday Singing Conventions, 141
Finney, Edward, 74, 75
Fire Hall Five, 59n.6
Fitzgerald, Ella, 18
Five Pennies, 41
Flaco, El, 10
*Flamenco,* 150
Floyd, Troy, 53, 81, 82
"Flying Home Number 2," 54, 64n.69
"Flying Home," 54
*Folk Music in the United States,* 175

Fontenot, Canray, 199
"For All the Saints," 143
Ford, Jimmy, 54
Fox News Service, 68
Fox, Oscar J., 73
*Fra Diavalo,* 122
Franco, Francisco, 168
Franer, James, 198
"Frankie and Albert," 101, 109, 110
"Frankie and Johnnie," 101
"Frankie's Man, Johnny," 101
"Freddie," 108, 109
*Freischütz, Der,* 123
Friederici, Marie, 122
Frizzell, Lefty, 26, 87, 87n.1
Frohsinn Männerchor, 132
"Funeral March," 134

Gabbenelli, John, 211
Gallien, Clarence, 197, 212, 213
*Gang's All Here, The,* 159
Garcia, Adelina, 163
Garcia, Jose, 157
Gardner, Fred, 44–48
Gardner, Jack, 53
Gardner, John, 47
Gardner, Steve, 45, 59n.6
Garland, Red, 54
Garlow, Clarence "Bon Ton," 206, 207
Garrido, Pablo, 39
Gaspard, Octave, 42
George R. Smith College, 135
George, Nelson, 203
German Casino Club of San Antonio, 123
*Gesangverein Germania,* 124
*Gesangvereine,* 120, 123, 127, 132
"Get Up in the Morning," 101
Ghost Dance, 5
Gibbona, Robert, 40
Gillespie, Dizzy, 49, 55, 58, 159
Gilliland, Henry, 67
"Git Along Little Dogies," 75
"Git on Board," 105
"Give Me Central 209," 115
"Give the World a Smile Each Day," 142
Gjuranovic, Mato, 185
Glaser, Joe, 44
Glenn, Tyree, 58

Glind, William, 42
Glinn, Lillian, 42, 61n.18
*Glory and Praise,* 144
*Go Down Old Hannah,* 106
"Go Down Old Hannah," 107
"God Bless America," 144
"Going Away Blues," 42
"Going Home Blues," 112
"Going Back to Georgia," 111
"Going Down Slow," 108
Gold Chain Bohemians, 188
Gold Chain Flour, 82
Gold Star Records, 112, 113, 206, 212
Gomez, Johnny, 58
"Gone With What Draft," 51
Gonzalez, Pedro J., 161, 162, 163
"Goodbye Old Paint," 74
Goodman, Benny, 11, 17, 40, 49, 52, 53, 56, 58, 208
"Goodnight Irene," 15, 100, 101, 107
Govenar, Alan, 197, 207, 210
"Governor O. K. Allen," 101
"Governor Pat Neff," 102
*Graceland,* 214n.1
Grand German Opera Troupe, 122
Grau, Henry, 122
Grauman Chinese Theatre (Los Angeles), 168
Grauman, Sid, 168
"Green Corn," 102, 106
*Green Grow the Lilacs,* 73
"Green Grow the Lilacs," 173n.17
Green, Willie, 208, 209
Greene, Victor, 183, 184, 187
Greenwall, Henry, 122
Grieg, Edvard, 143
Griffin, Reverend "Sin Killer," 100
Grout, Donald J., 171
"Growling Baby Blues, The," 98
Guadalupe Theatre (San Antonio), 168
Guerrero, Lalo, 160, 165, 168, 169
Guillory, Wilbert, 210
Gulf Oil Refinery, 209, 211
Guralnick, Peter, 84
Guthrie, Woody, 15, 103, 104, 107
*Gwine Dig a Hole to Put the Devil In,* 102
"Gwine Dig a Hole to Put the Devil In," 106

*H.M.S. Pinafore and Madame Butterfly,* 69
"Had a Gal Named Sal," 116
Haggard, Merle, 26, 27
Hahn, Carl, 131
Haiduk, Charlie, 177
Haley, Bill, 115
"Hallelujah Chorus," 131
Hampton, Lionel, 54
Hancock, Logan, 53
Handel, George Friedrich, 131
Handy, John, 58, 65n.81
Handy, W. C., 155
Hann, Al, 61n.31
Happy Black Aces, 38, 39
Hardee, John, 61n.19
Hardee, Stanley, 44, 61n.19
"Haricots, Les," 22
"Harlem Renaissance," 17
Harlem Square Club (Houston), 54
*Harmoniemusik,* 127
Harvard University, 100
Haverly's United American European Minstrels, 101
Hawkins, Coleman, 40
Hayden, Franz Joseph, 130
Hayden, Russell, 86
Haywood, Cedric, 54
"He Arose," 143
"He Knew All the Answers," 85
"Headin' Down the Wrong Highway," 81
*Hee Haw,* 102
Heerbruger, Emil, 121
"He'll Have to Go," 26
Henderson, Fletcher, 48
Hendrix, Jimi, 16
Henley, Don, 4, 27
"Henny Penny Blues," 114
Herald Records, 115
Herman, Woody, 49
Hermann Memorial Auditorium (Houston), 185
Hernandez, Little Joe, 30n.31, 170
Hernandez, Luis, 157
Henderson, Fletcher, 62n.35
Hermanos Banuelos, Los, 159
Hermanos Eliceiri, Los, 159
Hermanos Padilla, Las, 163

Hermanos Sanchez y Linares, Los, 160
Hertzberg, Eli, Mrs., 131
Hill, Teddy, 51
"Hindenburg Disaster, The," 105
Hines, Earl, 42, 48, 49
Hines, Frankie, 52
*History of Music,* 171
*History of Texas, The,* 28
*History of Western Music, A,* 171
"Hittin' the Bottle," 50, 62n.45
Hofner, Adolph, 20, 77
Hogan, G. T., 55
Hokum Kings, 45
Holder, Terrence, 53
Holly, Buddy, 4, 27
"Holy Ghosts," 103
"Holy, Holy, Holy," 144
"Honey Child," 61n.31
"Honky-Tonk Blues," 79
Hook, Jonathan B., 28
Hooper, Stix, 55
Hopkins, Sam "Lightning," 16, 96, 98, 99,
    107, 108, 111–16, 206, 207
*Hora del Soldado, La* (Hour of the Sol-
    dier), 164
Horn Palace (San Antonio), 39
"Hot Rock," 54
Hotel Tyler Orchestra, 43–44
"House of the Rising Sun," 15
"Howard Hughes," 103
Howell Brother's Moonshine Orchestra,
    45, 46, 59n.6
Howell, Bill, 46
Howell, F. N. "Tommy," 45, 46
Howell, Hilton, 46
Howell, Jay, 46
Howell, Lee, 44, 46, 47, 61n.31
Howell, Thomas Alva, Jr., 44–48, 59n.6
Howell, Thomas Alva, Sr., 45
Hudson, Estelle, 183, 184, 185
"Huerfano, El," 157
Huerta, Baldeman "The Bebop Kid." *See*
    Fender, Freddy
Hunt, Prince Albert, 69
Hurley, Clyde, 57
Hutchenrider, Clarence, 52, 53
Hutchingson, Bob, 47, 48

"I Ain't Bothered a Bit," 104
"I Ain't Got Nobody," 50
"I Asked the Bossman," 116
"I Got Stripes," 105
"I Gotta Have My Baby Back," 81
"I Let a Song Go Out of My Heart," 52
"I Love You So Much, It Hurts," 81
"I Once Was a Gambler," 114
"I Want to Do Something for You," 110
"I Would If I Could," 114
Ideal Records, 11, 12
"If It Wasn't for Dicky," 102
"If You've Got the Money, I've Got the
    Time," 26
"I'll Fly Away," 142, 143
"I'll Keep on Loving You," 80
"I'm a Ding Dong Daddy from Dumas,"
    61n.31
"I'm Coming Virginia," 46
Immigration and Naturalization Service
    (INS), 163
Imperial Records, 162, 165
"In the Garden," 142
"In the Mood," 57
"In the Pines," 15
"In the Sweet By and By," 142
Independencia Theater (Monterrey), 161
Infante, Pedro, 164, 168
International Theatre (San Antonio), 168
Irene's Café (Houston), 208, 209
Irvis, Charlie, 58
Isabela, 149, 150
"It Makes No Difference Now," 80
*It's Time For "T": The Story of Jack Tea-
    garden,* 40
Ives, Burl, 15, 107

"Jack O Diamonds," 74
Jackson, George Pullen, 139
Jackson, Michael, 170
Jackson, Milt, 55
Jacquet, Illinois, 53, 54
Jacquet, Russell, 54, 55
"Jäger Abschied, Der," 124
James, Harry, 52, 53, 56
James, Jesse, 114
Jazz Bandits, 39

Jazz Crusaders, 55
*Jazz in Texas,* 47
Jazz Messengers, 55
Jazz Prophets, 56
Jefferson, Blind Lemon, 14, 15, 16, 37, 52, 96–99, 101, 104, 108, 109, 111, 116
"Jelly Jelly," 48
Jennings, Waylon, 87, 87n.1
Jerome, Jerry, 52
"Jeszcze Polska nie zginea (Poland is Yet Alive)," 176
Jimenez, Flaco, 4, 30n.26
Jimenez, Jose Alfredo, 164
Jimenez, Santiago, Jr., 30n.26
Jimenez, Santiago, Sr., 10
Jimeunez, Jose Alfredo, 168
Jimmie's Joys, 59n.6
"Jimtown Blues," 59n.4
"Jitney Man, The," 55, 64n.71
Jocque, Beau, 213
"John Hardy," 107
"John Henry," 106
Johnson Brothers, 49
Johnson, Budd, 41, 43, 48, 49, 50, 56
Johnson, Bunk, 38, 53, 59n.2
Johnson, Charley, 209
Johnson, Gus, 56
Johnson, Jack, 102
Johnson, Keg, 41, 48, 56, 62n.35
Johnson, Pete, 49
Johnson, Robert, 99, 194
Johnson's Lounge (Houston), 203, 209
"Jole Blon," 23, 208
Jones, George, 26, 87, 87n.1
Jones, Grandpa, 102
Jones, Jack, 61n.31
Jones, Maggie, 38
Jones, Spike, 85
Jones-Smith, Inc., 53
Joplin, Florence, 135
Joplin, Giles, 135
Joplin, Janis, 4, 16, 27
Joplin, Scott, 4, 17, 37, 134–35
Jordan Company, 46
"Joyful, Joyful, We Adore Thee," 143
"Juan Soldado," 157
*Jubel,* 130

Jumano, 5
"Jumpin' at the Woodside," 63n.59
*Jure,* 199
"Just As I Am," 144
"Just Over in the Glory Land," 142

Kapp, Dave, 84
Karankawa, 5
"Katie Mae," 112, 113, 115
*Katolicka Jeanota Texaska, The,* 183
*Kazdy Check de Musikant* (Every Czech is a Musician), 183
KCOR (San Antonio), 167
Keepnews, Orrin, 97
Kelly, Peck, 39
Kempenski, Fred, 178
Kenton, Stan, 168
Kessel, Barney, 18
KGKO (Fort Worth), 82
Kickapoo, 5, 6
"Kidney Stew Blues," 54
King, Freddie, 116
Kiowa, 5
*Kiowas, The,* 28
Kittredge, George Lyman, 100
KMPC (Los Angeles), 162
"Knocking Down Windows," 109
Kolenda, 181
*Kommers,* 127
Koster, Rick, 30, 95, 111
KPRC (Houston), 187
Kreissig, Hans, 132
Krenek, Ignac, 187
KRLD (Dallas), 68
*Krusha Amerika: A Study of Texas Czechs,* 184
KTAT (Fort Worth), 76
KVOO (Tulsa), 77

La Vere, David, 28
La Vere, Stephen, 40
Langford, Thomas A., 139
Lara, Augustin, 168
Larkin, Milt, 53, 54, 55
Latinaires. *See* Hernandez, Little Joe
Laubin, Gladys, 28
Laubin, Reginald, 28

"Laughin' Louie," 48

"Lavaplatos, El (The Dishwasher)," 159

Laws, Hubert, 55

Lead Belly, 4, 14, 15, 37, 96, 99–109, 115, 116

Ledbetter, Huddie. *See* Lead Belly

Lee, Clois "Cub," 41

Lee, George, 48

*Let It Shine on Me,* 102

"Let It Shine on Me," 103

Lewis, Texas Jim, 84

"Liberian Suite," 58

*Life Among the Texas Indians: The W.P.A. Narratives,* 28

"Life's Evening Sun," 142

"Light Cavalry Overture," 130

Light Crust Doughboys, 25, 76, 77

"Lightning Don't Feel Well," 115

Linares, Fernando, 161

Lipscomb, Mance, 15, 96, 98, 107–11, 112, 116

"Little Darling," 166

Little Joe and the Latinaires. *See* Hernandez, Little Joe

Llamas, Lucio, 161

"Lockstep Blues," 99

Lomax, Alan, 15, 32n.40, 100, 102, 103

Lomax, John, 15, 32n.40, 73, 74, 75, 100, 104, 106, 107

Lone Star Cowboys, 84

Lone Star Hall, 122

"Lone Star Trail," 84

"Lonesome Home," 113

"Lonesome House Blues," 98

Long, Hubert, 87n.1

Long, Jimmy, 71

Longoria, Valerio, 12, 170

Lopez, Isidro, 11, 12, 169

"Loretta Blues," 112

Lornell, Kip, 100, 101, 102, 103, 104

Lou, Eddie, 43–44

Lou, Sugar, 43–44

Louis, Joe, 113

"Love Like a Fire Hydrant," 114

"Loveless Love," 44

Lozano, Ignacio, Sr., 156

*Lucayanos,* 149

Lummis, Charles F., 156

Lunceford, Jimmie, 18, 50, 51 54

Luther, Martin, 143

McAuliffe, Leon, 50, 51, 77, 62n.46

McClendon, Doris, 209

McCormick, Robert Burton "Mack," 96, 107, 108, 109, 116, 205, 206, 212

McDowell, John Holmes, 29

McGee, Dennis, 201

McGhee, Brownie, 103, 107

McGuire, James, 179

Machann, Clinton, 183, 184, 185

Machito, 159

McKinley, Ray, 57

McKinney, B. B., 143

McLean, Duncan, 69

McShann, Jay, 56

Macy's Records, 207

Madero, Francisco, 155

Madrugadores, Los, 159, 161, 162

*Magic Flute, The,* 122

"Magic in the Moonlight," 168

Magon, Ricardo Flores, 155

Mahaffey, J. Q., 99

"Mahogany Hall Stomp," 48

"Maid Freed From the Gallows," 102

"Mal Hombre (Bad Man)," 10, 161

Malone, Bill, 68

Maloney, Jimmy, 59n.6

*Männergesangverein,* 124

"Maple Leaf Rag," 17, 37

*Mardi Gras,* 154

Maresh, Henry, 183, 184, 185

Maria and Margarita, 163

Maria, Panna, 175

Mariachi Vargas de Tecatitlan, 168

Marin, Alfredo, 158

Marin, R. J., 39

Marlbrough, Frank, 210

Marschner, Adolf, 124

Marshall, Brian, 176–78, 181

Marshall, Ed, 177

*Martha,* 122, 123

Martin, Bill, 109

Martin, Fatty, 39, 59n.4

Martinez, Lupe, 157

Martinez, Narciso, 10, 169, 170
*Mas Canciones,* 165
*Matachines, Los,* 152
"Matchbox Blues," 14, 97, 98, 101
Mayan, 148, 170
Mayhall, Mildred P., 28
Maynard, Ken, 24, 25
Mazewski, Adam, 181, 182
Meiners, Carolyn, 184, 186
*Melody Ranch,* 71
Memphis Minnie, 110
Mendelssohn, Felix, 131
Mendl, James, 184, 185
Mendoza Sisters, The, 170
Mendoza, Beatriz, 161
Mendoza, Francisca, 161
Mendoza, Francisco, 161
Mendoza, Leonor, 161
Mendoza, Lydia, 4, 10, 160–61, 162, 169, 170
Mendoza, Teofila, 161
Menger, Simon, 124
"Mercy," 113
Messengers, The, 55
*Messiah,* 131
"Mexicali Rose," 72
"Midnight Special, The," 15, 100, 101, 115
"Mighty Fortress, A" 143
Miller, Glenn, 11, 18, 57, 58, 168
Miller, Hugh M., 171
Miller, Roger, 26
Miller, Sodarisa, 101
Millet, Fred, 42
Million Dollar Theatre (Los Angeles), 168
Mills Merry Makers, 41
Mingus, Charles, 55, 58, 65n.81
"Minifalda de Reynalda, La," 165
Minton, John, 193, 197, 208, 209
Minton's Playhouse (New York), 51
"Miss Molly," 86
Mitchell, Alfonse Lonnie, 208–209
Mitchell's Lounge (Houston), 209
Moffett, Charles, 57
"Mojo Hand," 115, 116
*Mojo Hand: The Lighting Hopkins Anthology,* 115
"Momma Did You Bring Any Silver," 102

Monk, Thelonious, 56, 58, 63n.55
Montgomery, Marvin "Smokey," 25
"Mood Indigo," 47
Moonshine Orchestra, 45, 46, 59n.6
Moore, Alex "Whistlin," 16
Moore, Bill, 108, 111
Moore, Oscar, 56
Moore, Tom, 107, 108, 112
Moors, 149
Morroguin, Armando, 11
Morthland, John, 75
Morton, Ferdinand "Jelly Roll," 17, 38, 54, 59n.2, 64n.65
"Mosquito Moan," 99
Moss, Anderson, 197, 204, 208
Moten, Bennie, 41, 44, 49, 50
"Moten's Swing," 44
*Mozarabic,* 150
Mozart, Wolfgang Amadeus, 131
"Mr. Hitler," 103, 104
Mraz, Bill, 187
Muller, Professor, 130
Mullican, Moon, 80
Mulroy, Kevin, 28
*"Mundo Artistico and Social,"* 156
Murrieta, Joaquin, 160
Musical Brownies, 50, 76, 77
Muszynski, Fruman, 178
Muszynski, John, 178
Muszynski, Leonard, 178
"My Blue Ridge Mountain Home," 70
"My God and I," 144
Myers, Augie, 30n.26

Nanton, Sam "Tricky," 58
"Narodil se Kristus Pan," 185
National Association of Broadcasters, 86
National Endowment for the Arts, 165
National Heritage Award, 165
National Zydeco Society, 214
Navarro, Fats, 55
Naylor, Ken, 61n.31
Neff, Pat, 100, 102
Negrete, Jorge, 164
Nelson, Romeo, 97
Nelson, Willie, 4, 26, 81, 82, 83, 87, 87n.1
Nettl, Bruno, 175, 179, 181

Nevarez, E., 159
New Orleans Jazz and Heritage Festival, 193
New Orleans Theater Orchestra, 130
"New San Antonio Rose," 77, 80
"New Vine Street Blues," 62n.45
Newman, David "Fathead," 18, 64n.72
Newman, Paul, 17
Newman, Roy, 77
Nichols, Red, 40, 41
"No Good Rider," 103
"No Mail Blues," 114
"No Trumps," 44, 45, 46
"No Way, Jose," 165
*Nobody Knows the Trouble I've Seen,* 105
"Nobody Knows the Trouble I've Seen," 106
Nooner, Ray, 61n.31
*Norma,* 130
North American Regional Broadcasting Agreement (NARBA), 166
"Nubes, Las (The Clouds)," 170
"Nunca jamas," 160

"O Lord I Am Not Worthy," 144
Oberstein, Eli, 202
Obregon, Manuel, 155
"Ode to Joy," 143
"Oh, Susannah," 19
OKeh Phonograph Corporation, 160, 161
OKeh Records, 77, 187
Oklahoma Blue Devils Band, 43, 44, 49
Okonski, Steven, 176, 177, 181
"Old Joe Clark," 102
Old Phillips Frairs, 53
"Old Rattler," 102
*Old Santa Fe,* 25
"Old Woman Blues," 114
Oliver, Joe "King," 38, 41, 42, 54
Olmec, 147, 148, 170
"On Jordan's Stormy Banks I Stand," 143
*Onda, La,* (La Onda Chicano), 12, 30n.31, 170
"One Dollar Bill Won't Buy You No Shoes," 106
"One Thin Dime," 109
"Onward Christian Soldiers," 100, 143

"Operation Wetback," 167
Orbison, Roy, 4, 27
Original Dixieland Jazz Band (ODJB), 38
Osorio, Jesus, 159
Otis, Johnny, 166
Otten, Professor, 123
Our Mother of Mercy Catholic Church (Houston), 213
"Our Native Spirit," 28
"Outshine the Sun," 106
"Overture to *Die Zauberflöte,*" 131
"Overture to *Egmont,*" 130
"Overture to *Fidelio,*" 131
"Overture to *Tannhäuser,*" 131
Owens, Alvis Edgar, Jr., "Buck," 26–27, 87n.1
Ozuna, Sunny, 170

"Pachuco Boogie," 165
Pachuco Boogie Boys, 165
Page, Oran "Hot Lips," 43, 44, 49, 50
Page, Walter, 56
Panchos, Los, 160
"Papa's Gone," 44
Paramount Records, 14, 97
Paredes, Americo, 29
Parker, Charlie "Bird," 18, 40, 48, 49, 50, 55, 56, 58, 62n.42
Parker, John "Knocky," 25
"Paseo Street (Strut)," 49
Pass, Joe, 18
*Pastores, Los,* 152
Patek Band, 20, 188
Patisca, Claude V., 171
Pavlas, Julius, 188
Paycheck, Johnny, 26
Pecos Commercial Club Band, 128
Peeples, Stephen K., 116
Peer, Ralph, 70
Peña, Manuel, 28, 29, 30, 169
"Penitentiary Blues," 98
"Pepiky (Little Joe)," 186
Perez, Fernal, 150
Perkins, Carl, 14
Peterson, Richard, 68
Pharr, Blondy, 59n.6
Pharr's Fire Hall Five, 59n.6

Pietrowski, Alec, 178
Pietrowski, George, 178
Pinson, Bob, 78
"Pistol Packin' Mama," 79
Pittman, Portia, 48
"Play With Your Poodle," 115
"Please Release Me," 26
Polcos Revolt, 153, 169
"Police Station Blues," 110
Polish Hall (Houston), 182
Polish National Alliance, 182
*Polish Texans, The,* 179
"Polish Wedding Polka," 180
Polka Ambassadors, 184
Polka Kings of Texas, 187
Pollack, Ben, 39, 40, 41, 53
Porterfield, Nolan, 106
Powell, Bud, 55
Prado, Perez, 168
Prazka Prout, 21
*Preciosa,* 123
*Prensa, La,* 160
Presley, Elvis, 14, 16, 98, 166
"Pretty Baby," 52
Price, Ray, 26, 87, 87n.1
"Prison Cell Blues," 98
"Prisoner's Song, The," 70
Protola, Gaspar de, 151
Pugh, Ronnie, 82

Quaker Avenue Church of Christ (Lub-
     bock), 139
*Quartier Francias, Le,* 195
"Queen Mary," 102
Quevas, Cresencio, 159
Quinn, Bill, 112, 113, 206
Quintanilla, Selena, 4

Rabago, Andres. *See* Russell, Andy
"Rabbit Foot Blues," 97
"Race Is On, The," 26
Raley, Leo, 80
Ramey, Gene, 43, 49, 56
Ramirez, Arnaldo, 164
Ramsey, Doug, 55
"Rancho Grande," 156
Rausch, Leon, 94n.40

Real Jazz Orchestra, 38
"Red Cross Store," 106
Red Hot Sizzling Band, 209
Redford, Robert, 17
Redman, Dewey, 57
Reed, Jimmy, 109
Reeves, Jim, 26, 87, 87n.1
Reinhardt, Django, 51
Republic Pictures, 71, 75
Revard, Jimmie, 77
Reyes, Lucha, 160
Reyna, Jose R., 29
Reyna, Juan, 159, 160
Reynolds, John, 101
Reynolds, William J., 140
Richardson, J. P. *See* Big Bopper
*Ride Tenderfoot Ride,* 84, 86
Rideau, Step, 213
Ritter, Dorothy Fay, 86
Ritter, Woodward Maurice "Tex," 25, 71,
     73–75, 77, 86, 87n.1, 90n.12
Robertson, Alexander Campbell "Eck,"
     67–69
Roca, Pedro, 157
Rock and Roll Hall of Fame, 79
"Rock Around the Clock," 115
"Rock Island Line," 105
Rodgers, Carrie, 82
Rodgers, Jimmie, 25, 70, 71, 73, 82, 103,
     106, 107, 110
Rodgers, Robert W., 134, 135
Rodriguez, Jose, 10
Rogers, Harrison, 151
Rogers, Kenny, 4
Rogers, Roy, 75, 164
Ronstadt, Linda, 165
"Roosevelt Song, The," 103
Roosevelt, Teddy, 128, 154
Rosales y Robinson, 157
*Rose Maiden, The,* 131
Rosetti, Anna, 123
Ross, Doc, 39
Rossini, Gioacchino, 130, 131
Rounder Records, 100, 101, 102, 106
*Routes of Rhythm,* 154
Royal Aces, 56
Royal Orchestra, The, 39

Royal Room (Hollywood), 41
Rudy and the Reno Bops, 169–70
Rushing, Jane Gilmore, 140
Rushing, Jimmy, 47
Russell, Andy, 168–69
Russell, Bud, 115
Russell, Ross, 49
Russell, Tony, 77
Rust, Brian, 42, 44, 47
Ruthania, 186
"Rye Whiskey," 74, 75
Ryman Auditorium (Nashville), 79

Sacred Harp, 138, 140, 141, 142, 144
*Sacred Harp, The,* 138
Sahm, Doug, 27, 30n.26
"Sail on Little Girl," 105
Saint Edward's University, 157
Saint Francis of Assisi (Houston), 213
Saint John's Catholic Church (Fay-
    etteville), 185
Saint Joseph's Society (Bremond), 182
Saint-Saens, Camille, 131
"Sallie Gooden," 67, 68
"Sam Hall," 75
Sample, Joe, 55
San Antonio Opera Club, 123
San Antonio Philharmonic, 132
"San Antonio Rose." *See* "New San An-
    tonio Rose"
San Antonio Symphony Orchestra, 131,
    132
San Gabriel Mission (Los Angeles), 151
Sanchez, Jesus, 161
Sanchez, Victor, 161
Sängerbund, 19, 125
*Sängerfest,* 124, 125, 126, 127, 129,
    130, 131
Santa Anna, Antonio Lopez de, 153
"Santa Fe Blues," 110
Satherley, Art, 71, 72, 74–75
Savoy, Ann Allen, 210
Savoy, Ashton, 204–205
Schilz, Thomas F., 28
Schnell, Helen Valcik, 185
Schnell, Steven, 185
Schuller, Gunther, 42, 48, 49, 51, 52

Scottish Rite Temple (Houston), 185
Scottsboro Boys, 103
"Scottsboro Boys, The," 103
"Se acabo el WPA (The WPA is Over)," 159
*Seasonal Missalette: Worship Resource,*
    144
"See That My Grave Is Kept Clean," 14, 97
Seeger, Pete, 104, 107
Seekatz, Chester, 45
Sellers, J. R., 69
Seminole, 5
"Send My Child Home to Me," 115
"Seven Beers with the Wrong Man," 84
"Seventh Avenue Express," 53
"Shake It Down, 61n.18
"Shake, Shake Momma," 109
Shaw State Prison Farm (De Kalb), 99
Shaw, Artie, 44
"Shining Moon," 113
"Shoo Fly," 106
"Short Haired Woman," 112
"Shorty George," 105
Showler, Joe, 40, 41
"Shreveport Jail," 104
*Siboney,* 149
Sifuentes, Leonardo, 157
Signorelli, Frank, 46
"Silver City," 110
Silver, Horace, 55
Silver Slipper (Houston), 198
"Silver Spurs (On the Golden Stairs)," 86
Simon, Bill, 51
Simon, Paul, 214n.1
Sinatra, Frank, 83, 107, 168
*Singin' Texas,* 139
"Singin' The Blues," 46
"Six Pack to Go, A," 26
Skrabanek, Robert, 184, 186, 188
Slaughter, Marion Try, II. *See* Dalhart,
    Vernon
"Slavery Time," 114
Slavic Benevolent Order of the State of
    Texas (SPJST), 183, 186
"Slippin' Around," 26, 81, 83
*Slovanska Podporujici Statu Texas, The,*
    183
Smalls' Paradise (New York), 44

Smetana, Bedrich, 185
Smith, Ben, 48
Smith, Thunder, 111
Smith, Alena Collins, 134
Smith, Carl "Tatti," 52, 53, 63n.57
Smith, Floyd, 92n.27
Smith, Henry "Buster," 18, 43, 49, 50
Smith, Jeremiah, 151
Smith, Kate, 144
Smith, Robert W. *See* Wolfman Jack
Smithsonian Institution's National Museum of American History, 100
Snyder, Jared, 202
"So Different Blues," 110
*Sol de Texas, El,* 167
"Soldier's Last Letter," 83
Solis, Javier, 160
"Solo Flight," 52
"Some of These Days," 42
"Sometimes I'm Happy," 49
*Song of the Gringo,* 74, 75
*Songs of the Saddle,* 24
Sons of the Pioneers, 87n.1, 90n.12
Soul Stirrers, 13
Sousa, John Philip, 57
"South of the Border," 72
Southern Pacific Railroad, 197
Southwest Museum (Los Angeles), 156
Southwest Trumpeters, 39
Southwestern Baptist Theological Seminary's School of Music, 140, 141
*Spanish Songs of Old California,* 156
Speciality Records, 212
Spell, Lota, 183
Spivey, Victoria, 38
Sprague, Carl T., 24, 90n.12
"Squabblin," 44
"St. Louis Blues," 108
*Stabat Mater,* 130
Stafford, Will, 99
Stamps-Baxter Music and Printing Company, 141, 142, 143
Stansfield, W. C., 134
"Star Dust," 52
Starrett, Charles, 83
"Steel Guitar Rag," 51
Stevenson, Robert, 29

"Still ruht dein Herz," 134
Stills, Stephen, 4
*Sting, The,* 17
"Stormy Monday," 204
*Story of Sacred Harp, The,* 139
Strachwitz, Chris, 107, 108, 109, 110, 111, 112, 113, 114, 200, 206, 211–12, 213
Strait, George, 26, 87
Strauss, Johann, Jr., 127
Stricklin, Al, 77, 93n.35
Studewood Hall (Houston), 185
Stuart, Marty, 93n.36
Suarez, Sara, 167
"Sugar Babe (It's All Over Now)," 108
"Sugar Moon," 86
Suppe, Franz von, 130
"Sweet Home Chicago," 194
"Swing Low Sweet Chariot," 106
"Swing to Bop," 52, 63n.55
"Syn Bozi se nam narodil," 185

"T. B. Blues," 106
*T de Monterrey, La,* 157
*Tainos,* 149
"Take a Whiff on Me," 101
"Take Up Thy Cross and Follow Me," 143
"Taking Off," 50
"Talk to Me," 170
Tamburash Orchestra, 185
"Tampa Shout," 42
*Tancredi,* 130
Tate, Buddy, 53, 54
Teagarden, Charlie, 40, 41
Teagarden, Helen "Mama," 41
Teagarden, Jack "Big T," 18, 39–41, 56, 58
Teagarden, Norma, 41
"Teddy Bear Blues," 14
"Teddy Bear," 14, 98
Teotihuacana, 148
Terry, Sonny, 103, 107
Teutonia Singing Association, 123
*Texas & Tennessee Territory Bands,* 47, 48
*Texas Blues,* 114
Texas Christian University, 57
Texas Collegians Varsity Peacocks, 59n.6
Texas Hotel (San Antonio), 201
Texas Medley Quintet, 17

*Texas Music,* 95
Texas Playboys, 26, 50, 77, 78, 79
Texas Quality Network, 188
Texas Rangers, 9, 159
*Texas Songster,* 107, 108
Texas Southern University, 55
Texas Tornados, 30n.26
Texas Troubadours, 83, 84, 86
Texas University Troubadours, 45, 47, 59n.6
Texas Wanderers, 80
"That Old Time Religion," 106
"That Silver Haired Daddy of Mine," 71
"That's a Plenty," 40
"That's the Way Love Goes," 26
"There'll Be Some Changes Made," 44
"They Call It Stormy Monday," 16
"They Will Know We Are Christians by Our Love," 144
Thieleman, Louise, 120, 121
"Thin Man, The," 55
"This Cold War with You," 81
Thomas, George W., 54
Thomas, Hersal, 37, 54
Thomas, Jay "Bird," 47, 59n.6
Thomas, Lorenzo, 192
Thompson, Hank, 26, 87, 87n.1
Thompson, Henry, 44
Thornton, Willie Mae "Big Mama," 4, 16
"Tight Like That," 104, 106
Tigua, 5, 6
Tillman, Floyd, 26, 80–82, 87n.1
"Tim Moore's Farm," 112
"Time Out," 50, 62n.45
Tin Pan Alley, 72, 78, 79
Tisserand, Michael, 194, 196, 206, 210
*Titanic, The,* 104
Tobin, Jack, 59n.6
Toltec, 148, 170
"Tom Moore's Farm," 111, 112
"Topsy," 63n.55
Tosches, Nick, 79, 81
Tosti, Don, 165–66,
"Toy Symphony," 130
*Treasury of Field Recordings, A,* 205
Treaty of Guadalupe Hidalgo, 153
Treaty of Utrecht, 22

*Treemonisha,* 135
Trent, Alphonese, 53
Trepina, 179
Tricolor Records, 162
Trio Aguirre del Pino, 157
Trio Gonzalez, 157
*Trovatore, Il,* 122
Trumbauer, Frankie, 46
Tubb, Ernest Dale, 26, 73, 81, 82–84, 86, 87n.1, 107
Tuesday Musical Club, 131
*Tumbling Tumbleweeds,* 71, 72
Turner, Grant, 87n.1, 93n.33
Tuska, Jon, 72
"12th Street Rag," 57

Universal Mills, 188
University of Indiana, 141
University of Texas Institute of Texan Cultures, 97
University of Texas, 40, 45, 73
"Unsuccessful Blues," 113
"Up from the Grave," 143

Valdez, Luis, 168
Valentino, Rudolph, 155
Vallee, Rudy, 72
Van Dyke, Henry, 143
"Vaterlandslied," 124
Vaughan, Stevie Ray, 15, 16, 116
Venth, Carl, 132
*Vereins,* 126
Vernon Fiddlers, 68
Viadurreta, Emilio Azcarraga, 157, 158, 166
Victor Records, 24, 68, 69, 70, 82, 156, 159, 162, 201
Victoria Talking Machine Company, 67
Villa, Beto, 11, 169
Villa, Francisco "Pancho," 155, 162
Villareal, Bruno, 10
Vinson, Eddie "Cleanhead," 54
Vocalion Records, 77, 78, 162
*Voz de America Latina, La* 157

Wagner, Richard, 131, 133
Wakley, Jimmy, 81

Waldman, Herman, 53
Walker, Aaron Thibeaux "T-Bone," 16,
    92n.27, 99, 116, 204, 207
Walker, Cindy, 66, 81, 84–87, 87n.1
"Walking the Floor Over You," 26, 83
Wallace, Beulah "Sippie," 4, 16, 38
Waller, Fats, 17, 40
"Wang-Wang Blues," 39
"Warm Red Wine," 81, 83, 86
"Washington Post March," 57
Washington, Booker T., 48
Waters, Muddy, 104
WBAP (Fort Worth), 24 68, 76
"We Can't Use Each Other Any More," 47
Weavers, The, 101, 107
Weber, Carl Maria von, 128, 130
Weiss, Julius, 134, 135
Welding, Pete, 96
*We're Czechs,* 184
"Were You There When They Crucified
    My Lord," 142
"West End Blues," 42
West Texanischer Gebirgs Sängerbund
    (West Texas Hill Country Singers
    League), 130
West Texas Fair, 128
West Texas Historical Association, 144
"What a Difference a Day Makes," 168
"What Can It Be," 113
"When I Can't Be With You," 48, 61n.31
"When I Was a Cowboy," 103
"When My Blue Moon Turns to Gold
    Again," 85
"When the Work's All Done This Fall," 24,
    90n.12
"Whiskey Blues," 113
"Whispering," 39
White, Benjamin, 138–39
White Eagles, 178
White, Josh, 107
"White Lightnin'," 26
Whiteman, Paul, 39, 41, 59n.6
Whiting, Margaret, 81
Whiz Antifreeze Company, 40, 41
WHN National Barn Dance (New York), 73
"Wild Side of Life, The," 26
Wiley College, 55

Wilkerson, Don, 63n.62
*William Tell,* 131
Williams, Hank, 83
Williams, "Big" Joe, 205
Williams, Leroy, 42
Williams, Ralph Vaughn, 143
Williams, Richard "Notes," 55, 58
"Willie and the Hand Jive," 166
Willis, Chuck, 102
Wills, James Robert "Bob," 4, 23, 25,
    26, 50, 73, 76–79, 86, 87n.1, 91n.21,
    93n.35
Wills, John, 76
Wilson, Teddy, 43, 56
*With His Pistol In His Hand,* 29
WLS National Barn Dance (Chicago), 71,
    72
Wolfe, Charles, 69, 101
Wolfekahn, Roger, 39
Wolfman Jack, 167
"Wreck of the Old 97," 24, 60, 70
Wright, Lammar, 41, 42
Wright, Leo, 58
Wright, Louis B., 120
WSB (Atlanta), 24
WSM (Nashville), 24, 83

XEAC (Baja California), 166
XEAW (Reynosa), 167
XED (Reynosa), 167
XEFW (Tampico), 166, 167
XEG (Monterrey), 166, 167
XELO ( Juarez), 166, 167
XEMO (Baja California), 166
XENT (Nuevo Laredo), 167
XEPN (Piedras Negras), 167
XER (Ciudad Acuna), 167
XERA (Ciudad Acuna), 167
XERB (Baja California), 166
XERF (Ciudad Acuna), 167
XERU (Tijuana), 163
XET (Monterrey), 167
XEXO (Nuevo Laredo), 166, 167

"Y tenia un lunar (And She Had a Mole),"
    39
"Yellow Rose of Texas," 19–20

Yoakam, Dwight, 27, 93n.36
"You Ain't Nothin' But A Hound Dog," 16
"You Don't Know My Mind," 101
*You Got to Reap Just What You Sow,* 109
"You Got to Reap Just What You Sow,"
   110
"You Got to Walk This Lonesome Valley,"
   106
"You Nearly Lose Your Mind," 83
"You Rascal You," 110
*You Were Lovelier,* 159

Young, Lester, 44, 48, 52, 53, 56, 57,
   63n.57
"You're the Only Star in My Blue Heaven,"
   72

Zapata, Emiliano, 155
"Zodico Stomp," 212
"Zolo Go," 206
Zydeco Hall of Fame, 214
"Zydeco Sont Pas Sale," 212
ZZ Top, 4, 27

ISBN 1-58544-221-6

90000